BEST RESUMES

for College Students and New Grads

Jump-Start Your Career!

Third Edition

Louise M. Kursmark

jist Works
America's Career Publisher®

Best Resumes for College Students and New Grads, Third Edition

© 2012 by Louise M. Kursmark

Published by JIST Works, an imprint of JIST Publishing
875 Montreal Way
St. Paul, MN 55102
Phone: 800-648-JIST   E-mail: info@jist.com

Visit our website at **www.jist.com** for information on JIST, free job search tips, tables of contents, sample pages, and ordering instructions for our many products!

Quantity discounts are available for JIST books. Please call our Sales Department at 800-648-5478 for a free catalog and more information.

Development Editor: Heather Stith
Cover Designers: Toi Davis and Leslie Anderson
Page Layout: Toi Davis and Jack Ross
Production Editor: Jeanne Clark
Proofreader: Chuck Hutchinson
Indexer: Joy Dean Lee

Printed in the United States of America
16 15 14 13 12   9 8 7 6 5 4 3 2

Library of Congress Cataloging-in-Publication data is on file with the Library of Congress.

ISBN 978-1-59357-887-9

About This Book

You're a soon-to-be college graduate. Or maybe you're still in college, looking for a co-op job or internship. Perhaps you're a nontraditional student, with years of work experience that's only marginally related to your degree. Even if you're finishing up an advanced degree, you're probably a beginner in your career.

Best Resumes for College Students and New Grads will help you make a successful move from college to the world of work. This step-by-step guide to writing an effective resume starts with some prep work (Chapter 1, "Proving Your Value to Employers") that will help you pinpoint what it is about you that is interesting and valuable to employers. Chapter 2, "Writing Your Resume," provides easy-to-follow guidelines, worksheets, and examples to draft your own unique resume. Once you've learned how to write your resume, use Chapter 3, "Managing Your Job Search—Online and Off," to gather the latest techniques on using social media and other online tools and resources to manage your job search and advance your career—now and into the future. Chapter 3 also has an in-depth discussion of traditional networking and other "old school" activities that you should include in your job search. Because you'll need a variety of job search letters to go along with your resume, I've included an overview of the types of letters you'll need and some good examples of each type (Chapter 4, "Writing Effective Job Search Letters"). Throughout these "how-to" chapters, I answer the questions and address the issues new grads raise most often.

In Chapters 5 through 10, you can browse through 123 resumes to get ideas for strategy, organization, language, and formatting. All of the resumes were written by professional resume writers for real people in college or with newly earned degrees from associate to doctoral level. Each student had unique circumstances, educational and work experiences, career goals, and areas of strength and weakness. I've provided comments that will tell you such things as how the strengths were emphasized, how shortcomings were downplayed, or why a particular approach was taken for this resume—information that can help you strategize, write, organize, design, and format your own resume.

As a professional resume writer, I believe wholeheartedly in the value of a good resume. But I'm well aware that the resume is only one piece of the puzzle—and maybe not even the most important piece. **Learning how to look for a job is probably the most valuable skill you can acquire as you start your professional career.** In addition to serving as a comprehensive guide to writing your resume, this book will also cover some job search essentials:

- How and why to look at the job search from the employer's perspective
- How to extract meaningful information from education and experiences that seem unrelated to your career goals
- How to make your resume and cover letters appealing to the "what's in it for me" mentality of hiring authorities
- Why networking is so important and how you can do it effectively

This book is an early step in what will be a lifelong journey. Just as you pursued your major field of study in college, you should devote the time and energy to build a solid base of knowledge in the field of job search and career self-management. The knowledge and skills you develop will make it easier for you to land jobs that will provide intellectual challenge, professional growth, financial reward, and personal satisfaction.

Fourteen Steps to an Effective Resume

This book is built on the framework of 14 steps to writing an effective resume that will get you interviews for the jobs you want:

1. Identify Your Job Target and Write Job Target Statements (see Chapter 1)
2. Identify Your Core Job Qualifications (see Chapter 1)
3. Compile Evidence of Your Hard and Soft Skills (see Chapter 1)
4. Start Strongly with Well-Organized Contact Information (see Chapter 2)
5. Sell Your Strongest Qualifications in a Powerful Skills Summary (see Chapter 2)
6. Emphasize Education as a Key Credential (see Chapter 2)
7. Describe Your Work Experience with a Focus on Skills and Achievements (see Chapter 2)
8. Add the Extras to Give You a Competitive Advantage (see Chapter 2)
9. Format, Edit, and Polish Your Draft (see Chapter 2)
10. Cross-Check Your Evidence Against Core Job Qualifications (see Chapter 2)
11. Proofread Your Final Resume (see Chapter 2)
12. Convert Your Resume for an Online Job Search (see Chapter 3)
13. Make Networking Work for You (see Chapter 3)
14. Write a Great Cover Letter to Accompany Your Resume (see Chapter 4)

Contents

PART 1

Working Toward Your New Career

Proving Your Value to Employers

Why would a company want to hire you?

Looking at hiring from an employer's perspective is an essential first step in preparing your resume and launching your job search. Generally speaking, companies hire people who have the skills needed to do a particular job and the attributes that will make them a good employee, one who will contribute to the mission and goals of the organization.

Don't assume that your new college degree automatically qualifies you for a great job. Yes, you've worked hard, learned a lot, and feel prepared to launch your career. Now you must show employers that you have skills, attributes, and abilities that will help them be more successful, and your resume is the tool to use to do just that. The purpose of the resume is to motivate employers to call you for an interview to better determine whether you are, in fact, a good fit for their needs. Your resume must clearly relate your education, activities, and work experiences to specific job qualifications—both the "hard" and "soft" skills that together paint the picture of the ideal candidate.

STEP 1: Identify Your Job Target and Write Job Target Statements

Before you can create an effective resume—one that presents your skills, abilities, and potential that will interest employers—you must know what kind of job you want.

FAQ

I'm not sure exactly what I want to do. I'm open to a lot of different jobs, and I'm afraid that if I pin down a position, I won't be considered for others. Won't that hurt my job search?

Companies aren't in business to help you figure out your career path. It's not enough to present yourself and your spanking-new degree to a company and expect the employer to determine where (or if) you fit in. Businesses have specific hiring needs. If your resume shows skills and attributes that fit those needs, you're likely to get an interview. But if your resume is vague and unfocused, the employer won't make the connection (and doesn't have time to try). Instead of being an attractive candidate for many opportunities, chances are you'll be attractive for none. As you continue in this chapter, you'll learn how to research job descriptions to find those that match your skills and education. And you'll see that you don't have to tailor your resume for a narrow target but can instead show yourself as a good candidate for a number of different jobs that call for similar skills.

Don't worry that by writing your resume for a specific job you'll be aiming for a target that's too narrow. The skills and accomplishments approach I recommend—which you'll be learning as you work your way through the exercises in this chapter and the next—will result in a versatile resume that you can use when applying for a variety of related jobs, or one that you can change quickly and easily to steer toward a slightly different target.

But if you're interested in several jobs that are quite diverse—say you're a business major torn between a job in human resources and one in retail sales management—you'll want to develop two different resumes so that you are a credible candidate for each position. Start by choosing one target and completing your resume. Then repeat the process for the second target. (It will be much quicker and easier the second time, and you will be able to use much of the same information.) You'll end up with a focused and effective resume for each target.

You can see how this works by looking at Resumes 27 and 28 and Resumes 29 and 30 in Chapter 7. Each pair represents two different, focused resumes for one individual seeking two different positions.

To write your job target statements, use the following form or open a new document in your word-processing program and label it "Job Targets." Write the specific jobs you're interested in. You might be definite about one particular goal ("design engineering position with a robotics manufacturer" or "med-surg nursing position in a teaching hospital"), or you might want to list three or four jobs that use similar skills, as in these examples:

1. Public relations position with a large corporation, ideally involved in writing press releases and newsletter articles

2. Marketing communications position (agency or corporate) with primary focus on writing marketing pieces

3. Reporting and copyediting job with a major metropolitan newspaper

Beware of confusing an industry or general profession with a job target! "Advertising" is an industry. "Accounting" is a profession. Neither is a specific job target. Do some research to find out what jobs are available in your chosen industry or profession, and work to refine those broad targets into something more specific, such as "account executive in an advertising agency" or "entry-level auditor for a Big 5 accounting firm." If you need help developing your specific job targets, the resources described on pages 5 and 6 will help you understand what different job titles mean and how specific jobs are defined. Keep in mind that your college or university career center can provide all of these resources and more—plus the expert advice of career professionals—to help you define your job targets, identify your skills, prepare your resume, and perform all of the other activities involved in a job search campaign.

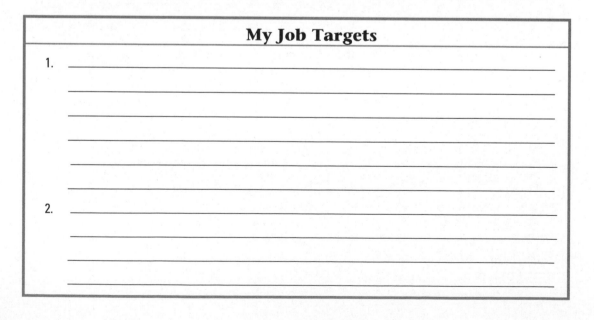

My Job Targets

1. _____

_____

_____

_____

_____

_____

2. _____

_____

_____

_____

3. _____

_____

4. _____

_____

Job Target Trouble

If you can't write a specific position for your job target, or if your desired positions are wildly different from one another, take a step back before moving forward with your resume.

Start by talking with the people in your college's career center. They have resources and knowledge that can help you figure out a variety of potential jobs that might fit your skills and interests. Next, meet with people who work at the jobs you're considering. Find out what they do all day, what they like about the job, what frustrates them, and what the opportunities for career advancement are. (Your career-center advisor can guide you in finding people to talk to and approaching them for advice.) If you're really stuck, consider hiring a career coach or counselor, someone who's an expert at helping people determine the best career fit for their talents.

If finding a job immediately is your first priority—if you don't have the time or money to invest in the career-planning process—pick one job that you can live with while you're figuring things out. Keep in mind that you'll be making several job and career changes during your working life, so this first step does not have to be your ultimate career path. But please don't abandon the career-planning process. Determining the best fit for your skills, personality, and interests is essential for long-term career happiness.

STEP 2: Identify Your Core Job Qualifications

The next step in the resume writing process is to identify the core qualifications for your specific job target—the combination of "hard" and "soft" skills that make up the ideal candidate.

Understand Hard and Soft Skills

Hard skills are the core knowledge and abilities needed to do the job. A C++ programmer must know how to program in C++. A social worker must be able to perform assessments, counseling, case planning, and case management. Hard skills are the kinds of things that can be proven through education and experience—you can do the job because you've been trained in the discipline or you've worked in a similar job. Or maybe both. **Your resume must show that you have the core knowledge and skills needed to do the job.**

Soft skills describe personal attributes—how you get things done. Soft skills are more difficult to measure and quantify. They include things such as teamwork, drive, leadership, a positive attitude, a good work ethic, attention to detail, or a customer-first attitude. **To be believable, your resume must *prove* your soft skills—not just list them.**

? FAQ

Aren't companies always looking for good employees? I know lots of people who have landed jobs when all they had going for them were good grades. They had no clue what jobs they were applying for when they met with potential employers.

There's always a chance that you'll get a job offer because your mother's college roommate is the CEO, or the hiring manager likes your positive attitude, or someone the company hired last year with a background just like yours has turned out to be one of its brightest and best employees. (This illustrates the power of networking! Learn more about it in Chapter 3.) But don't let your job search depend on happenstance or luck. Instead, use your resume to tell employers what you can do for them. Show that you understand their priorities. Let them know how what you've studied relates to their needs. That way, even when you don't have a heavyweight in your corner, you'll still capture their interest.

Find Job Qualifications

One of the easiest ways to unearth job qualifications is to look at want ads or online postings. Most ads specify a variety of required hard and soft skills. Let's take a look at some examples.

This listing for a Telesales Account Executive calls for specific hard skills and experience:

> **TELESALES ACCOUNT EXECUTIVE**
> The ideal candidate will have a Bachelor's degree and 3+ years of experience in outbound telesales. PC literacy, including Windows, Microsoft Office, and contact-management software needed. Prior recruiting experience is a PLUS.

This next ad, for an Executive Assistant, is much less explicit—it doesn't even specify what kind of computer skills are needed, nor does it demand a degree. But it clearly communicates the kind of attitude the company is looking for, along with some basic competencies (organization and follow-through; and administrative, clerical, and computer skills).

> **EXECUTIVE ASSISTANT**
> We are looking to hire a person who has not only the right basic skills but also the attitude we need. Are you a person with a "roll your sleeves up, happy to pitch in and help" attitude? If you answered YES, then this job is for you!
>
> You are a highly organized person with the confidence to see tasks through to completion with minimal supervision. You possess administrative, clerical, and computer skills.

Most postings specify a combination of hard and soft skills, as in these next examples. By communicating information about attitude, atmosphere, and expectations along with the specific competencies required for the job, employers are hoping to find the best match for their needs and the best fit for their culture and environment.

ENTRY-LEVEL APPLICATIONS DEVELOPER

The candidate should have knowledge of Microsoft Visual Basic, HTML, ASP.NET, C#, and database design. Strong communications skills are important to work in a highly interactive team environment. Candidate should be a self-starter who can work under a project manager. The candidate should understand and have practical software development knowledge of object-oriented environments, client/server environments, and a broad range of operating system platforms. Experience with SQL Server and Crystal Reports a plus.

SOCIAL WORKER

Under general supervision, a Social Worker IV provides social services requiring a high level of expertise and the application of advanced techniques related to the provision of protective services for children and adults. This position utilizes assessment, counseling, interviewing, case planning, and writing skills.

Minimum qualifications include the possession of an MSW or a Master's Degree from a two-year counseling program if the program's course of study emphasized vocational rehabilitation, family or marriage counseling, gerontology, or a closely related field.

PACKAGE DESIGNER

This position is with the department of Creative Services/Marketing. Our client operates on the idea that teamwork overrides ego—they seek designers who want to create, but who do not believe that artistic prima donnas rule.

Qualifications: Adept with Adobe Illustrator, InDesign, and Photoshop, multimedia and 3D.

3+ years of applicable experience as a package designer, ideally with consumer products, but also will consider graphic designers with strong portfolios.

QUALITY ENGINEER

Qualifications: Bachelor's degree; 1–2 years of experience in Quality in an ISO 9001 environment; exposure to machining, casting, and assembly a plus. Must be hands-on and have a real desire to grow in the Quality field. Must have good interpersonal skills and be a team player.

Beyond job postings, you can use other excellent sources to identify the hard and soft skills your target positions require:

- ***Occupational Outlook Handbook (OOH).*** This guide produced by the U.S. Department of Labor describes job duties, working conditions, required training and education, job prospects, and typical earnings for a wide range of occupations. The *OOH* is revised every two years and can be found online at www.bls.gov/oco/, in your college or public library's reference section, or in bookstores.

- **O*NET OnLine (www.onetonline.org).** Another top-notch resource from the Department of Labor, O*NET is described as "a tool for career exploration and job analysis." Numerous search options make it easy to learn about different jobs, find related professions, and identify specific job titles that match your skills.

- **Company job descriptions.** More complete than a want-ad posting, a job description is a comprehensive account of the activities and expectations for a specific job within a particular company. When you interview for a job, you can ask to see the job description. You can approach a company's human resources department and ask whether you can view a description. You can also request a copy from your employed friends and relatives, especially those whose jobs are related to your target position. Be aware that not all companies have formal job descriptions, and not all descriptions are up-to-date or an accurate reflection of the job as it really is.

- **Interviews with people who do that kind of job (also known as *informational interviews* or *field research*).** The information you get "from the horse's mouth" is probably the most valuable of all. People who are actually doing the work can tell you the ups and downs of the job, the level of knowledge and experience required, and the soft skills that they have found to be most valuable. How can you find people to talk to? Start by asking your friends and their parents, your parents and their friends, neighbors, and relatives. Social networking sites can be useful for this purpose as well. The professional networking site LinkedIn, for example, has an advanced search feature that you can use to search your connections and your connections' connections (or people who belong to the same LinkedIn groups as you do) by industry and profession. Your college career center also can help you find the names of college alumni who are working in your target field. Most people love to talk about their work and will be more than happy to spend a little time helping you define your career goal.

- **Resume sample books (like this one).** Look at resumes in the field you're interested in. Don't limit yourself to entry-level jobs or new-grad resumes. Take a look at the resumes of successful people who have advanced their careers. Their resumes should be chock-full of specific skills and traits that paved the way for their success.

- **"How to get a job in..." books.** Check your local library, bookstore, or college career center for guidebooks that are specific to the field you're interested in. Publications of this kind may also be available for free from the appropriate professional association (see the next item).

- **Professional associations.** Most fields have a professional association that provides such services as a newsletter, annual professional conference, and continuing-education opportunities. Associations also serve as the public "voice" of the profession and are often involved in publicity and lobbying for the benefit of members. Associations can be a great source of career information. At Job-Hunt.org (www.job-hunt.org/associations.shtml), you can search for an association in your field. For instance, under "Education & Teaching" you will find more than three dozen association names and links to their websites. In print, the *Encyclopedia of Associations* is the definitive source.

- **College career center resources.** In addition to giving you access to the resources mentioned previously, your college career center will provide one-on-one assistance if you're having difficulty getting the information you need. Don't expect the counselors to figure out your career path, write your resume, or find you a job; but do call on them for advice, guidance, and expertise.

Know the Skills That Are Always Valuable

Employers always value certain skills and attributes no matter what job they are trying to fill. These skills are found in the best employees, those who can handle a variety of challenges and succeed in just about any environment.

What are these important attributes? The National Association of Colleges and Employers (NACE) conducted a survey in 2011 about which soft skills employers value most. Here are the top responses from the more than 100 employers who participated:

- Verbal communication skills
- Strong work ethic
- Teamwork skills
- Analytical skills
- Initiative

Using these findings and adding a few more key items, I have developed a list of core attributes that are valuable for every type of job in every organization:

- Leadership and initiative
- Communication skills
- Interpersonal skills ("people" skills)
- Organization, time management, planning, follow-through
- Reliability and work ethic
- Problem-solving skills

These skills are included on the Core Knowledge and Skills worksheets in this book because they're so important. Try to communicate these skills in your resume even if the job description doesn't call for them specifically.

Put Together Your Core Knowledge and Skills Checklist

Now that you've reviewed a variety of resources, it's time to put together your own skills checklist for your target position. Here are two samples.

Core Knowledge and Skills Checklist
Target Position: Pharmaceutical Sales Representative

Hard Skills and Requirements

- Bachelor's degree (preferably BS), minimum GPA 3.0 ❏
- Proficiency in Microsoft Word, Excel, and PowerPoint ❏
- Driver's license and ability to travel throughout territory ❏

Soft Skills

- Presentation skills ❏
- Outgoing personality ❏
- Ability to work with limited supervision ❏
- Ambition and drive to succeed ❏

Added Value

- Sales experience ❏
- Master's degree in science-related field ❏
- Knowledge/experience in medical-related field (such as nursing or physical therapy) ❏
- Willingness to relocate ❏

Always Valuable

- Communication skills ❏
- Leadership and initiative ❏
- Interpersonal skills ("people" skills) ❏
- Organization, time management, planning, follow-through ❏
- Reliability and work ethic ❏
- Problem-solving skills ❏

Core Knowledge and Skills Checklist
Target Position: Mechanical Design Engineer, Aerospace

Hard Skills and Requirements

- Bachelor's degree in mechanical engineering or aeronautical engineering ☐
- PC skills ☐
- Experience with CAD (computer-aided design) software ☐
- Analytical skills ☐

Soft Skills

- Ability to work in a cross-functional team environment ☐
- Self-starter ☐
- Creativity ☐
- Ability to use technical data to sell ideas ☐

Added Value

- Design experience ☐
- Master's degree in engineering ☐

Always Valuable

- Leadership and initiative ☐
- Communication skills ☐
- Interpersonal skills ("people" skills) ☐
- Organization, time management, planning, follow-through ☐
- Reliability and work ethic ☐
- Problem-solving skills ☐

Now it's your turn. Use this form, or you can create a new word-processing file.

My Core Knowledge and Skills Checklist Target Position:
_____

Hard Skills and Requirements

- _____ ☐
- _____ ☐
- _____ ☐
- _____ ☐
- _____ ☐
- _____ ☐

Soft Skills

- _____ ☐
- _____ ☐
- _____ ☐
- _____ ☐
- _____ ☐
- _____ ☐

Added Value

- _____ ☐
- _____ ☐
- _____ ☐
- _____ ☐
- _____ ☐
- _____ ☐

Always Valuable

- Communication skills ☐
- Leadership and initiative ☐
- Interpersonal skills ("people" skills) ☐
- Organization, time management, planning, follow-through ☐
- Reliability and work ethic ☐
- Problem-solving skills ☐

STEP 3: Compile Evidence of Your Hard and Soft Skills

You've clarified your job target and defined the hard and soft skills needed to be considered a great candidate for that job. Now your resume needs to prove that you have those skills. In this step, you'll dig through your various experiences to find your proof—specific examples of when you used or demonstrated those skills and attributes.

At this point, don't worry about how to word your experiences or how they will fit into your resume. The notes you'll make in this section are the raw material that you'll mold into the polished resume in the next chapter.

Start by reviewing the list of core job qualifications that you created in Step 2. Use the boxes at the right of the form to check off the qualifications that you possess.

Skills Reality Check

Have you checked off all or most of the hard and soft skills required for the job you'll be seeking? Remember, these represent the core knowledge required for the position. You won't be able to write an effective resume for this job if you don't meet the basic requirements. Even more important, this might not be a good career choice for you. Your job target should not be a "pie in the sky" wish, but rather an appropriate, achievable goal that fits your education and personality.

If your skills don't match your job target, take a break from resume writing and do some career planning, as advised earlier in this chapter.

But don't worry if you can't check off every single skill on your list. With a resume that highlights your strengths and shows employers your potential, you'll be a viable candidate for your target position and other, related roles in the company, as long as you clearly communicate most of the core skills and other positive employee attributes that the job requires.

You can now start to put together your "evidence" information that shows you have what it takes to be successful in the jobs you're seeking.

Consider All Sources for Evidence of Your Abilities

Before starting to write, think about the sources you might consider in searching for this evidence. Your recent educational experience, of course, is a prime source for relevant material. But don't stop there! You've had many opportunities to develop and demonstrate specific skills, and you'll want to consider a wide variety of sources when compiling your proof.

Keep this list handy as you start the next section. It will help jog your memory and give greater depth to your resume than if you concentrated only on your most recent college experience.

Education

Degree
Major studies
Class/team projects
Theses
Case studies
Areas of concentration
Research

Academic honors and awards

Other honors and awards
>Leadership
>Contribution
>Peer recognition

Extracurricular activities
>Clubs and organizations
>Varsity and intramural sports
>Fraternities and sororities

Internship or co-op experience

Employment
>During the school year
>Summer jobs
>Prior professional experience if you're a nontraditional student

Volunteer activities
>High school
>College
>Community

High school
>Academic honors
>Significant activities

Travel

Family background

Special skills and interests

In addition to searching your memory, you might find evidence of your abilities in any of the following:

- Performance reviews from your various jobs
- Letters of recommendation from teachers, friends, and employers
- Your college application materials and application essay

Draft Your Skills Proof Statements

Consider each important skill and attribute for your job target and come up with specific examples of how you have demonstrated that skill. Review the list of potential sources of examples in the preceding section to be sure that you're not overlooking any important areas of your background.

Be specific! Vague generalities are not credible proof of your abilities. Don't worry that you're getting too detailed or including information that you won't use on your resume. Remember, this is your raw material. Cherry-picking examples from a large number of possible items is better than scrounging around to find evidence that supports a key skill area. As long as your examples are specific and credible, employers will be happy to consider them as proof of your qualifications.

The following example of a skills list with supporting proof is a good illustration of how varying areas of life—school classes and projects, part-time work experience, extracurricular activities, volunteer pursuits, and personal activities—can provide material for your resume. This example was compiled by a college sophomore looking for a co-op position in a medical research environment.

Skills Proof Statements
Target Position: Medical Research Assistant (Co-op)

Core Knowledge and Skills	Proof
Hard Skills and Requirements	
Two years of undergraduate studies in biology or psychology	Completed two years, psychology major, Northeastern University—3.9 GPA.
Research experience/ability to conduct research-quality phone interviews	Performed extensive research for National History Day project, 11th grade—won regional competition and advanced to state.
	Did biology, chemistry, physics, statistics, and behavioral research and lab projects as part of first- and second-year coursework.
Administrative abilities to manage follow-up mailings	Part-time work experience includes office assistant position. Filed papers, handled large mailings, and sorted and organized material for two books.
Soft Skills	
Teamwork skills	In ER volunteer position, work as part of the emergency team doing whatever is needed for doctors, nurses, and patients.
	Worked as part of sales/customer service team for Organized Living.
	Worked with teams on community cleanup projects with Circle K and President's Leadership Institute.
Added Value	
Experience in a health-care environment	Volunteer: N.E. Medical Center, Emergency Department 2006, Pediatric Department 2005.
	Volunteer: Children's Hospital, summers 2004 and 2005.
Always Valuable	
Communication skills	Gave winning oral presentation for National History Day project.
	Speak conversational Spanish.
Leadership and initiative	Selected for President's Leadership Institute at NU.
	Sought volunteer experience at NE Medical Center and initiated transfer to ER in second year.
Interpersonal skills ("people" skills)	Worked in retail/customer service job during high school. Interacted with many different kinds of customers.
	Interacted with sick children and adult patients as hospital volunteer for last three years.

Organization, time management, planning, follow-through	Planned and coordinated trips to New York City, Boston, Chicago, and Asheville involving plane, train, and auto transportation, hotel selection, activity scheduling, and syncing the schedules of people coming from different places.
	As high school senior, balanced heavy course load (all AP-level courses) with work and volunteer activities. Completed all assignments, papers, and projects on time.
Reliability and work ethic	Never missed work or was late in two and a half years at Organized Living.
	Worked part-time in high school, full-time summers, part-time in college as well as volunteering. Never missed scheduled volunteer dates.
	Mrs. Ellis' recommendation: "the most organized, observant, conscientious, and reliable person we have ever hired to care for our children."
Problem-solving skills	Working with children for more than five years (baby-sitting and hospital volunteering), used creativity and problem-solving skills to keep kids interested and active.
	In team project for Bio II, came up with creative solution that enabled us to identify results more quickly and gave us extra time to work on the report (earned an *A*).

Following are additional examples of proof statements for

- A new Business Administration graduate seeking an entry-level human resources position.
- A recent MSME graduate looking for a design engineering role with a major industrial manufacturer.
- A nontraditional student who recently completed a Bachelor of Liberal Arts degree, is planning to relocate, and wants to find a customer-service or account-management job in the health-care industry.

Skills Proof Statements
Target Position: Human Resources Generalist

Core Knowledge and Skills	Proof
Hard Skills and Requirements	
Bachelor's degree in HR or related field	Bachelor of Arts in Business Administration, concentration in Management.
Ability to handle confidential material	As Assistant Manager at Best Buy, have access to confidential employee information and the store's financial information.
Computer proficiency (MS Word, Excel, e-mail, Internet, database)	Used computers since grade school. In high school and college, prepared all reports and projects using MS Word, Excel, and PowerPoint.
	Trained new employees on computerized cash-register system.
Attention to detail and accuracy	At Best Buy, manage details of keeping inventory sorted, shelved, and tracked.
	Prepared financial reports of daily activity.
Business writing ability	Wrote college papers and reports.
Soft Skills	
Ability to work with diverse personalities	Had excellent relationships with all staff, whether subordinates, peers, or managers.
Added Value	
General office/administrative experience	Managed reports and paperwork in Assistant Manager role with Best Buy.
Always Valuable	
Communication skills	Extensive training experience. Able to adapt training methods to meet needs of staff. Take responsibility if they don't learn something—I need to find a more effective way to teach them.
	Able to solve customer problems.
Leadership and initiative	Promoted five times at Best Buy.
	Helped make hiring decisions.
	Chosen as part of regional training team for a new corporate training program.
	Selected to train new managers as well as new clerks.
Interpersonal skills ("people" skills)	Worked successfully in customer-service positions for five years.
	Able to get the most out of staff by finding what motivates them and creating rewards and incentives that fit their motivations.

Organization, time management, planning, follow-through	Worked full-time while in school and still managed to finish in only four and a half years.
	Set training schedules for entire region and followed through to be sure all training was complete.
Reliability and work ethic	Worked full-time while going to school almost full-time.
Problem-solving skills	Came up with a new way to organize stockroom to get products on the shelves more quickly.
	When employees weren't working hard, took a look at what motivated them and came up with new rewards and incentives.
	Can adapt management and communication style to very different people.

Skills Proof Statements
Target Position: Mechanical Design Engineer

Core Knowledge and Skills	Proof
Hard Skills and Requirements	
Bachelor's degree in mechanical or aeronautical engineering	BSME, 3.8 GPA; MSME, 3.9 GPA.
PC skills	Fully proficient in MS Word, PowerPoint, Outlook; some experience with Access; extremely strong Excel skills.
Experience with CAD (computer-aided design) software	Used CAD for numerous design courses and projects, both undergraduate and graduate.
	In two six-month co-op jobs, used CAD daily for engineering projects related to industrial machinery design and power systems design.
	Professor Burke's comments on senior design project: "You have a talent for conveying both the art and the precision of your designs—excellent CAD skills."
Analytical and problem-solving skills	Analytical skills essential to successful completion of master's degree project.
	Brainstormed and problem-solved with design team at Apex Power Systems and came up with more than a dozen ways to trim cost from our "legacy" system.

(continued)

(continued)

Core Knowledge and Skills	Proof
Hard Skills and Requirements	This will save the company $12 million per year and also make the product more efficient for customers to use.
Soft Skills	
Ability to work in a cross-functional team environment	Assigned to new product development team at Acme Industrial Systems. Worked with people from marketing, sales, manufacturing, and engineering to develop new FS-17 industrial motor.
	As part of campus program-planning committee, worked with diverse students and administrators to develop and carry out entertaining and educational programs for the entire student population.
Self-starting	At first co-op job (Travant Consulting), came up with new scope of responsibility for co-op assignment; developed overall plan and prioritized action-item lists; completed scope with minimal supervision.
Creative	Earned *A*s in all design classes.
	Compiled portfolio of original designs and class projects.
Ability to use technical data to sell your ideas	Supported master's thesis in oral and written presentation.
	Proved value and cost benefit of using titanium in FS-17 motor; convinced design team to adopt that material.
Added Value	
Design experience	Two six-month co-op assignments in design engineering role.
Master's degree in engineering	MSME
Always Valuable	
Communication skills	With Apex Power Systems, drafted all initial reports for the new product design team. Most were approved with only minor changes.
	Columnist for *Campus Chronicle*—"Geek Speak," commentary from engineering/science viewpoint to balance liberal arts focus of newspaper.

Leadership and initiative	See notation re: designing co-op job.
	Elected to leadership positions (campus program-planning committee, finance committee for frat house).
Interpersonal skills ("people" skills)	See "leadership positions," above; worked with diverse teams and people in a variety of jobs and activities.
	As part of fraternity outreach, mentored high-school students considering engineering careers.
Organization, time management, planning, follow-through	Fulfilled all expectations for co-op assignments, "going the extra mile" when needed to get the job done.
Reliability and work ethic	Worked part-time through high school and full-time summers until beginning co-op.
	Asked to return to Acme based on excellent performance, reliability, and work ethic.
Problem-solving skills	Covered in "Hard Skills and Requirements," above.

Skills Proof Statements
Target Position: Health-Care Account Manager

Core Knowledge and Skills	Proof
Hard Skills and Requirements	
Bachelor's degree in business, allied health, or a related field	Bachelor of Liberal Arts degree.
PC skills	Daily use of MS Office products and proprietary CRM system.
Knowledge of medical terminology	Daily use of medical coding and medical terminology in resolving claims with health-care providers.
Experience in account management or customer service within health-care environment	15 years of experience in health-care claims, billing, and account management (managed care).
Soft Skills	
Planning work and carrying it out with minimal supervision	Have decision-making authority for a wide variety of customer issues and problems. When backup is needed, manager always approves of my decision to call her in.
Customer-service skills	Meet or exceed all performance goals for customer satisfaction and call volume while handling heavy call load.

(continued)

(continued)

Core Knowledge and Skills	Proof
Hard Skills and Requirements	
Ability to work in a team environment	Recognized for exceptional teamwork skills in most recent performance evaluation.
Added Value	
Team leadership experience	Co-led Policy and Procedure team—administered survey, led team in reviewing results, and presented proposals to management.
Always Valuable	
Communication skills	Able to de-escalate issues—often called on by other claims specialists to help with difficult calls.
	My job calls for constant written and verbal communication with health-care providers, other team members, and management.
Leadership and initiative	Policy and Procedure project was my idea.
	Recognized by manager for expertise and ability to complete extra projects while maintaining heavy call volume.
Interpersonal skills ("people" skills)	Frequently complimented by customers on ability to calm them down when they're upset about a claim.
Organization, time management, planning, follow-through	Went back to school and finished degree while working full-time and raising two children as a single mother.
Reliability and work ethic	See above.
Problem-solving skills	When dealing with sticky claim situations, able to keep focus on the issue and what we can do about it. Can come up with "workarounds" when the regular methods won't work.
	Manager received two complimentary letters last year on my ability to help customers with difficult problems.

Now it's your turn. Open a new word-processing document or use the following form to list the evidence for your skills. Complete a separate proof statement list for each type of position you are considering.

My Skills Proof Statements
Target Position: _____

Core Knowledge or Skill	Proof

Hard Skills and Requirements

_____

_____

_____

_____

_____

Soft Skills

_____

_____

_____

_____

_____

Added Value

_____

_____

_____

_____

_____

Always Valuable
Communication skills

_____

_____

_____

_____

Leadership and initiative

_____

_____

_____

_____

Interpersonal skills
("people" skills)

_____

_____

_____

(continued)

(continued)

Core Knowledge or Skill	Proof
Always Valuable Organization, time management, planning, follow-through	_____ _____ _____ _____
Reliability and work ethic	_____ _____ _____ _____
Problem-solving skills	_____ _____ _____ _____

Spend some time developing your skills proof statements. You'll end up with lots of great material to use as you construct the first draft of your resume in the next chapter.

Chapter 1 Checklist

You're ready to move on to Chapter 2, "Writing Your Resume," if you have done all of the following:

❑ Identified one or more specific job targets that are a good fit for your qualifications and your interests

❑ Made a list of the core qualifications for your target positions and matched these with your education, skills, and experience

❑ Written proof statements that provide evidence that you possess the core qualifications for your target positions

Writing Your Resume

You've done your background work, and now it's time to put together the pieces you've assembled into a resume that "sells" you to an employer.

That's right—resume writing is selling. Your resume is an advertisement for what you can bring to an employer. Similar to newspaper and TV advertising, to be effective your resume must do the following:

- Capture attention in the first few seconds.
- Establish credibility—a reason for the reader to believe that you can do what you say.
- Inspire the reader to want to know more.

When you're making a big purchase, an ad alone will not usually inspire you to act. (Have you ever bought a car or a computer based solely on a magazine, TV, or online ad?) But a good advertisement will create interest in the product and make you want to know more. That's what your resume should do for you. Your goal in sending your resume is to get the employer to become interested enough to contact you for an interview.

But your resume can do more than just get you in the door for an interview! It will also serve as a basis for the questions and discussions you'll have with the hiring managers. So for your interviews, you must be prepared to explain every item on your resume in a way that continues selling the "product"—you!

In this chapter, you'll start by creating a powerful introduction that quickly draws notice to your most important qualifications. You'll move through the other sections of the resume, detailing your credentials, and you'll learn the importance of adding numbers, results, and accomplishments as further support to the evidence you compiled in the preceding chapter. And finally, you'll proofread and polish your draft to perfection.

? FAQ

Where do I start?! Writing a resume seems overwhelming.

Take a deep breath and relax! If you followed the guidelines in Chapter 1, you have already gathered the raw material you'll need for your resume. In this chapter, I'll guide you through the process, step by step, and you'll see how smoothly everything falls into place.

Resumes are incredibly flexible documents. There are no "rules" about what you must or cannot include, how or where to present the information, or any real taboos except that your resume must not contain any spelling, grammatical, punctuation, or factual errors. You can select and present the most positive, impressive things about you—things that relate to the employer's needs, as you've identified them in your Core Knowledge and Skills checklist. But because a good resume is concisely written and tightly formatted, it's important that you start out with a good organizational structure so that you can include just the right information, arranged for maximum impact.

To create that structure, resumes are sectioned into five principal categories:

- **Header/Contact Information:** A well-organized presentation of your name and contact information (one or more mailing addresses, telephone numbers, e-mail addresses, and other ways of reaching you).
- **Objective and/or Skills Summary:** A section at the top of your resume that immediately identifies what you're looking for and highlights your most important qualifications.
- **Education:** Presents all facets of your recent college experience, such as coursework, academic honors, internships, and activities.
- **Work Experience:** Chronicles the details of your employment experience, whether co-op or internship; part-time during school year or summers; or full-time experience before, during, or since you graduated from college.
- **Extras:** In this category go the many bits of information that you'd like to include but that don't fit neatly into any of the prior categories.

You can start with the easy stuff and work your way through the process in the following steps.

? FAQ

I've been told I need a "functional" resume. What is it and how do I get it?

A functional resume groups and emphasizes related skills (functions) instead of presenting every fact within a chronological category on the resume. The functional style is a great way to pull together proof from different areas of your background. For instance, you might create a Leadership Skills section that includes examples from your college activities, part-time work experience, and volunteer activities—proof that might be overlooked if each stood alone in a purely chronological history. For experienced employees, a chronological resume usually works best, because employers can see at a glance their career progression and the specific responsibilities and achievements of each position. But if your work experience is not your strongest qualifier (and it usually isn't for new grads), a functional style may work better. Most of the resume samples in this book use a combination style that groups strengths into a skills summary at the top and then follows with a roughly chronological listing of education, experience, and activities.

Don't worry whether your resume is strictly "functional" or strictly "chronological." Create a strong summary (as described later in this chapter) and then organize your other information into sections that make it easy for readers to pick up relevant information.

STEP 4: Start Strongly with Well-Organized Contact Information

Give potential employers the information they need in a format that makes it easy for them to find what they're looking for. Your name should be prominent. Use bold and/or larger type to catch the reader's attention.

Because a resume is a fairly formal business document, it's traditional to use your full given name (Richard J. Williams, not Ricky Williams). But you might want to consider using a nickname in the following circumstances:

- If no one ever uses your full given name (for example, you go by Jay Vasipoli rather than Mortimer J. Vasipoli III).
- Your name appears difficult to pronounce (for example, you might want to use Shayna O'Riordan instead of Séadhna O'Riordan).
- You want to use an Americanized name or nickname in place of or to supplement your traditional name (for example, Manh "Mike" Nguyen).

It's becoming more and more common to omit your physical address from your resume and simply provide email and phone contacts. However, if you are looking for jobs in a specific area and you have an address (either home or school) in that area, do include the address because it will signal that you are a "local," and this can give you an advantage over someone from outside the area.

I recommend that you include only your cell number on your resume, assuming that is the most reliable way to reach you. Be certain your voice mail greeting is professional.

You must have an e-mail address that's professional, permanent, and reliable. Consider getting a separate Gmail or Yahoo! address just for your job search (this is especially important if your everyday e-mail address is something like fratparty@bigu.edu).

Finally, if you have a web portfolio or if you have a profile on a professional networking site such as LinkedIn, by all means include the URL as part of your contact information.

Create a new word-processing document or use the resume-development worksheet in the appendix to organize your contact information. Here are a few sample formats to consider:

Meredith Johnson

meredithj@yahoo.com
(513) 555-9049

4520 Hillsview Circle
Cincinnati, OH 45249

Tyler Van Aark

tylervanaark@hotmail.com
615.942.4493

EDWARD J. NILSSON III

ejIII@tampabay.rr.com
257 West Shell Court, Bradenton, FL 34201
941-459-3890 Home — 941-709-3490 Mobile

Dale Okenga, MD

Telephone	781-523-0909
Email	dokenga@att.net
Residence	7 Willow Drive
	Winchester, MA 01890

MORGAN VALLENCOURT

415-552-0983 • m.vallencourt@ucla.edu

STEP 5: Sell Your Strongest Qualifications in a Powerful Skills Summary

This important introductory section of your resume should present a quick "snapshot" of who you are and what you have to offer. Whether you use a formal objective statement, use both an objective and a skills summary, or combine the two into some kind of summary/ profile, be sure you do the following for greatest impact:

- Instantly communicate just what kind of job you're looking for.
- Highlight your strongest qualifications.

This essential information must be crystal-clear in just a quick glance at the top part of your resume. Equally important, you must write this section with the employers' interests in mind. Stating *what you want* is not nearly as effective as telling employers *what you can do for them.*

There are many interesting ways to communicate your job target and key skills. To make it easy for you, first I'll walk you through a step-by-step process of creating an objective statement and simple skills summary. Then, if you're feeling creative or would like to consider a different way of presenting this information, I'll review a variety of options and examples.

Possible Titles for Your Objective/Skills Summary Section

Accomplishment Summary	Key Credentials	Selected Accomplishments
Areas of Interest	Key Qualifications	Skills and Accomplishments
Capabilities	Objective	
Career Focus	Position Sought	Skills
Career Interests	Professional Qualifications	Skills Summary
Competencies	Profile	Skills Synopsis
Core Competencies	Proven Capabilities	Summary
Goal	Qualifications Summary	Summary of Qualifications
Highlights of Skills and Experience	Qualifications	Value Offered
Immediate and Long-Range Goals	Related Skills and Achievements	
Job Target		

Write an Objective Statement

Although it's not strictly necessary to lead off your resume with an objective, I do recommend it for new graduates. An objective is a quick, easy way to focus the employer's attention on your areas of interest. Otherwise, because you probably don't have a lengthy or relevant employment history, it might be difficult for the employer to understand what jobs you're qualified for.

When writing your objective, be specific, brief, and direct; avoid meaningless statements such as "Seeking a challenging, rewarding position with the opportunity for career advancement." Refer back to the job target statements you wrote in Chapter 1 to get started, but make sure that you word them to focus on the employer's needs.

Here are a few examples:

OBJECTIVE

To be one of the 15 transfer students selected this year for Florida State University's School of Motion Pictures, Television, and Recording Arts.

Seeking an entry-level position in the capacity of

MARKETING ASSOCIATE

OBJECTIVE

An entry -level position in investment banking or financial services that will capitalize on education, strong interpersonal skills, and excellent organizational capabilities.

CAREER FOCUS

Entry-level, Full-time Law Associate
▪ Corporate ▪ Labor ▪ Civil ▪

Goal	Internship: Summer 2012
	Public Relations / Marketing / Media Production

Objective

A **Contract Design Internship** utilizing communication and organizational skills in a team-oriented environment. Qualified by a unique blend of design knowledge and a business administration background.

Write your objective statement directly below your contact information on your resume.

Create a Simple Skills Summary

Review the core knowledge and skills checklist you created for your job target in Chapter 1. Narrow this list to the four or five skills or credentials you possess that you feel are *most* important for your job target and correlate *most strongly* to your qualifications.

Next, take a look at the proof statements you drafted in Chapter 1 for those skills. These form the basis of your skills summary.

For example, a recent college graduate who wanted a management trainee position with an emphasis in human resources decided the following core knowledge and skills were most important and connected best with his qualifications:

- Bachelor's degree in business or management
- Reliability and work ethic
- Management knowledge or experience
- Human resources or training experience
- Leadership skills

This skills summary describes his evidence for each of these requirements:

SUMMARY OF QUALIFICATIONS	• Bachelor's degree in Business Administration, with concentration in management and additional coursework in organizational behavior. • Track record of advancement based on capabilities, work ethic, and enthusiasm. • Management experience in a fast-paced retail environment. • Training responsibility for all new employees and new managers for 12-store retail district. • Ability to effectively supervise and motivate staff to high performance levels. • Understanding of bottom-line priorities and the importance of customer satisfaction.

This graduate student pinpointed the following skills as being the most important for her target position as a counselor, teacher, or case manager for special-needs youth:

- Experience diagnosing and treating developmental disabilities
- B.S. or M.S. in Social Work or Special Education
- Communication skills

Her finished skills summary provides the proof for these important skills:

PROFESSIONAL QUALIFICATIONS_____

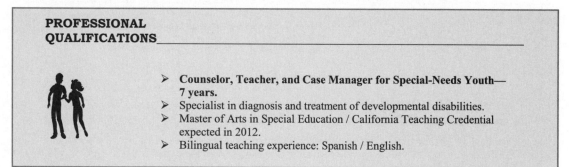

> **Counselor, Teacher, and Case Manager for Special-Needs Youth—7 years.**
> Specialist in diagnosis and treatment of developmental disabilities.
> Master of Arts in Special Education / California Teaching Credential expected in 2012.
> Bilingual teaching experience: Spanish / English.

Lastly, this undergraduate identified the following key skills for an internship in public relations, marketing, or media production:

- Knowledge of media production
- Presentation and communication skills
- Leadership
- People skills

The bold headings in the finished skills summary emphasize the connection between her skills and the internship requirements:

Skills	**Media Production:** Two hands-on summer internships with a multimedia producer of major corporate programs and events.
	Presentation and Communication: Comfortable speaking before groups and in business settings. Model, spokesperson, guide, and peer advisor. Strong writing and editing skills.
	Leadership: Repeatedly took on leadership roles in school and community activities. Demonstrated initiative, drive, and ability to manage multiple priorities.
	People Skills: At my best when interacting with others and working in a team environment.

Now it's your turn. Assemble the proof statements for your most important skills into a single bulleted list, starting with the proof statement for the most important or relevant skill. Place this skills summary just below the objective statement in your resume document.

Consider Objective and Skills Summary Alternatives

An objective statement and skills summary combination like the one you've just written is a relatively easy and usually effective way to highlight your most important qualifications. But it's not the only way! The sample resumes in this book show dozens of different ways to start off your resume. If you're not fully satisfied with your skills summary or want to consider a different approach, consider these ideas or flip through the samples for more inspiration.

■ With or without a category title, describe the value you offer in your target position:

What I bring to the Wastewater Department as an Entry-Level Civil Engineer:

✦ **Drive** to solve difficult problems— for the fun of doing it.　✦ **Discipline** to handle complex challenges well.　✦ Natural **aptitude** for advanced mathematics.

■ Fold your objective into a summary paragraph:

SUMMARY

Economic Analyst with MA in Applied Economics and real-world research, analysis, and consulting experience—an effective combination of theoretical and practical knowledge and a solid understanding of how economic principles and policies affect business, social, and political programs.

Key strengths include communication skills, leadership, and the ability to complete projects and deliver results in both individual and team assignments. Proficient in business and statistical software, including MS Excel, SAS, SPSS, and Statistix.

■ Combine an objective with a brief summary paragraph and a keyword list of core competencies:

Seeking an entry-level position in the capacity of

MARKETING ASSOCIATE

Offer a Bachelor's degree in marketing, diverse experience, and a solid understanding of marketing strategies illustrated through academic projects and an Internet venture that continues to develop and test theoretical marketing strategies and business management skills in the areas of

– Conceptual Planning	– Web-Based Marketing	– Advertising Campaigns
– Strategy Development	– Market Penetration	– Media/Client Relations
– Project Management	– Competitive Analysis	– Ad Copy Creation

---

■ Include an objective and create a profile that describes your strongest capabilities:

OBJECTIVE	Sales Associate—Retail Sales
PROFILE	☑ College student with more than 4 years of retail sales experience.
	☑ Professional and approachable manner. Talent for identifying customers' needs and presenting solutions that drive purchases.
	☑ Highly motivated team player—willing to take on added responsibilities.
	☑ Proven skills in problem solving and customer relations. Fluent Spanish.

★ RECAP

The Objective/Skills Summary section of your resume should provide a quick snapshot of who you are and the best you have to offer as it relates to your target positions. Organize and format your material to create a cohesive introduction and capture immediate attention.

STEP 6: Emphasize Education as a Key Credential

Because you've just completed a degree, the Education section of your resume is quite important. As you mature in your career, this section will become less prominent and will simply take its place, in abbreviated form, toward the end of your resume. But for now, create a section that communicates the value of your education in terms of your career target and a company's desired core qualifications.

Use the resume-development form in the appendix or work directly on your computer draft. Start by listing your degree (you can use abbreviations such as BS, BA, MS, or JD if you like), major, minor if applicable, year of graduation (it's not necessary to list the year you started), and your school's name and location (city and state).

If you've earned a license or credential as a result of your education, be sure to list it. You can also include relevant training that you completed outside the scope of your degree. For instance, you might have taken sales-training courses or earned CPR certification.

Next, review the evidence you compiled in Chapter 1 and pull out any education-related information to add to this section. If you find a theme—for instance, three examples that show strong leadership skills—consider creating a subheading to group together these items and call attention to them. Take a look at the "Possible Education Section Subheadings" box for ideas.

Possible Education Section Subheadings

Academic Honors	High School	Relevant Coursework
Area of Concentration	Honors and Awards	Research
Athletics	International Study	Scholarships
Co-op Experience	Internship Experience	Thesis
Extracurricular Activities	Leadership Experience	Volunteer Activities
Fellowships	Licenses/Credentials	
	Major Projects	

Education FAQs

Should I include my GPA?

That depends. If it's good (generally speaking, 3.0 or above), include it. Sometimes an effective strategy is to list your "GPA in Major," if it's higher than your overall GPA. If your GPA is unimpressive, omit it; including it on your resume can only harm you. Sure, the first question you're asked in an interview might be, "What was your GPA?" But you might not even be in that interview if you had listed a low GPA on your resume. Don't get yourself screened out of consideration by including a low GPA.

I spent my first two years at a community college and then transferred to State U. Should I list both?

It's not necessary to list any school except the one granting your degree. Include other institutions only if you have a specific reason for doing so—say you're going to network with alumni of your first school, or your first school has higher prestige than your graduating school. Two years at Harvard are valuable even if you finished up at Nondescript U.

How do I indicate my graduation date if I haven't finished my degree yet?

If you're starting your job search within a few months of graduation, it's not necessary to qualify the date—a resume with "Bachelor of Fine Arts, June 2012" that is circulated in March does not need to be explained. But if you're using your resume while still in college (say for an internship, co-op job, or part-time employment), use the word "projected" or "anticipated" along with the graduation date: "BA anticipated 2012."

Should I list my courses?

In general, I don't recommend taking up valuable space on your resume with an entire course listing. But consider adding "Relevant Coursework" or "Highlights of Courses" if you took unusual or advanced classes or if your degree or major course of study is not well known. Course listings can also be helpful for students applying for internships or co-op jobs where employers will not know which of the undergraduate courses in your major you've already completed.

Should I include high school information?

In most cases, you can omit high school information. But it's acceptable to include high school information that's relevant, adds to your qualifications, or gives you a competitive advantage. Perhaps you went to an out-of-state college but are now back in your hometown hoping to make connections with fellow graduates of Midtown High. Or you might be a younger student seeking an internship or co-op job who has earned some notable honors and awards during high school. But don't overload your resume with high school activities—you don't want to appear as if you peaked at age 18 and have done nothing memorable since! Be sure that any high school activities that you do include are balanced by more recent examples of your success.

There are many acceptable ways to format education information in a resume. The following sample Education sections are taken from the resumes in this book.

EDUCATION		
Medical	**Baylor College of Medicine,** Houston, TX M.D.	2006
Undergraduate	Washington & Jefferson College, Washington, PA B.A. Biology	1994

EDUCATION

Bachelor of Arts, English, May 2012
Saint Thomas Aquinas College, Spring Valley, NY
Alpha Sigma Lambda Honor Society

■ EDUCATION

Bachelor of Arts, Psychology (Magna Cum Laude)   2012 Graduate
VANDERBILT UNIVERSITY; Nashville, Tennessee
Coursework included Childhood Psychopathology, Abnormal Psychology, Psychology of Women, Multicultural Communications, Racial and Ethnic Diversity, and numerous other Human Service courses.

Education

BS, Iowa State University
Ames, IA (May 2012)
AGRICULTURAL STUDIES

TEAM PROJECTS:
Nutrient Management

Fly-Ash Environmental Soil Management

AAS, Des Moines Area Community College
Ankeny, IA (2009)
AGRICULTURAL BUSINESS

Education

BOSTON COLLEGE, Chestnut Hill, MA
Bachelor of Arts in Business Administration, December 2012
Area of Emphasis: Management

Relevant Coursework:

Accounting	Organizational Management	Administrative Personnel Systems
Economics	Organizational Behavior	First Line Supervisor
Finance	Small Business Management	Quantitative Methods for Business
Business Law	Operations Management	High Performance Teams in Business

Accomplishments:

- Personally financed 100% of college education through full-time employment; completed bachelor's degree in 4½ years.
- Won Coach's Award as member of track team, freshman year.

★ RECAP

Your resume's Education section might be a brief one-liner, or it could take up a large part of the page. Choose information that is relevant to your career goal and paints a picture of you in the way you want to be perceived—perhaps as a leader, a high achiever, an involved citizen, a hard worker, or someone respected by peers and administrators.

STEP 7: Describe Your Work Experience with a Focus on Skills and Achievements

Even if your jobs have been totally unrelated to your current goal, they gave you the chance to learn and practice specific skills. When you describe your work experience, relate what you did to a skill you learned or a contribution you made to the business. Try to phrase your work experience in the form of achievements rather than job duties.

For instance, instead of simply listing your job duties as an Admissions Representative for your college, communicate the achievement and importance of that role in a sentence like this:

> **Admissions Representative:** Chosen through competitive interview process to work with Admissions Office and represent Boston University to prospective students.

Wherever possible, support your achievement statements with specific numbers and results. Numbers add substance and credibility and are 10 times more effective at selling your capabilities than words are. (Doesn't that last sentence have greater impact and believability than if I just said "much more effective"?)

Even if you can't add numbers, demonstrate that you contributed to the success of the organization where you worked. Did you save money or increase efficiency? Multiply sales? Improve customer service or customer satisfaction? Think of a better way to do things? Help coworkers be more productive? Save a sale or placate an unhappy customer? Come to the rescue when the business was short-handed? Come up with an idea for a partnership with another business that added to the success of both? Your achievement statements don't have to be earthshaking; even small things that you did on the job will demonstrate your value as an employee.

? Work Experience FAQs

I don't have any real work experience. Why would an employer be interested in me?

By now, following the guidelines in Chapter 1, you should have compiled plenty of raw material to write a resume that will sell you for the job you want. Prior work experience is only one thing employers look for. They realize that most new grads will not have work history that is really relevant to their professional careers. However, the employer might rely on an employment history to prove work ethic, time-management skills, reliability, interpersonal skills, and other attributes that make a good employee, so if you don't have prior paid work experience, make sure you document these important traits from other areas of your background. Volunteer activities, unpaid work experience, leadership of student organizations, extensive personal travel, and even undocumented work experience such as babysitting can all be used to provide evidence of valuable, provable skills.

Use your diverse experiences to prove you have the attributes of a good employee. But don't worry too much about what you don't have. Instead, put your best foot forward with what you do have to offer and feel confident about your abilities!

All of my work experience is from part-time retail sales jobs. Does this really count to an employer?

Yes, indeed! As noted above, employers will look for evidence of your "good employee" traits by looking at your past work experience. If you can prove you were a good employee for someone else, the employer can guess that you're likely to repeat that success in another job. Every job exists for a reason and is important to the organization. So even though you might not think much of your part-time cashier job at Megastore, you learned some valuable skills (customer service, teamwork, and flexibility, for instance).

When writing about your past positions on your resume, don't inflate your responsibilities or importance (don't make your pizza-delivery job sound like you were the CEO), but do communicate the value you brought to the organization and the kinds of skills you used every day.

Possible Titles for Your Work Experience Section

Career Highlights	Experience	Internship Experience
Career History	Experience and	Professional Experience
Co-op Experience	Accomplishments	Relevant Experience
Employment	Experience Summary	Relevant Work History
Experience	Highlights of	Work Background
Employment History	Experience	Work Experience

Write Your Work Experience Section

List your job titles, dates of employment, and the name and location of the company where you worked. Add statements that convey the skills you learned and the ways you contributed to the business. You can use the resume-development form in the appendix or enter this section directly into your draft resume on your computer.

Don't go overboard trying to make your positions sound impressive. Generally, employers know what's involved in the typical retail sales, restaurant service, office administration, and customer-service jobs many students hold during high school and college years. Focus on the things that are unique to you and those that demonstrate skill or achievement.

If you have experience that is related to your career target—perhaps through a co-op job, internship, or position you held between attaining your bachelor's and master's degrees—you can provide more detail of your job duties. These duties relate to your current goal and position you as a person with experience rather than an entry-level employee. In these positions, too, you should focus on skills and achievements instead of simply listing the duties of the job. What did you learn or do that will make you an even more valuable employee? What were your unique contributions?

Sample Work Experience Phrasings

The following examples demonstrate how you might phrase your job experiences to add impact and value to your resume. All of these examples were taken from the resumes in this book. Most of the statements refer to part-time employment that is typical of many new college graduates.

- Developed loyal clientele and increased sales through personal attention to customers' needs. Resolved customer complaints diplomatically.
- Supported the pharmacy operations as necessary, fulfilling the role of pharmaceutical technician.
- Generated a list of 160 sales leads and contacts through aggressive cold-calling from a database of 1,100 companies.
- Devised 13 on-site strategies to effectively meet and recruit more than 750 Multi-Campus Hillel members in 18 months.
- Implemented creative learning techniques that resulted in student passing exams.
- Kept events running smoothly through effective problem solving and good decision making.
- Successfully completed the project on time to specification with full user interactivity.
- Publicized an urban youth organization to the media, the general community, and potential supporters. Wrote and designed a brochure for the organization.
- Defrayed college expenses and gained problem-solving, decision-making, communication, and leadership skills through diverse customer service, training, and supervisory positions.

Include awards, honors, recognition, and other evidence that you were a standout employee. Here are a few examples:

- Earned perfect job evaluation.
- Won three contests for selling the most dinner specials from among 15 servers.
- Received Outstanding Service Award, 2007–2008.
- Was requested to return for third summer internship.

> ★ **RECAP**
>
> Write a Work Experience section that demonstrates your employability by sharing your achievements and success as an employee.

STEP 8: Add the Extras to Give Yourself a Competitive Advantage

What makes you special? Each person has unique attributes, knowledge, and experiences that might not fit into the standard resume sections or match a list of job requirements. Perhaps you speak fluent Urdu, have backpacked across Europe for a summer, or devote hours and hours of time to disadvantaged kids. Sometimes these "extras" are related to your job target in significant ways, even though they might seem to be irrelevant on the surface. They say something unique about you and can set you apart from other candidates.

Write Your Extra Section(s)

List the unique points that make you special. Organize them into separate sections (with their own headings) or combine them under one umbrella heading. Just as you did in the Work Experience section of your resume, try to communicate skills and accomplishments, with results where possible, when detailing these "extras." If you volunteered, what were the benefits of your efforts? If you held a leadership role with an organization, did you introduce new programs that boosted membership or increased member involvement? Did you self-finance a summer of travel through nine months of part-time work? Use this section of your resume to continue the message of capability and success you've communicated throughout your resume.

Possible Category Titles for Your Resume "Extras"

Additional Information/Additional Qualifications

Community Involvement/Community Service/Volunteer Experience

Computer Capabilities/Computer Skills/Technical Expertise/Technical Proficiency

Affiliations/Membership/Organizations/Professional Associations

Languages

Military Service

Personal Information

Travel

Use What Others Say About You

If you have performance evaluations, letters of recommendation, customer letters, or other written commendations that sing your praises, consider incorporating one or a few quotes from these sources into your resume. This kind of third-party endorsement is extremely powerful, adds credibility to your resume, and lets you boast about yourself by using the words of others.

If you're using quotes, select one or a few that say the most relevant and positive things about you and determine the best place on your resume to put them. Quotes can be inserted on your resume in a number of places with great effect:

- As part of your Skills Summary, add a quote as a separate item or in a box to one side.
- Position quotes from professors in the Education section; place quotes from employers in the Work Experience section.
- Arrange your quotes in a narrow left or right column running the length of the page.
- Add a quote as a final, powerful footnote at the end of the resume.

★ RECAP

The "extras" make your resume more memorable, may hit on a helpful but not "required" job attribute, and can provide interesting material for an interview discussion.

STEP 9: Format, Edit, and Polish Your Draft

Now that you've finished drafting the material for your resume, it's time to wordsmith your draft copy, and then organize and format the material to create an attractive, easily skimmed document. Use the samples in this book for inspiration, if you like, or come up with something uniquely your own.

? FAQ

Does my resume have to be just one page?

Whereas most new college graduates can fit their most compelling and relevant information onto one page, some simply cannot—and it would be a mistake to try. There are absolutely no rules about resume length. Most of the samples in this book are one page; some are two pages. In each case, the decision about length was made after the resume was written, based entirely on the amount and type of information to be presented.

Write your resume first, following the guidelines in this chapter. Organize and format the information, and then see whether you can fit everything comfortably on one page. Use the samples in this book to inspire you to create a layout and design that will provide maximum impact and readability within a fairly concise format. Strive for one page—edit your first draft—but don't sacrifice information that is truly important.

Use Formatting to Guide the Reader

Use formatting to guide readers through your document and focus attention where you want it. Create a "structural hierarchy" similar to the outline format you would use when planning a research paper. Use indents, different type styles and enhancements, and different type sizes to create a consistent and logical flow for your resume while drawing the reader's eye to the information you consider most important.

Here's a structural hierarchy you might use in your resume:

CATEGORY TITLE

Subhead

Paragraph Text

- Bullet Text

And here's how that hierarchy would look with text inserted into it:

WORK EXPERIENCE

Sales Associate: Tower Records, New Haven, CT   5/10 to 6/11

Filled custom orders and assisted retail customers of full-service music store. Managed store opening and closing in manager's absence.

- "Sales Associate of the Month" 6 of 13 months—top performer among 12 part-time sales staff.
- Trained all new employees in online research for custom orders.

Use Type Creatively Yet Appropriately

Most word-processing applications offer dozens of font choices. Experiment to find one or two that you like and that contribute to the impact and readability of your resume. But don't go crazy with unusual or ornate fonts. A resume is a business document, and readability is key!

When choosing fonts, keep these tips in mind:

- Both *serif* (with little decorative lines or "feet" attached to the edge of each letter, such as Times New Roman) and *sans serif* (plain, clean fonts lacking decorative flourishes, such as Arial) fonts can be used effectively and can be highly readable.
- Use a font that is widely available on most computers. If the recipient of your resume is viewing it on a computer that doesn't have the fancy font you chose, your resume will default to something plain and possibly ugly or hard to read.
- Consider using two different fonts, one for your name, headlines, and other material that needs to stand out and the other for maximum readability in the text sections.
- Because Times New Roman and Arial are the fonts most used in resumes and other business documents, you can make your resume stand out from the others simply by choosing a different font.
- As a general rule, choose a text size between 10 and 12 points.

FAQ

Can I use a resume template in Microsoft Word or another word-processing program? It would make formatting much easier.

The problem with resume templates is that they force you to fit your unique background into a rigid organizational structure. Thumb through the resume samples in Chapters 5 through 9 and you'll see numerous ways to organize and present your qualifications. Drafting your material without a template yields better results because you are not confining yourself to the template's categories and layout. Another point against templates is that they are widely used by do-it-yourself resume writers. The person reading your resume has probably seen dozens if not hundreds of resumes with the identical template format. Why not create something unique for yourself?

Keep It Short

Avoid overly long paragraphs—dense text is hard to read and even harder to skim for essential information. To break up text-heavy sections, do the following:

- Write concisely.
- Divide a long paragraph into two or more paragraphs.
- List key points in short bullet-point statements.
- Use subheadings to grab attention and divide long lists into shorter, more manageable groupings.

Write Using "Resume Language"

Resumes have a style all their own. As you write yours, keep these key points in mind:

- Write in the first person, but omit the subject (I).
- Use present tense for current activities and past tense for past activities and achievements.
- For concise writing, omit articles (*a, an,* and *the*) and the possessive adjective *my*. Here are some examples:

> - [I] Completed [my] bachelor's degree in 3.5 years while working more than 20 hours weekly.
> - [I was] Elected president of [a] 60-member student organization and created [a] new program that boosted membership 20%.
> - [I] Cultivate cooperative, team-oriented relationships with [my] coworkers and managers.

- Summarize and trim to reduce wordiness and increase impact. For example, change this:

> While I was in college, I took a full course load of Honors-level courses while holding down a part-time job, volunteering 5 hours weekly, and actively participating in several organizations on campus.

To this:

> Combined intensive Honors curriculum with employment, regular volunteer work, and active participation in student organizations.

- Begin sentences with strong action verbs; avoid passive phrases such as "responsible for" or "duties included." For example:

> - Exceeded goals for speed and accuracy of data entered after just two days on the job.
> - Completed bachelor's degree in 3.5 years; earned 3.7 GPA.

- Write using parallel structure for consistency and comprehensibility. For instance, avoid listings like this:

SUMMARY OF QUALIFICATIONS (nonparallel structure)

- Creative problem-solver
- Work ethic
- Earned CPA while still a senior in college
- Strong analytical skills
- Energetic, industrious, and ambitious

Instead, make the items parallel:

SUMMARY OF QUALIFICATIONS (noun format)

- Creative problem-solving skills
- Work ethic
- CPA designation—earned while still a senior in college
- Strong analytical skills
- High energy, industriousness, and ambition

Or perhaps:

SUMMARY OF QUALIFICATIONS (verb format)

- Solve problems creatively.
- Work hard.
- Possess CPA (earned while still a senior in college).
- Demonstrate strong analytical skills.
- Display energy and drive in all endeavors.

★ RECAP

The way you organize and present your resume material will have a big effect on readability and impact. Be consistent and clear, and make sure that the format helps readers understand and absorb your capabilities.

STEP 10: Cross-Check Your Evidence Against Core Job Qualifications

You've finished your resume...almost. Before you start circulating it, review your resume with a critical eye to be sure that it does the following:

- Clearly communicates skills and capabilities that match the core job qualifications.
- Adds credibility through accomplishments and results.
- Uses a clear organizational structure and hierarchy for maximum readability.
- Draws attention to important facts and categories.
- Conveys employability—communicates that you have what it takes to be a good employee.
- Presents information that is meaningful to employers and shows that you understand business priorities (profitability, customer service, and other contributions to business success).

? **FAQ**

How will I know when my resume is right?

Perhaps the number-one misconception is that there is a "right" and a "wrong" way to write your resume. There are no rules! You can include what you like (as long as it's truthful), emphasize the most important information, and organize and present the material in any way that makes sense to paint the perfect picture of who you are and what you have to offer. You'll know your resume is right for you when it helps you define and organize your skills and attracts interviews for jobs you're interested in.

STEP 11: Proofread Your Final Resume

When you have finished writing, formatting, and polishing your resume, proofread it carefully! Errors in your resume are unacceptable. Don't rely totally on your computer spell-checker—it won't pick up common errors (for example, "advise" instead of "advice," "lead" instead of "led," and so on), nor will it check for consistency in your formatting and presentation. A careless error can cost you a job interview.

Ask others to review your resume, too—friends, parents, career-center advisors, and professors. They might pick up errors or inconsistencies that you overlooked or important items you omitted.

Before sending out your resume, take the time to proofread it one last time. Don't let a simple mistake derail your job search.

? **FAQ**

I have finished my resume; what do I do next?

Put your resume to work by getting it out to potential employers and networking contacts (you'll read more on this in Chapter 3) and creating an action plan that will keep you on track as you move from new grad to newly employed. Seek help and guidance from your college career center, parents, friends, and other advisors. The more you learn about the process of looking for a job, the more successful you'll be in every job transition of your working life.

Chapter 2 Checklist

You're ready to start your job search by reading Chapter 3, "Managing Your Job Search—Online and Off," if you have completed these steps in writing your resume:

- ❑ Created a resume header that displays your name and all of your pertinent contact information for easy availability to hiring managers
- ❑ Written a skills summary or other introduction that clearly communicates your job target and emphasizes your strongest qualifications
- ❑ Created an Education section that tells readers the most important things about your recent educational experiences and credentials
- ❑ Developed a Work Experience section that is appropriate for your background and emphasizes your accomplishments and contributions, not just your job duties
- ❑ Edited, formatted, polished, and proofread your draft resume so that it creates a positive first impression

Managing Your Job Search—Online and Off

The Internet has revolutionized job search—hasn't it? After all, with thousands of jobs listed, and the chance to post your resume to sites that are scanned daily by recruiters and employers, isn't the whole thing much simpler than it used to be?

The answer is…yes and no.

Yes, it's simpler to distribute your resume than in the past. Yes, it's easier to make your credentials available to a wider selection of employers. And yes, the process of doing so is faster, easier, and much cheaper than traditional methods.

But in reality, only a small percentage of people find jobs through Internet postings, just as only a small proportion of job seekers find positions through recruiters or want ads. In fact, job search continues to operate most productively when candidates use the centuries-old tradition of personal networking.

But because much of your job search activity will take place online, it's essential that you know how to use these important resources and channels as efficiently and effectively as possible—and how to truly accelerate your search by combining online tools with all-important in-person networking activity.

This chapter will help you get started.

STEP 12: Convert Your Resume for an Online Job Search

Undoubtedly you will visit some of the thousands of resume-posting sites, job sites, and company career pages during your job search, and you'll be uploading and posting your new resume in response to the opportunities you find. In addition, you'll use e-mail to send a resume, follow up on a lead, or reach out to an old or new contact.

Up to this point in this book, you've created a traditional resume—meant to be printed and read on paper. It can also be read onscreen, provided that the person you send it to has compatible word-processing software. But your traditional resume has a few limitations:

- It won't flow easily into an online resume bank or job application.
- Depending on format, it might not scan cleanly into a company's resume-scanning system.
- Formatting problems can occur for any number of reasons when you e-mail it.

Clearly, then, you'll need to adapt your resume for an online search. You will need a text (also known as ASCII) version, and you may need a PDF version and possibly a web resume. Here's when you'll use each of the different resume formats:

- **Traditional (Word .doc file):** You can use this format when you send your resume as an attachment to an e-mail message. You may also be able to upload the traditional format to a resume bank or online application—but often it makes better sense to use the text version, as discussed next.

- **Text (.txt file):** Use this format when pasting your resume into an online application, as a copy-and-paste source for data for online profiles, or any time you want to be 100 percent certain that the content of your resume transmits without formatting flaws that can occur with many Word files.

- **PDF file:** If your resume is highly designed and the design is an integral element of the document, this format is preferable. PDF files may be attached to e-mail messages or uploaded. However, not all companies will accept a PDF file, and some will not be able to scan the content of your PDF resume into their applicant tracking systems. When in doubt, use a text file.

- **Web resume (or online portfolio):** To provide an expanded resource for companies and contacts, you might list the URL of your web portfolio on your traditional resume, in your e-mail signature, or in any of your online social media profiles and postings.

Convert Your Resume to Text Format

A text resume contains all of the content of your traditional resume but none of the formatting or graphics—no font variations, no bold or italic type, and no boxes or rules or bullets. It's text, pure and simple. A text resume is ugly but effective, in that any computer can read it without file-conversion issues or formatting problems that often occur with word-processing (Microsoft Word) files.

Here's how you can convert your resume to this useful version:

1. Using the Save As feature in your word processor, choose "Text Only" as the file format and rename your document.

2. Close the file, open the renamed version, and you'll see that an automatic conversion has taken place—your resume now appears in Courier font, with most of the formatting stripped out.

3. Review the resume to fix any odd formatting glitches. If you've used tables, columns, or other unusual formatting, take extra time to be sure that all the text is in the right place.

4. Add extra blank lines before key sections, if necessary, and use lines of the available "typewriter symbols" to create graphic separators. (Typewriter symbols include ~, !, @, #, $, %, ^, &, *, (,), <, >, and /.)

5. Don't worry about how long your resume is or whether it breaks oddly between pages. It's not intended to be printed; rather, you will paste it into online applications or enter it into a resume database.

Figure 3.1 is a resume in the traditional printed format. Figure 3.2 is the converted text version of the traditional resume in Figure 3.1.

Gerald T. Clark

909 Main Street, Reading, MA 01867 • 781-942-0040 • geraldclark@mac.com

---

CAREER TARGET   **Human Resources/Employee Assistance Programs (EAP)**

SUMMARY OF QUALIFICATIONS

- **Education:** Earned advanced degree in Industrial and Organizational Psychology and Organizational Development; can diagnose and design remedies for organizational issues that affect productivity, employee retention and satisfaction, and bottom-line results.
- **Multicultural/international background:** From six-plus years living outside the U.S., appreciate diverse cultures and understand the challenges faced by relocating employees.
- **Communication skills:** Can build rapport with people at all levels of the organization, speak confidently before business and academic groups, and train and supervise employees.
- **Organization and leadership:** Can take ideas from concept to reality.
- **Adaptability:** Able to adapt quickly in new and changing business, social, and cultural environments.

EDUCATION

UNIVERSITY OF KANSAS, Manhattan, KS
Master of Science in Industrial/Organizational Psychology, 2011
Concentration: Organizational Development

- GPA 3.98/4.0: Dean's List all quarters.
- Completed coursework in Organizational Development, Organizational Behavior, Counseling in the Work Environment, and Industrial/Organizational Psychology.
- Student Affiliate, Society for Industrial and Organizational Psychology (SIOP).
- Member, OD Network National Conference Committee: Worked with OD professionals to plan and manage 2010 national conference.

BOSTON UNIVERSITY, Boston, MA
Bachelor of Science in Psychology, 2009
Minor: Spanish

- GPA 3.27/4.0.

UNIVERSITAT DE BARCELONA, Barcelona, Spain
Semester Abroad, 1/08–5/08

- Attended college classes that emphasized European culture and heritage.
- Resided with a European family and traveled extensively throughout Europe.

WORK EXPERIENCE

Defrayed college expenses and gained problem-solving, decision-making, communication, and leadership skills through diverse customer service, training, and supervisory positions.

- **Security Guard,** CLUB MARDI GRAS, Manhattan, KS: 10/10–5/11
- **Crew Trainer and Supervisor,** WENDY'S, Manhattan, KS: 9/09–5/10
- **Ski Technician and Rental Clerk,** CANYONS SKI RESORT, Park City, UT: 11/08–3/09
- **Doorman/Crowd Control,** THE RATHSKELLAR, Boston, MA: 10/07–6/08
- **Doorman,** BOSTON UNIVERSITY CLUB PUB, Boston, MA: 1/07–6/07
- **Sales Associate,** RADIO SHACK, Peabody, MA: Summers 2004, 2005, 2006

ADDITIONAL INFORMATION

- Fluent in Spanish; conversationally proficient in Italian.
- Lived overseas from 1994–2000: Japan (grades 3–4), Peru (grades 5–7), and Canary Islands (grade 8).
- Proficient in using Microsoft Office, SPSS, and SAS.
- Available for national or international relocation.

Figure 3.1: A traditional printed resume.

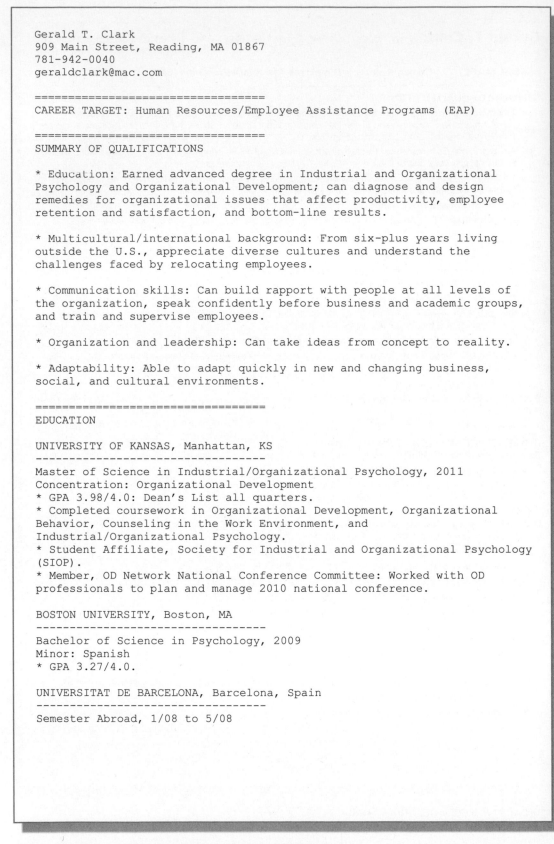

```
Gerald T. Clark
909 Main Street, Reading, MA 01867
781-942-0040
geraldclark@mac.com

===================================
CAREER TARGET: Human Resources/Employee Assistance Programs (EAP)

===================================
SUMMARY OF QUALIFICATIONS

* Education: Earned advanced degree in Industrial and Organizational
Psychology and Organizational Development; can diagnose and design
remedies for organizational issues that affect productivity, employee
retention and satisfaction, and bottom-line results.

* Multicultural/international background: From six-plus years living
outside the U.S., appreciate diverse cultures and understand the
challenges faced by relocating employees.

* Communication skills: Can build rapport with people at all levels of
the organization, speak confidently before business and academic groups,
and train and supervise employees.

* Organization and leadership: Can take ideas from concept to reality.

* Adaptability: Able to adapt quickly in new and changing business,
social, and cultural environments.

===================================
EDUCATION

UNIVERSITY OF KANSAS, Manhattan, KS
-----------------------------------
Master of Science in Industrial/Organizational Psychology, 2011
Concentration: Organizational Development
* GPA 3.98/4.0: Dean's List all quarters.
* Completed coursework in Organizational Development, Organizational
Behavior, Counseling in the Work Environment, and
Industrial/Organizational Psychology.
* Student Affiliate, Society for Industrial and Organizational Psychology
(SIOP).
* Member, OD Network National Conference Committee: Worked with OD
professionals to plan and manage 2010 national conference.

BOSTON UNIVERSITY, Boston, MA
-----------------------------------
Bachelor of Science in Psychology, 2009
Minor: Spanish
* GPA 3.27/4.0.

UNIVERSITAT DE BARCELONA, Barcelona, Spain
-----------------------------------
Semester Abroad, 1/08 to 5/08
```

Figure 3.2: The text version of the resume in Figure 3.1.

(continued)

(continued)

```
* Attended college classes that emphasized European culture and heritage.
* Resided with a European family and traveled extensively throughout
Europe.

===================================
WORK EXPERIENCE

Defrayed college expenses and gained problem-solving, decision-making,
communication, and leadership skills through diverse customer service,
training, and supervisory positions.

* Security Guard, CLUB MARDI GRAS, Manhattan, KS: 10/10 to 5/11
* Crew Trainer and Supervisor, WENDY'S, Manhattan, KS: 9/09 to 5/10
* Ski Technician and Rental Clerk, CANYONS SKI RESORT, Park City, UT:
11/08 to 3/09
* Doorman/Crowd Control, THE RATHSKELLAR, Boston, MA: 10/07 to 6/08
* Doorman, BOSTON UNIVERSITY CLUB PUB, Boston, MA: 1/07 to 6/07
* Sales Associate, RADIO SHACK, Peabody, MA: Summers 2004, 2005, 2006

ADDITIONAL INFORMATION
===================================
* Fluent in Spanish; conversationally proficient in Italian.
* Lived overseas from 1994 to 2000: Japan (grades 3 to 4), Peru (grades 5
to 7), and Canary Islands (grade 8).
* Proficient in using Microsoft Office, SPSS, and SAS.
* Available for national or international relocation.
```

Note: You probably won't need to create the so-called scannable resume that was required in the early days of automated resume systems. But if you are ever asked for a resume that's scannable, just use your text resume.

Convert Your Resume to PDF Format

A PDF (Portable Document Format) file is practical, easy to create, and will ensure the integrity of your resume design. However, the PDF format may not be fully integrated with resume-scanning software, and some employers have a strong preference for Word files. So I recommend that you use the PDF format only when design is of paramount importance.

Follow these guidelines for creating the PDF version of your resume.

- PDF files are created using Adobe Acrobat (the full version, not just the Acrobat Reader). If you have this software on your computer, you can use it to create your PDF file.

- If your computer is a Mac, you can create PDFs from any file by using the Print command and selecting PDF.

- Windows users can find free PDF converter applications that integrate with Word. PDFCreator and PrimoPDF are two popular tools.

- Free online services such as PDFonline.com and freePDFconvert.com and can perform the conversion for you.

? FAQ

What are keywords and what do they have to do with my resume?

Keywords are important words that relate to your job target. They are the words that a recruiter uses to search online resume banks for good candidates, or the words an employer enters into its applicant-tracking system when looking to fill a position. There is no defined set of keywords for any given position, but it makes sense to include many possible keywords in your resume to maximize your chances of being found in an online search.

Because you've taken the time to match your abilities to the requirements of your target jobs, your resume probably contains just the right keywords. To make sure, go back and review relevant job postings and observe which terms come up over and over, and then make sure that exact terminology appears in your resume. It's not necessary to create a separate section of your resume for keywords; you can simply include the words as part of the text.

Post Your Resume on the Internet

Once your resume is in text format, you can post it to both popular and specialty websites where employers go to look for candidates. There are thousands of career sites on the Internet, and no matter how specialized your field or narrow your interests, you can probably find a site to meet your needs.

Each site has its own protocol for posting resumes, so just follow the directions on the site. In most cases you'll fill in a few text boxes and then paste your *text* resume in its entirety into the spot indicated. If asked to provide keywords, pick out the words and phrases from your resume that exactly match the job descriptions you've been looking at; this will increase the chances of having your resume selected for review.

But a word of caution...simply posting your resume will not guarantee interviews or a job. A few years ago, the respected career site 6FigureJobs estimated that there were more than *30 million* resumes online! You can certainly add yours to the throng, but it's absolutely essential that you supplement your posting with other job search efforts—such as direct application to companies, response to print and online ads, and active networking to find out about unadvertised jobs or gain an advantage through a personal referral.

To get you started, here are posting sites appropriate for many new grads. You're sure to find dozens more as you negotiate the world of online job searching:

- **www.monster.com and www.careerbuilder.com:** These are two of the oldest and largest general career sites. You can post your resume, search literally millions of job postings, research salaries, and read a host of articles on career management.

- **http://college.monster.com:** MonsterCollege is a specialty site from the Monster company that is designed to help college students and alumni find jobs and internships. To use the site, you must be a student or graduate of one of its many participating colleges.

- **www.wetfeet.com:** This site offers information on careers, industries, and specific companies.

- **www.collegegrad.com:** Billed as "The #1 Entry-Level Job Site," CollegeGrad.com is designed specifically for people about to enter the professional workforce.

- **www.campuscareercenter.com:** Join up at this free site and you can apply for jobs, get information on companies, and get job interview and resume-writing tips.

- **http://student.fins.com:** This service of the *Wall Street Journal* provides information for new-grad job seekers in the fields of finance, technology, sales, and marketing.

- **www.collegerecruiter.com:** CollegeRecruiter.com bills itself as "The leading job board for college students searching for internships and recent graduates hunting for entry-level jobs and other career opportunities."

- **www.tenstepsforstudents.org:** This site is extremely helpful for students and new graduates who are considering careers with the federal government.

- **www.aftercollege.com:** As its name implies, this site focuses on new grads, and it claims more than 500,000 students and alumni.

- **Your college or university's career site:** Often an untapped resource, college and university career centers and websites can be a great source of relevant, free, up-to-date information and customized one-on-one services. Be sure to check out what your school has to offer.

Build Your Online Image

Where do you turn when you want to find out more about someone or something? The Internet, of course! Employers, recruiters, and network contacts are no different, and it's likely you'll be googled numerous times during your job search. So it's important that you know what they'll find and do your best to build a relevant, positive, and appropriate online presence that supports your professional image.

Establish Your Professional Persona

Who are you? Are you a sales professional, mechanical engineer, radiologic technician, accountant? Are you passionate about the arts, deeply interested in a specific field of technology, or dedicated to environmental sustainability?

As you move from college to career, you'll make decisions about what kind of work you want to do and where you want to do it. I've already discussed how important those decisions are when you write your resume. As you build your online image, keep that "who you are" information at the top of your mind and look for opportunities to enhance your professional image and visibility. Then, when employers do an online search for you, they'll find content and references that support what you've told them about yourself.

Do an Online Audit

The first step in building your image is to do an "online audit." And that's as simple as typing your name in Google and seeing what comes up. Several possibilities exist:

- **You're invisible online.** Either you have no online image or your listings are so far down the list of search results that it's unlikely anyone will make it that far. This could happen if you have a common name or if you share your name with a well-known person.

■ **Material that comes up is irrelevant.** It's nice that you ran a 10K race or set a video game scoring record, but this kind of information might lead an employer to conclude that you're not a serious professional or that your professional claims are just not true.

■ **Negative information rises to the top.** Whether it's as serious as a criminal record or as commonplace as a frat party, information about you that exists online will be used by employers in evaluating you as a candidate.

■ **Your search results are relevant and appropriate for a young professional.** Employers don't expect you to have published a book about your profession, won a major industry award, or established yourself as an expert in your field. But it's a plus if they find that you have shared an opinion, attended a professional meeting, or competed in a relevant academic competition that relates to your profession.

What you find in your online audit dictates your next move. But whether you need to do some serious damage control or simply build on a good foundation, it's important to keep monitoring and adding to your online image as you advance your career.

? FAQ

How can I prevent employers from finding negative online information about me?

Purge your Facebook page of any negative, suggestive, or questionable posts and photos. Of course, you can't control your friends' pages that might mention you, but if you know of a post that could be particularly damaging, you can ask them to pull it down as a favor to you. If you have a serious negative result from a search of your name, be sure to check out services such as Reputation.com that can help you "scrub" such references from the web so they don't derail your job search.

Improve and Highlight Your Online Image

One of the best things you can do to build your online image is to create a LinkedIn profile. LinkedIn (www.linkedin.com) is the premier professional networking site, and it's a prime source for employers and recruiters looking for candidates with specific knowledge and expertise. Not only that, but LinkedIn also has very high Google rankings so your LinkedIn profile is likely to jump to the top of search results for your name. Use these tips to maximize your use of LinkedIn:

■ Use your resume as the foundation for a strong profile that highlights your education, experience, and career interests.

■ Pack as many keywords as possible into the Specialties section.

■ Upload an appropriate, businesslike photo.

■ Join LinkedIn Groups that relate to your field. Ask questions and add comments as appropriate.

■ Ask for recommendations from former bosses, college professors, and any other contacts in your professional field.

You can build up your online image in other ways, too:

■ Keep your eyes open for Facebook fan pages or BranchOut pages that relate to your field. "Like" and comment as appropriate.

■ Join a professional association in your field. Look for one that has an online member directory so you can appear there.

■ Share your opinions via Twitter and follow others who speak intelligently about your profession.

- Visit blogs written by people in your field. Share your own opinions and comments.
- Go to Amazon.com and write a short review of a book that relates to your field. You can add the book review link to your LinkedIn profile.

In all of these efforts, be sincere and genuine. Don't pretend to have an expertise you don't have, but do feel free to share your thoughts and opinions. Employers want to see someone who is engaged and passionate about her work.

Once you've beefed up your presence, make sure that employers are able to find all of these positive and appropriate things about you. If a Google search still confuses you with others or pushes pertinent results below the second page, you can give your contacts a "cheat sheet" of prescreened Google results using a tool called Vizibility (http://vizibility.com).

Vizibility lets you group your top five most relevant search results in a distinct URL that you can add to your resume, e-mail signature, and other communications. You can also create a QR code that can be scanned by mobile devices to bring up your Vizibility home page. In a nutshell, Vizibility lets you present the most pertinent search findings to an interested audience.

★ RECAP

Web-based technologies and resources are the foundation for your job search—but not the entire structure. Master the tools you need, build your online image and visibility, and then move on to an even more critical activity: networking. Networking will help you in your job search today and in managing your career throughout your lifetime.

STEP 13: Make Networking Work for You

With the ease of online search strategies, a lot of job seekers reach no further than their computers when starting to look for jobs. Don't make this mistake! Instead, spend most of your time talking to people you know who can give you advice, suggestions, leads, and referrals that will bring you to the notice of people who can hire you.

Today, of course, you can combine traditional in-person networking with online social platforms and tools such as Facebook, LinkedIn, Twitter, Google+, and many more. The secret to making these tools work for you—and for your career—is to be smart, strategic, and thoughtful about what you say and the image you create. Your network can open doors for you, provide valuable inside information, connect you to your dream job or dream company, and transform your job search from online drudgery and frustration to a series of positive and helpful interactions. Sounds great, doesn't it? Let's explore networking in more detail.

There's nothing mysterious or frightening about networking. What it means, quite simply, is talking to people. One contact often leads to another, and in this way your web of contacts grows and your visibility expands tremendously beyond your own inner circle. You can make new contacts through people you know in person and people you know online, and often the two overlap and your means of communications mix and mingle.

For example, you send an e-mail message to a friend of your mother's who used to work at a company you're interested in. That e-mail message leads to a phone call and a referral to someone who still works at the company. You reach out to the new contact via e-mail and are referred to HR for a telephone interview and ultimately an in-person interview. You send an e-mail thank-you to your mother's friend and your new contact. After your interview, you print and mail a more formal written thank-you to the hiring manager. The point is that you should be flexible about how you connect with people and always look to extend one contact to another.

There are several keys to successful networking:

- **Don't ask for a job.** Most people you talk with will not be able to give you a job, and they'll feel bad if they can't help you. Instead, ask for their advice or suggestions. Tell them you respect their expertise and would appreciate their advice and assistance. And don't worry—if they're looking for someone with your skills, they'll be sure to let you know.

- **Don't assume anyone won't be able to help.** You never know how people are connected, so make a point to mention your job search to everyone you know and everyone you meet. It's surprising how often a casual comment will lead to a solid job lead.

- **Prepare and practice your introduction.** To approach each phone call, e-mail contact, or meeting with a feeling of confidence, prepare a one- or two-paragraph introduction that tells your contacts who you are (if they don't already know), why you're contacting them, and what specifically they can do for you. Here are three examples:

  "Mr. Smith, this is Patti Dillon. You might remember meeting me at my parents' New Year's Day brunch, when we talked about the advertising business. I'm about to graduate from Wilberforce University with a degree in media communications, and I'm looking for my first professional job. Would you have a few minutes to share with me? I'd love to get your advice on my resume and your ideas for people I should contact in the media, advertising, or PR who might know of potential job openings for someone with my qualifications."

  "Hello, Ms. Andrews, this is Paul Gonzalez. Sheila Wilkins in the career center at Northeastern gave me your name and said you might be willing to talk with me. I'm just finishing up my degree in physical therapy, and since you've been in the field for a few years, I hope you might be willing to help me pinpoint my career direction. Specifically, I'd love to know more about the differences between hospital-based and outpatient PT from the therapist's viewpoint."

  "Sally, this is Rita Hanscomb. I wanted you to know that I took the advice you gave me years ago—I finally went back to school and finished my degree. It's in accounting, and I'm excited about looking for a new job with this new credential. I'm looking for an opportunity with a company that will also value my years of retail sales experience, and I thought you could give me some suggestions. You seem to know everybody in the financial world in Sioux City! Can we get together for a cup of coffee next week?"

- **Try to set up an in-person meeting, whenever possible.** A personal meeting is more formal, usually lengthier, and more memorable than a phone conversation. If meeting in person is out of the question (your contact is in Detroit and you're in Mobile), set up a time for a formal phone meeting. In either case, e-mail your resume prior to the meeting and reiterate how you think your contact can help you. Be specific. Always be on time for your meetings. Dress appropriately in business attire for an in-person meeting.

- **Don't expect your contacts to run your job search for you.** Your job search might be *your* number-one priority, but it's not that high on the list for most of the people you talk with. Keep the ball in your court and follow up regularly with people you've contacted.

- **Be clear about your job target and how your contacts can help you.** Asking contacts to "help you find a job" doesn't give them much information to go on. Instead, tell them you're interested in Megacorporation and ask whether they know someone there. Tell them you're thinking about a career in marketing—do they have any suggestions, or can they refer you to someone in that field? Make it easy for them to help you, and they'll be delighted to do so.

- **Use powerful social media to extend your contact network.** LinkedIn is an incredibly powerful tool for finding direct contacts at your target company. With Facebook, you can share news and questions with your entire personal network at the same time. Google+ lets you create different circles of contacts—such as family, college friends, professional contacts, social contacts, and any other group you can think of. Then you can craft different messages that are appropriate for each unique group.

- **Make a great impression.** No matter how casual your everyday communications with friends and family, a more formal style is appropriate for job search and professional networking. You never know how or when one of your messages will be referred on to an influential person. Avoid profanity at all costs, and use proper spelling and grammar.

- **Follow the #1 rule of networking: "Give to get."** That means you should always be ready and eager to help your contacts, trusting that when you need help they'll give it to you. If you approach each network outreach with a giving mindset, you won't feel like you're "begging your friends for help," and networking will be a much more comfortable experience for you.

- **Follow up on all leads and let your contacts know how helpful they've been.** If your contact gives you a referral, be appreciative, follow up, and then get back to your original contact to let him know how it went. When you've landed your job, send thank-you notes to everyone who helped you in your search. And once you're employed, be ready to help others when you can!

★ RECAP

Traditional and online networking are powerful tools in your career management toolkit. Don't be afraid to ask people for help, but be clear and specific about just what they can do. Don't make the mistake of asking for a job or expecting your contacts to manage your job search. Keep your network alive throughout your working life—you'll benefit immensely.

Chapter 3 Checklist

You're ready to move on to cover letters in Chapter 4, "Writing Effective Job Search Letters," if you have mastered these important concepts in Chapter 3:

❑ Converted your resume to text format for electronic applications

❑ Performed an online audit and strengthened your online identity with appropriate content and connections

❑ Carefully reviewed the information on networking and included this tactic as a critical element of your job search

Writing Effective Job Search Letters

During your job search, you'll be writing lots of letters and e-mail messages:

- Cover letters to potential employers when you send your resume for consideration
- Letters to network contacts and the referrals that arise from those contacts
- Thank-you letters as follow-up to networking meetings and interviews

In this chapter, you'll learn how to quickly and easily write targeted letters to help you find job openings, get interviews, and land the job.

? FAQ

How do I write a job search letter that shows confidence and professionalism without sounding boring and fake?

When writing your job search letters, use a natural tone and simple writing style. Avoid stilted, outdated phrases like "per your request" and "enclosed please find." Of course, because these are business letters, they should sound more formal than a quick note or e-mail message you'd send to a friend, and they must be absolutely correct in grammar, spelling, and punctuation.

When writing your letters, focus on the employers' concerns (what you can do for them) and don't overstate your own needs and goals. Keep in mind that employers like people who really want to work at their company. Don't be afraid to show interest in your industry and enthusiasm about starting your career. These are among the most positive qualities you bring to the workplace.

STEP 14: Write a Great Cover Letter to Accompany Your Resume

Cover letters—letters that accompany or "cover" your resume each time you send it out—are essential partners to your resume. Because they can be customized for each person to whom you write, they give you the opportunity to highlight the information that is most relevant for that particular audience. But hiring managers may not read cover letters thoroughly (or at all), so don't count on your cover letter to communicate essential information that's not in your resume. Instead, your cover letter is an opportunity to sell yourself in a different way than your resume does.

Think of your cover letter as having three parts: a beginning (A), a middle (B), and an end (C). The following sections discuss this A-B-C cover letter format in detail.

A: Attention!

Your opening paragraph should tell readers why you are contacting them. To capture attention and make readers want to know more about you, use interesting language.

The following example shows the attention-getting introduction of a letter written to the manager of a retail store where the candidate hopes to become assistant manager:

Mark Strong, Manager
Bethpage Books
255 Seaview Street
Bethpage, NY 11714

Dear Mr. Strong:

If you are looking for a hardworking, dedicated, literate assistant manager, please consider me!

B: Because...

The middle section of your cover letter should answer the question "Why should I hire you?" by communicating your key qualifications for the job you're seeking. You can convey this information in one or two short paragraphs or in three or four bullet-point statements. Don't copy phrases or achievements word-for-word from your resume. Instead, write a summary statement about related achievements or tell a brief story that illustrates your strengths.

Here's the middle section of the letter introduced previously:

My education, work history, and personal activities all point to a successful career in retail management—specifically in the book business. I have recently completed my Bachelor of Business Administration (concentration in Marketing) from Hofstra University, and for five years I have worked part-time as a retail sales associate. This experience led to my decision to pursue a career in retail management. I understand retail sales concepts, merchandising, and general business management. Most of all, I am a true book lover and would be able to communicate my knowledge and enthusiasm to your customers.

C: Close

Neatly wrap up your letter with a polite yet assertive closing that asks for an interview; here's an example:

Thank you for your consideration. I am enthusiastic about working at Bethpage Books and will call within a few days to see whether we can schedule an appointment to meet.

Sincerely,

Sample Cover Letter

Figure 4.1 is a cover letter that demonstrates a good A-B-C format and clearly communicates key selling points. Written by a student seeking a co-op job at a children's hospital, the letter is a follow-up to a phone conversation. Note the three selling points in the middle section of the resume: a strong academic record, personal attributes shown in prior jobs and volunteer positions, and a hard-to-quantify but important interest in children that is essential to the job.

Meredith Johnson

meredithj@yahoo.com
(513) 555-9049

4520 Hillsview Circle
Cincinnati, OH 45249

August 29, 2012

Peter Andrews, M.D.
Children's Hospital Medical Center
Administrative Director: Research
3333 Burnet Avenue
Cincinnati, OH 45229

Re: **Co-op Position, April–September 2013**

Dear Dr. Andrews:

As you suggested, I am forwarding my resume to you for consideration for a six-month co-op position at Children's Hospital beginning next spring.

I am about to begin my second year at Northeastern University in Boston. My major is psychology, but my career goal is medicine, and I would welcome any kind of hospital-based position that provides either laboratory experience or patient contact.

My record of school work, employment, and volunteer activities demonstrates attributes that make me a valuable employee:

- **Strong academic skills:** First-year college GPA of 3.96 with a rigorous honors-level course load emphasizing math and science.
- **Reliability and work ethic:** In all my employment and volunteer positions, I have maintained an excellent record of being on time, prepared, and eager to take on new responsibilities.
- **Deep interest in the care and welfare of children:** In addition to volunteering at Children's Hospital for the past two summers, I have extensive experience caring for children, including a full-time summer nanny position. I relate well with children, truly care about their interests, and intend to pursue a career in pediatric medicine.

I will be at home in Cincinnati until September 15 and would be glad to meet with you. After that, I am easily reachable by phone or e-mail and will be home again during the holiday break (December 14–January 3).

Thank you for your consideration. I am enthusiastic about returning to Children's Hospital next year and believe I will be a valuable co-op employee.

Sincerely,

Meredith Johnson

Enclosure: Resume

Figure 4.1: A cover letter for a co-op job.

E-mail Cover Letters

Many if not most of the cover letters you send will go by e-mail. These letters need to be relatively short and crisp so that readers can quickly browse the contents on a computer screen or smartphone.

When you send your resume and cover letter by e-mail, place your cover letter in the body of the e-mail message and attach the resume as a Word (.doc) file. Write a descriptive subject line for your e-mail message. To fit many keywords into the subject line, you might want to abbreviate.

Here are a few examples of descriptive subject lines:

PR Assoc (Job #A-924) - BA Northwestern, NBC internship, strong writing skills

Med Rsrch Co-op - UCLA Bio major, hosp. exp., great work ethic

App Developer - Visual Basic, C++, database - recent training - team player

MSW – strong assessment & counseling skills – program mgmt exp

Figure 4.2 is an e-mail cover letter. Note that it is shorter than the previous sample letter—it gets right to the point and quickly communicates key information.

Subject: Marketing candidate - creative & focused - BSBA

Dear Mr. Andrews:

Are you looking for an enthusiastic, hardworking person for your marketing team?

As a marketing major (graduating with a Bachelor of Science in Business Administration degree in May), I gained a thorough understanding of the concepts of effective marketing, advertising, and merchandising. My activities during college expanded on my classroom learning--I had the chance to take leadership roles that demonstrated my ability to get things done while working effectively with both students and administrators.

I have identified your company, its products, and its culture as a good match for my qualifications and interests.

Can we schedule a time to explore your needs and my qualifications? My background, professionalism, and enthusiasm will make me an effective member of your team.

Sincerely,

Tyler Van Aark

Figure 4.2: An e-mail cover letter.

Make Contact Through Networking Letters

Your network—your friends and relatives, your parents' friends, your friends' parents, and anyone else you can connect to through anyone you know—is a powerful source of job information, and you should dedicate most of your time during your job search to reaching out to these people. Most people—50 percent to 85 percent, according to informal opinions from career professionals—find jobs through someone they know, not through online or print advertisements.

Networking letters are written to people you know or people you have been referred to. You might be contacting these people about a specific job or simply to ask for their help with your job search. These letters are easy to write because you already know the person or have been referred to him or her, so it's not a "cold call." In general, the tone is more informal and less "hard sell" than other types of cover letters.

Figure 4.3 is an example of a networking contact letter. The writer of this letter doesn't know the person he's writing to, but because he has been referred by a mutual friend, he can assume his letter will get a positive response. You can assume this, too, when you're writing to someone you know or someone you've been referred to.

Subject: Referred to you by Joe Sanders

Dear Ms. Rolfson:

Joe Sanders at All-Sports Marketing suggested that I contact you about my job search.

I am about to graduate from Ohio State with a BS in Athletic Training. When a knee injury ended my competitive baseball career two years ago, I found athletic training to be a good fit for my abilities and my interest in helping athletes achieve top performance.

I was fortunate to land an internship at All-Sports Marketing last year. I couldn't have asked for a better experience! Mr. Sanders offered me a full-time job upon graduation, but I've decided to pursue training rather than marketing. Mr. Sanders thought your connection with Dr. Samuels and the rest of the Pirates' training team could be helpful to me.

Would you be willing to spend a few minutes giving me your advice and suggestions? I would greatly appreciate it. I'll be in Pittsburgh the first week in April and can meet with you anytime that week, whenever is most convenient for you.

Sincerely,

David McChesney

Figure 4.3: A networking contact letter.

Follow Up with Thank-You Letters

It's common courtesy to thank people who have helped you, so be sure you send a thank-you letter to each networking contact who shares time, advice, or contact names with you. After an interview, use a thank-you letter to reinforce your candidacy, reiterate key points, and make a positive impression on the interviewer. Many job candidates don't take the time to write thank-you letters, so just by doing so you'll give yourself a competitive advantage.

You can send thank-you letters by e-mail as an immediate follow-up, but they make a stronger impression when you send them by postal mail. Don't try to hand-write your thank-you letters unless they are very short (one or two sentences) and you have exceptionally clear handwriting. Instead, use your word processor and compose a neat letter with information that will keep on "selling" you even when you're no longer in front of the interviewer.

Figure 4.4 is a follow-up letter to a networking contact who provided helpful advice and referrals. It demonstrates some "golden rules" of networking. Note that Dale has followed up on referrals that were provided. And, at the end, he offers to be a networking resource for Dr. Grandin's niece.

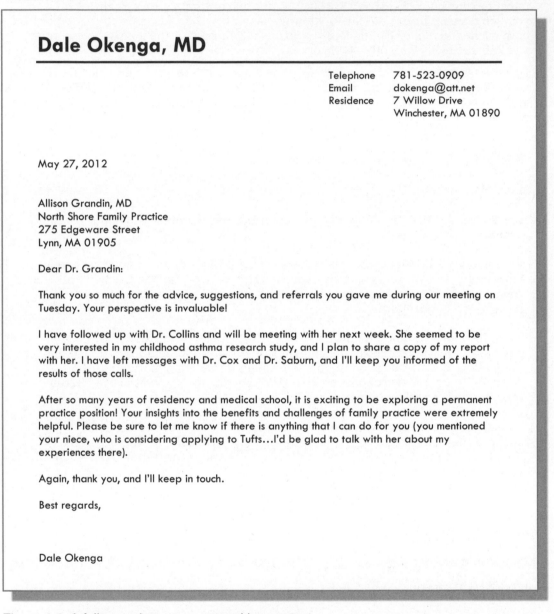

Figure 4.4: A follow-up letter to a networking contact.

Figure 4.5 was written as a follow-up to an interview. It recaps key qualifications and expresses enthusiasm about joining the company. Notice how a timetable for response is set up in the last paragraph. If this candidate doesn't hear back by the time stated, he should give Mr. Lin a call.

EDWARD J. NILSSON III

ejIII@tampabay.rr.com
257 West Shell Court, Bradenton, FL 34201
941-459-3890 Home — 941-709-3490 Mobile

July 27, 2012

Rick Lin
Engineering Manager
Suncoast Systems, Inc.
4527 Monument Street
Bradenton, FL 34201

Dear Mr. Lin:

Thank you for taking so much time on Friday to tell me about the engineering opportunities at Suncoast Systems.

I am excited about working on your leading-edge power systems and believe that my engineering education and co-op experiences have prepared me well to be a productive member of your company.

As we discussed during our meeting, I made significant contributions to several key projects at Simco Systems and Apex Environmental. After a brief orientation, I quickly became a contributing member of the design team and enjoyed adding my abilities to the group projects, while continuously learning from the senior engineers.

I am committed to working hard, working smart, and doing my best in every endeavor, and I would like to help Suncoast Systems become even more successful.

You mentioned that you would get back to me next week about the next step in the interviewing process. I look forward to hearing from you.

Sincerely,

Edward J. Nilsson III

Figure 4.5: A thank-you letter written after an interview.

? RECAP

All of your job search communications should carry the same message as your resume: that you are a skilled, qualified, employable person with lots to offer. Don't be afraid to show the enthusiasm you feel about launching your professional career.

Chapter 4 Checklist

You're ready to launch your job search in earnest if you have completed these essential activities from Chapter 4:

❑ Reviewed the A-B-C sections of a cover letter and drafted some letters for your job search

❑ Learned the differences between mailed and e-mailed cover letters

❑ Learned what makes an effective thank-you letter and planned to write your own letters immediately after any interview or networking meeting

PART 2

Sample Resumes for College Students and Graduates

CHAPTER 5

Resumes for Associate Degree Graduates

Resume Number	Degree	Job Target
1	AS, Paralegal Studies	Paralegal/legal secretary
2	AA, Paralegal Studies	Office assistant
3	AA, Criminal Justice	Police officer
4	AS, Nursing	Critical-care nurse
5	AAS, Occupational Therapist Assistant	Occupational therapist assistant
6	Certificate in Dental Hygiene	Dental hygienist
7	AAS, Equine Training and Management	Horse trainer
8	Certificate in Computer Systems Technology	Computer systems technician/field service technician/help desk technician
9	AAS, Hospitality Management	Hotel manager

1

Degree: AS, Paralegal Studies.
Job Target: Paralegal for SC Bar Association.
Strategy: Positioned this job seeker as "candidate of choice" by highlighting internship experience and magna cum laude distinction at graduation.

Lydia C. Hendricks

65 Thorn Hill Court
Greenville, South Carolina 29607
Mobile (828) 516-4548 • Residence (828) 236-9925 • Email lydiac@earthlink.net

PARALEGAL / LEGAL SECRETARY

Dedicated to providing superior, uninterrupted administrative support to legal and non-legal staff.

Confident, articulate, and results-oriented legal-support professional offering a strong foundation of education and experience. Looking to join an established team that rewards hard work and personal achievement with stability and the opportunity for increased responsibility.

IMMEDIATE VALUES OFFERED

- Highly skilled in MS Word, Excel, PowerPoint, and Access and Dictaphone transcription. Typing rate 80 WPM with consistently superior levels of accuracy.
- Organized, efficient, and thorough; proven record of success in prioritizing and processing heavy workflow without supervision.
- Perform well under stress, taking pressure off superiors and peers.
- Proficient in the planning and execution of projects in time-critical environments.
- Dependable and successful problem-resolution and time-management solutions.
- Creative and cooperative, working equally well individually or as part of a team.
- Outstanding record of performance, reliability, confidentiality, and ethical business standards.

LEGAL EXPERIENCE

Criminal / Civil	Powers of Attorney	Complaints
Domestic Relations	Divorce	Exhibits / Witness Lists
Affidavits	Adoption	QDRO
Subpoenas	Probate	Personal Injury
Motions	Wills	Client Interviewing
Orders	Estates	Real Estate
Research	Worker's Compensation	Mortgages / Deeds

SUMMER INTERNSHIP EXPERIENCE

Paralegal, **Tranter & Tranter, Attorneys and Counselors At Law,** Greenville, SC 2011
(Temporary) Legal Secretary, **Elmer George, Attorney At Law,** Spartanburg, SC 2010–2011

EDUCATION AND SPECIAL CERTIFICATIONS

Associate of Science Degree, Paralegal Studies, 2012 — Sullivan College, Greenville, SC
Magna Cum Laude Distinction
Dean's List

Attended South Carolina Business College, 19 credit hours accumulated, Legal Writing
Attended Hutchinson Community College, 24 credit hours accumulated, Criminal Justice

Commissioned Notary Public, South Carolina State-at-Large — Status, current

2

Degree: AA, Paralegal Studies.
Job Target: Office assistant.
Strategy: Described job activities in some detail because they relate to current job targets. Included an extensive summary detailing both hard skills and personal qualities.

JIM DELANO

845 South Lake
Anaheim, CA 92804

jimdelano@yahoo.com
714-699-4587

EXPERIENCED OFFICE ASSISTANT

PROFILE

Resourceful and dedicated paralegal student offering a combination of education and business support skills and experience. Proven ability to build and manage relationships with customers, team members, peers, and coworkers. Professional demeanor and strong commitment to professional growth.

- Successful working in fast-paced, deadline-oriented environments.
- Proficient in MS Word, Excel, Access, and PowerPoint.
- Accurate keyboarding (65 wpm).
- Adept at handling multiple telephone lines, filing, and performing Internet research.
- Tactful, patient, and courteous. Enthusiastic, efficient, and effective. Calm under stress.

EMPLOYMENT HISTORY

Customer Service Representative
Sunshine Instrument Corporation, Buena Park, CA   2008 to Present

Sunshine is a world leader in the design and manufacture of ham, shortwave, and CB radio instruments and accessories.

- Promoted from data entry to customer service rep after only six weeks.
- Act as point of contact for, and respond to, all telephone, e-mailed, and faxed inquiries.
- Serve as direct liaison for customers visiting the Anaheim facility to ensure prompt, courteous, and effective attention to their needs.
- Handle multiline telephone system.
- Perform other administrative activities as needed, including photocopying, burning software CDs, and filing.

Customer Service Clerk   (part-time)
Kmart, Irvine, CA   2007 to 2011

EDUCATION, HONORS, AND ACHIEVEMENTS

- **Candidate for AA in Paralegal Studies**   2013
  Orange Coast College, Costa Mesa, CA (evening studies)
  4.0 GPA
- Eagle Scout, Boy Scouts of America
- High School Honor Roll and Citizenship Awards

3

Degree: AA, Criminal Justice.
Job Target: Police officer.
Strategy: Equally balanced education and relevant experience as a security officer to paint the picture of a well-qualified police officer.

Melanie Cross

melanie.cross@network.net
1923 Bigelow Drive
Broomfield, CO 80023
303-555-6912

PROFILE

Commitment to a career in law enforcement with ultimate goal of canine officer. Training in and understanding of law enforcement fundamentals—to protect the community, reduce crime, and enforce laws—supported by ability to respond, investigate, resolve, report, and communicate. Hands-on technical training in crime scene investigation, forensics, and fingerprinting. Experience using Microsoft Office.

EDUCATION & TRAINING

**Associate of Applied Science
in Criminal Justice** (April 2012) ....Colorado Technical University • Denver, Colorado
Recognized for Academic Achievement

Highlights of course work:
- ☒ Principles of Policing & Law Enforcement
- ☒ Policing Techniques: Interviewing & Interrogation
- ☒ Criminal Investigation
- ☒ Forensics & Crime Scene Investigation
- ☒ Criminalistics of Cybercrime
- ☒ Criminology

Certificate in Veterinary Medicine (2009).....................ACO Vocational School • Broomfield, Colorado

Highlights of course work:
- ☒ Animal Handling/Restraint
- ☒ Basic Animal Care
- ☒ Infectious Disease (including bloodborne pathogens)
- ☒ Emergency Medicine
- ☒ Animal Nursing Care
- ☒ Human Animal Bond

Internships:
- ☒ Lakewood Veterinary Hospital
- ☒ Haute Dog Grooming

EMPLOYMENT & LIFE EXPERIENCE

Security Guard (2009–2010)....................................HSS Security Services • Denver, Colorado

Assignment sites:
- ☒ Office Building
- ☒ Manufacturing Complex
- ☒ Retail Store
- ☒ Home Improvement Supplier

Monitored interiors and exteriors of single and multiple building sites for suspicious activity. Patrolled parking lots. Controlled access and checked identification of individuals entering sites. Inspected personal property and vehicles. Alerted police and medical responders during emergencies. Communicated with clients. Created logs and generated incident reports.

Secretary (Summer 2009) ....Granger Insurance Agency • Berkley, Colorado
Intern Veterinary Assistant (2008–2009)............ Lakewood Veterinary Hospital • Lakewood, Colorado
Intern/Volunteer (2008).. Haute Dog Grooming • Denver, Colorado
Volunteer Animal Caretaker (2007) .... Cresset Community Farm • Denver, Colorado

4

Degree: AS, Nursing.
Job Target: Critical-care nursing position with a major hospital.
Strategy: Highlighted extensive health-care experience (as a medical assistant, CNA, and EMT) that adds value to recently completed nursing degree. Emphasized work ethic (working full-time while going to school full-time).

Ann-Margaret O'Leary

2479 Oceanview Terrace, Miami, FL 33132   (305) 491-1010 • ann-margaret@hotmail.com

---

REGISTERED NURSE: Critical Care / Medical / Oncology

Dedicated, hardworking nurse with 7 years of diverse healthcare experience and recent nursing education/RN certification. Recognized by supervisors, peers, and professors for team orientation, high-level critical-thinking skills, and desire for continuous learning. Record of initiative in alerting healthcare team to changing patient status. Exceptional work ethic.

Hospital and clinic experience includes

- Monitoring vital signs
- Administering EKGs and X rays
- Initiating oxygen therapy
- Caring for ventilated patients
- Bathing and tube-feeding
- Administering injections
- Educating patients and families

- Providing compassionate end-of-life care
- Using cardiac monitors/interpreting cardiac rhythms
- Drawing blood and initiating intravenous lines
- Assisting MDs with examinations and sterile procedures
- Operating autoclave/conforming to sterilization protocols
- Training new healthcare and administrative staff
- Communicating patient information to the healthcare team

EDUCATION

Associate Degree in Nursing/RN Certification, May 2012
Miami-Dade Community College (NLN-accredited program), Miami, FL
- Held full-time nursing positions while carrying full course load.

Medical Specialist Course, 2006
Army Medical Department (AMEDD) Center and School, Ft. Sam Houston, TX

HEALTHCARE EXPERIENCE

MEDICAL ASSISTANT: Hialeah Urgent Care and Family Clinic, Hialeah, FL   2011–Present
Serve a diverse patient population, beginning with triage and covering full range of urgent and ongoing care. Work cooperatively with physicians and other members of the healthcare team. Provide extensive patient education.
- Took on added responsibilities: taking X rays and EKGs, performing lab work, calling in medication renewals, and arranging consultations with specialists.
- Selected to train all new employees, identifying and filling in knowledge gaps to build overall staff capability.

PATIENT CARE ASSISTANT (CNA II): Miami-Dade Community Hospital, Miami, FL   2011–Present
On a combined medical/oncology unit, provide high level of care to patients—monitoring vital signs, bathing and tube-feeding patients, communicating patient status to the nursing team, and delivering end-of-life care with empathy and compassion.
- Recognized for ability to identify significant changes in status based on observation, intuition, and patient interaction.
- Effectively prioritized care during periods of staff shortages, dealing appropriately with patient concerns and complex medical issues.

CNA I and UNIT SECRETARY: South Florida Memorial Hospital, Miami, FL   2010–2011
Assisted nurses with care of critically ill patients on an emergency unit.
- Monitored cardiac monitors, interpreted rhythms, and notified nursing staff of changes in rhythm, oxygen saturation, respiratory rate, and blood pressure.
- As unit secretary, input physician orders into computer, answered phones, and paged physicians.

MEDICAL SPECIALIST: United States Army Reserves, Miami, FL   2005–2011
Provided preventative and emergency care including air and land evacuation of injured soldiers.
- Earned EMT certification.

EMERGENCY MEDICAL TECHNICIAN: Dade County Rescue Squad, Miami, FL   2008–2009

Fluent in Spanish. Proficient in a variety of computer applications.

5

Degree: AAS.
Job Target: Occupational therapist assistant.
Strategy: Capitalized on his extensive internship experience.

JONATHAN P. SADOWSKI, OTA

1984 Miller Pass ▸ Linden, MI 48452 ▸ 810-555-2399 ▸ bdybldr@yahoo.com

---

EDUCATION

BAKER COLLEGE • Flint, Michigan
Associate of Applied Science — Occupational Therapist Assistant   2012
COTA Certification   June 2012

HIGHLIGHTS OF SKILLS AND EXPERIENCE

▸ Plan and implement treatments and activities appropriate to individual patients, helping them increase capacity and attain their highest levels of functional independence.
▸ Experience working with pediatric and adult patients in outpatient and inpatient settings, individually and in groups.
▸ Basic knowledge of Neuro-Developmental Treatment (NDT) and Proprioceptive Neuromuscular Facilitation (PNF).
▸ Incorporate knowledge of and experience with body-building techniques into OT practices.
▸ Assess and treat patients regarding these issues:
   — Cognitive   — Mobility and motor   — Perceptual skills
   — Social/behavioral   — Sensory integration   — Communication
   — Community integration   — Activities of daily living (ADLs)
▸ Experience with patients with varying diagnoses:
   — Brain injuries   — Cerebrovascular accidents   — Orthopedic
   — Hand injuries
▸ Familiarity with these and other treatment methods:
   — Iotophoresis   — Electrical stimulation   — Ultrasound
   — Phonophoresis   — BTE

CLINICAL EXPERIENCE

GENESYS REGIONAL MEDICAL CENTER • Flint, Michigan
Student Intern [320 hours]   Jan.–Mar. 2012

HEARTLAND REHABILITATION SERVICES • Lapeer, Michigan
Student Intern [320 hours]   Oct.–Dec. 2011

HURLEY MEDICAL CENTER • Flint, Michigan
Student Intern [120 hours]   Sept.–Oct. 2011

MARION D. CROUSE INSTRUCTIONAL CENTER • Flint, Michigan
Student Intern [60 hours]   July–Aug. 2011

AFFILIATIONS

▸ AOTA (American Occupational Therapy Association)
▸ National Physique Committee *(for competitive bodybuilders)*

OTHER EXPERIENCE

JAY'S POTATO CHIPS • Flint, Michigan	**Route Driver**	2009–Present
EXPEDX PAPER & GRAPHICS • Flint, Michigan	**Shipping Clerk**	2006–2008
AIRBORNE EXPRESS • Lansing, Michigan	**Courier**	2003–2006
GM PROVING GROUNDS • Milford, Michigan	**Vehicle Test Driver**	2002–2003

Degree: Certificate in Dental Hygiene.
Job Target: Dental hygienist.
Strategy: Capitalized on her experience in the dental field as a chair-side assistant.

Juanita P. Morales

3482 McCandlish Road
Grand Blanc, MI 48439
810-555-2396 • jpmsmiles@home.net

Profile

- ❖ Certification and training as **Dental Hygienist.**
- ❖ Experience as chair-side **Dental Assistant** in general and periodontal practices.
- ❖ Ability to earn **trust** and develop **rapport** with patients.
- ❖ Strong patient **assessment** and **education** skills.
- ❖ Training and experience in using **Prophy Jet** and **ultrasonic scalers.**

Dental Experience

CARO PERIODONTAL ASSOCIATES • Caro, MI	2012–Present
FAMILY DENTAL • Clarkston, MI	2008–2012
DR. ROGER ANDERSON • Rochester, MI	2007–2008
MACKIN ROAD DENTAL CLINIC • Lapeer, MI	2003–2007

Education

MOTT COMMUNITY COLLEGE • Flint, MI
Certificate in Dental Hygiene   2012
— Graduated in Top 10% of class
— Passed state and national exams
— Past President, MCC Dental Students Association

Selected Classes & Training

- ❖ "Infection Control in a Changing World"
- ❖ "Advanced Techniques in Root Planing and Instrument Sharpening"
- ❖ "AIDS: Oral Signs, Symptoms, and Treatments"
- ❖ "Periodontal Diseases in Children and Adolescents"
- ❖ "Periodontal Screening Record"
- ❖ "Strategies for Teamwork and Communication Skills"

Community Involvement

- ❖ International Institute — Event Assistant
- ❖ Spanish-Speaking Information Center — Volunteer Tutor
- ❖ Big Brothers Big Sisters of Greater Flint — Big Sister

7

Degree: AAS, Equine Training and Management.
Job Target: Horse trainer.
Strategy: Communicated specific horse-related knowledge gained through training and experience.

Michael A. Viner
44811 WCR 33, Pierce, CO 80650
(H) 970-238-1718 ● (C) 970-504-6184
viner@hotmail.com

EDUCATION

Associate of Applied Science in Equine Training and Management
Laramie County Community College, Cheyenne, Wyoming
2012

RELEVANT COURSEWORK

Basic Management and Training, Equine Science I and II, Advanced Horse Management
and Training, Equine Evaluation, Equine Breeding, Equine Health Management,
Advanced Training Techniques, Internship, Equine Sales and Service

EXPERIENCE

Training

- Halter-broke weanlings for ranches and individuals.
- Started colts under saddle.
- Taught ground manners to weanlings and yearlings.

Breeding

- Assisted with mare care and exercise.
- Prepared mares for breeding.
- Handled stallions in barn.

Management and Maintenance

- Successfully managed up to 45 employees for 12 years.
- Maintained health and breeding records.
- Administered vaccinations and de-wormers.
- Organized and managed barn.

EXPERIENCE HISTORY

Trainer/Handler	TR Paints and Quarter Horses, Laramie, Wyoming	2009–2010
Office Manager	Brooks and Associates, Cheyenne, Wyoming	2008–2009
Trainer/Handler	Happy Hollow Ranch, Pierce, Colorado	2006–2008
Manager	Dairy Queen, Pierce, Colorado	1995–2006

PROFESSIONAL AFFILIATIONS

Laramie County Community College Equine Show Team, Secretary, 2010–2011
Block and Bridle Executive Council, 2010–2011
Southern Colorado Horse Activities, Vice President, 2007–2008
Westernairs, 1985–1995

8

Degree: Certificate in Computer Systems Technology.
Job Target: Computer systems technician/field service technician/help desk technician.
Strategy: Because job experience, although relevant, was only limited part-time work, emphasized recent education and coursework more heavily.

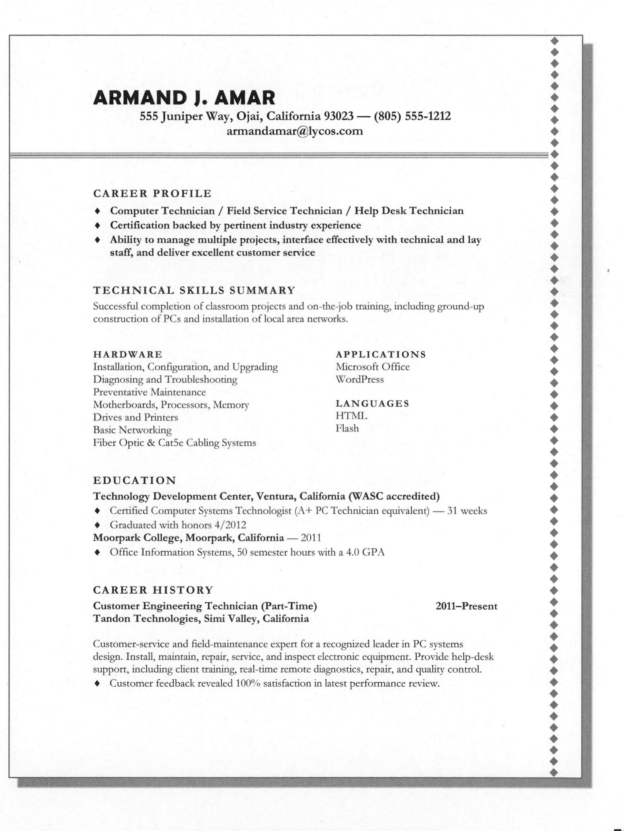

ARMAND J. AMAR

555 Juniper Way, Ojai, California 93023 — (805) 555-1212
armandamar@lycos.com

CAREER PROFILE

- Computer Technician / Field Service Technician / Help Desk Technician
- Certification backed by pertinent industry experience
- Ability to manage multiple projects, interface effectively with technical and lay staff, and deliver excellent customer service

TECHNICAL SKILLS SUMMARY

Successful completion of classroom projects and on-the-job training, including ground-up construction of PCs and installation of local area networks.

HARDWARE
Installation, Configuration, and Upgrading
Diagnosing and Troubleshooting
Preventative Maintenance
Motherboards, Processors, Memory
Drives and Printers
Basic Networking
Fiber Optic & Cat5e Cabling Systems

APPLICATIONS
Microsoft Office
WordPress

LANGUAGES
HTML
Flash

EDUCATION

Technology Development Center, Ventura, California (WASC accredited)
- Certified Computer Systems Technologist (A+ PC Technician equivalent) — 31 weeks
- Graduated with honors 4/2012

Moorpark College, Moorpark, California — 2011
- Office Information Systems, 50 semester hours with a 4.0 GPA

CAREER HISTORY

Customer Engineering Technician (Part-Time)   **2011–Present**
Tandon Technologies, Simi Valley, California

Customer-service and field-maintenance expert for a recognized leader in PC systems design. Install, maintain, repair, service, and inspect electronic equipment. Provide help-desk support, including client training, real-time remote diagnostics, repair, and quality control.
- Customer feedback revealed 100% satisfaction in latest performance review.

9

Degree: AAS, Hospitality Management.
Job Target: Management position at a major hotel.
Strategy: Showed transferable skills, solid work ethic, and academic accomplishments for this 54-year-old man recovering from major illness and looking for a second career. Demonstrated prior experience in management. Listed extensive honors and professional development training.

DONALD C. DUDEK

267 French Road   (315) 839-6504
Syracuse, New York 13135   DonCDude@att.net

OBJECTIVE: Position utilizing skills, training and experience in supervision and hospitality management.

SUMMARY:
- Demonstrated solid knowledge and hands-on skills in front office, lobby/front desk, room service, restaurant and housekeeping operations.
- Hired, trained, motivated, evaluated, disciplined, dismissed, promoted and supervised up to 60 employees.
- Scheduled personnel, oversaw purchasing and coordinated outside contracting.
- Revised tour planner's guide, updated database of tour guides and planners, scheduled appointments for international show, collected tourist information regarding local sites, planned itineraries and evaluated quality of services.
- Gained firsthand experience in all aspects of running and maintaining an upscale, high-occupancy hotel serving business and leisure clientele.
- Participated in banquet planning, preparation and execution.
- Assisted in a variety of marketing projects designed to promote tourism.
- Supervised full- and part-time staff comprising maintenance workers in a 325-bed hospital and major apartment complex.
- Maintained 184 apartment units with responsibility for plumbing, heating, air conditioning and electrical repairs.

EDUCATION: Cazenovia College, Cazenovia, New York
Associate in Applied Science — Hospitality Management, 2012
Dean's List   GPA: 3.5

Courses included:

Introduction to Hospitality	Accounting Principles
Human Resource Management	Front Office Operation
Hospitality Management	Macroeconomics
Rooms Division Management	Urban Promotion and Marketing
Effective Business Communications	Cultural Diversity
Microcomputer Applications	Ethics
Food, Beverage and Banquet Operations	Convention Sales, Trade Shows and Gaming Operations

INTERNSHIPS: Syracuse Convention & Visitors Bureau, Syracuse, New York (3/2012–5/2012)
Travel and Tourism Intern

Syracuse Marriott, Syracuse, New York (10/2011–12/2011)
Front Desk/Kitchen/Housekeeping Intern

(continued)

9 *(continued)*

DONALD C. DUDEK   Page Two
(315) 839-6504 • DonCDude@att.net

ADDITIONAL
TRAINING: Kaset International — "The Foundation for Creating Loyal Customers," "Caring
                     Responses for Extraordinary Service," "Understanding Behavior to Create
                     Successful Service Encounters and Skills" and "Strategies and Choices for
                     Handling Challenging Situations"
                     Syracuse University — Emerging Leaders Forum with workshops in "Person-
                     Centered Language" and "The Many Sides of People"
                     Fulton Community College — Courses in building and maintenance management
                     Northgate Nursing Home — Courses in "Supervisory Management Development,"
                     "Implementing Change" and "Assertiveness"
                     Service Engineering Associates — Seminar in housekeeping management and
                     supervision
                     New York State — Class 2 HVAC License

HONORS: President of Student Union Board, 2009–2011
                     Phi Theta Kappa, International Scholastic Order
                     Guest Speaker at Friends of Cazenovia Dinner
                     Cazenovia Hospitality Student Scholarship
                     Carrier Foundation Scholarship
                     Certificate of Recognition for Service as Student Orientation Leader

EMPLOYMENT: Colonie Apartments, Syracuse, New York (1994–2008)
                     Director of Maintenance

                     Northgate Nursing Home, Syracuse, New York (1993–1994)
                     Interim Director of Maintenance

                     Brown Barron Lounge, East Syracuse, New York (1991–2002)
                     Maintenance Manager/Bartender

CHAPTER 6

Resumes for Internship and Co-op Applicants

Resume Number	Degree	Job Target
10	BS, Communications	Media production intern
11	BA, Advertising	Advertising intern
12	BA, Communication Studies	Communications intern
13	BS, Exercise and Sports Science	Sports industry intern
14	BA, Sports Management	Sports management intern
15	BS, Accounting	Accounting co-op position
16	BS, Management	Marketing/management intern in construction industry
17	AAS, Construction Management	Construction management intern
18	BFA, Interior Design	Contract design intern
19	BS, Neuroscience	Research intern
20	BS, Biological Sciences	Clinical laboratory intern
21	BS, Political Science	Congressional intern
22	BA, Political Science	Congressional intern
23	BA, Criminal Justice	FBI Honors intern
24	BS, Chemical Engineering	Engineering intern or co-op position
25	BS, Chemical Engineering	Chemical engineering co-op position

10

Degree: BS, Communications.
Job Target: Internship in media production.
Strategy: Demonstrated consistent record of leadership, initiative, and achievement supported by relevant work experience in media production, modeling, and sales. High school information is included (on page 2) because it is relevant to the current goal and supports the strategy.

Corinne Sanderson

Permanent Address		**School Address**
119 Old Stone Trail	203-248-0973	139 Bay State Road
Guilford, CT 06437	csanderson@bu.edu	Boston, MA 02115

Goal

Internship: Summer 2012
Public Relations / Marketing / Media Production

Skills

Media Production: Two hands-on summer internships with a multimedia producer of major corporate programs and events.

Presentation and Communication: Comfortable speaking before groups and in business settings. Model, spokesperson, guide, and peer advisor. Strong writing and editing skills.

Leadership: Repeatedly took on leadership roles in school and community activities. Demonstrated initiative, drive, and ability to manage multiple priorities.

People Skills: At my best when interacting with others and working in a team environment.

Education

Boston University, Boston, MA
BS Communications — anticipated 2014
Concentrations: Public Relations / Film & Television

Leadership

Admissions Representative: Chosen through competitive interview process to work with Admissions Office and represent Boston University to prospective students.

- Greet and assist visitors and prospective students as front-desk representative for Admissions Office; weekly assignment.
- Lead tours for visiting high school students and their families and for visiting alumni during Reunion Weekend.
- Served on Recruitment Team; interviewed potential admissions representatives.
- Conducted recruitment events at Cheshire Academy, Connecticut, 2010.

Alumni Bridge: Recommended by faculty member and approved through alumni interview process.

- Volunteer at special alumni events such as new student receptions, athletic events (home and away), and Reunion Weekend.
- Chosen for Recruitment Team; interviewed prospective members.
- Nominated and elected to Executive Board position — VP of Publicity, 2011

Membership
Public Relations Student Society of America (PRSSA)

Volunteer
Special Olympics Volunteer, 2009, 2010, 2011

Experience

Media Production Internship

Production Assistant, Shoreline Productions, Madison, CT, Summers 2010, 2011
Participated in every aspect of producing corporate media programs for major events. In fast-paced, demanding work environment, performed tasks from PowerPoint programming and tape dubbing to running errands, serving as production crew, and modeling for corporate promotions. Also assisted with office administrative duties.

- **Major projects:** Major corporate convention for $1 billion Mega Products Company (2010 and 2011) and corporate event for Good Stuff, Inc., a $100 million direct-sales company (2011).
- **Media production duties:** Creating and editing PowerPoint presentations; programming TVL; scanning; researching footage; dubbing tapes; propping sets; operating TelePrompTer; assisting with production footage.
- **Requested to return** for third summer internship.

continued

---

10 *(continued)*

Corinne Sanderson
Page 2   csanderson@bu.edu   203-248-0973

Experience

Modeling   *(continued)*
Sales   **Model,** East Coast Talent, West Haven, CT, 2007–Present
                  Sales Associate, Ann Taylor, Boston, MA, 2010–Present
                  Sales Associate, The Gap, Meriden, CT, 2007–2009

High School

Cheshire Academy, Cheshire, CT
Graduated with Distinctive Honors, 2010

Academic Honors

National Honor Society, inducted 2008

French Honor Society, President

Second Place, French, Connecticut Scholastic Achievement Test (team competition)

Center for the Advancement of Academically Talented Youth / Johns Hopkins University
- Chosen in junior high school based on academic achievement and promise; participated for 6 years.

Founders Award in History

Faculty Award in Languages (French)

Leadership

Elected to Student Council, 2 years

Prom Committee, 3 years; co-chair, senior year

Yearbook Editor, senior year

Peer Counselor

Volunteer

School-based: Educational Assistance Program (classroom aide for local elementary school); annual Book Drive for schools in underprivileged neighborhoods; Famine Relief fund-raising initiative

Community: American Heart Association, Madison Hill Nursing Home, Shoreline Association for Retarded and Handicapped (SARAH)

Special Project: SARAH Ambassador: Delivered presentations at more than a dozen area schools to promote participation in programs benefiting SARAH and the people it serves.
- Influenced the launching of SARAH chapters at 7 schools.
- Named "Ambassador of the Year" (among 20 Ambassadors) for outstanding achievement in community service.

Athletics / Modeling / Travel

Varsity soccer player — 4 years

Dance — jazz, tap, ballet, pointe

New England Talent Expo — Model (placed in all 3 categories entered)

Travel abroad — Australia, most of Europe, Ghana

11

Degree: BA, Advertising.
Job Target: Internship in advertising with direction in creative strategy and graphic design.
Strategy: Elevated student's candidacy by highlighting his background, which includes business experience as well as college classes. Included interests in skiing, wakeboarding, and in-line skating to promote him as a risk-taker with a thirst for adventure.

Franklyn North

Permanent address: 9669 N. Heatherbrook Bloomfield, MI 48335	northfrank@wmu.edu • 248-555-6101 *portfolio available at:* www.FrankNorth.com	*Current Address:* 1221 University Avenue Kalamazoo, MI 49008

GOAL INTERNSHIP — Business/Advertising with core direction in Creative Strategy, Account Planning, and Graphic Design

COMPETENCIES Highly proficient computer skills in Adobe Photoshop and InDesign; Microsoft Word, PowerPoint, and Excel applications; and Internet business strategies

Web page development and design skills

Advertising Communications • Brand Strategy • Creative Services • Electronic Media
Market Research • Radio & Television Media • Press Releases • Marketing Statistics
Advanced Mass Media • Consumer Research • Creative Writing • Branding

---

EDUCATION

WESTERN MICHIGAN UNIVERSITY, Kalamazoo, Michigan
Major: **Advertising** — Bachelor of Arts degree *(anticipated)* 12/2013
Curriculum includes: **Graphic Design/Studio Art**

EXPERIENCE

BRADLEY ENTERTAINMENT PRODUCTIONS; Kalamazoo, Michigan
Creative & Design Director, 9/2011–present
Design, develop, and produce advertising material and promotional tools for nonprofit student-run business promoting entertainment groups.
- Developed business identity logos for the company and bands; designed graphics for advertising promotions.

GROUNDWATER ENTERPRISES, INC.; Royal Oak, Michigan
Internship, 6/2010–8/2010
Designed websites and updated Internet-based graphics for company that provided Business Continuity services and expertise. Assigned to Now&Again.com account.
- Designed business website including navigation strategies. Developed all logos, graphics, icons, and routing.

ACTIVITIES

Member — American Advertising Federation; Western Michigan University, 2009–present
Developed ideas and advertisements for the creative department. Also conducted campaign work in the community relations department. Currently organize fund-raising efforts and social events.

Member — Alpha Tau Omega Fraternity, Epsilon Eta Chapter
Attained positions as House Social Coordinator and Philanthropy Chair.

OTHER INFORMATION

Involved in snow skiing, water skiing, wakeboarding, in-line skating, and mountain biking. Highly knowledgeable and accomplished in weight training, fitness, and nutrition. Skilled in drawing, painting, ceramics, and sculpture. Talented guitar player.

12

Degree: BA, Communication Studies.
Job Target: Communications internship.
Strategy: Highlighted business and customer service skills; de-emphasized hairstyling expertise without sacrificing her creativity.

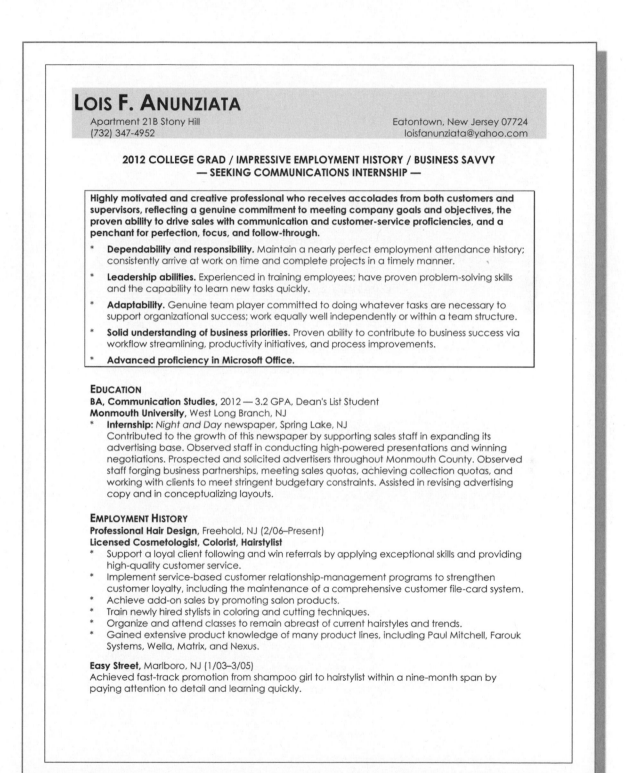

LOIS F. ANUNZIATA

Apartment 21B Stony Hill   Eatontown, New Jersey 07724
(732) 347-4952   loisfanunziata@yahoo.com

2012 COLLEGE GRAD / IMPRESSIVE EMPLOYMENT HISTORY / BUSINESS SAVVY
— SEEKING COMMUNICATIONS INTERNSHIP —

Highly motivated and creative professional who receives accolades from both customers and supervisors, reflecting a genuine commitment to meeting company goals and objectives, the proven ability to drive sales with communication and customer-service proficiencies, and a penchant for perfection, focus, and follow-through.

* **Dependability and responsibility.** Maintain a nearly perfect employment attendance history; consistently arrive at work on time and complete projects in a timely manner.

* **Leadership abilities.** Experienced in training employees; have proven problem-solving skills and the capability to learn new tasks quickly.

* **Adaptability.** Genuine team player committed to doing whatever tasks are necessary to support organizational success; work equally well independently or within a team structure.

* **Solid understanding of business priorities.** Proven ability to contribute to business success via workflow streamlining, productivity initiatives, and process improvements.

* **Advanced proficiency in Microsoft Office.**

EDUCATION

BA, Communication Studies, 2012 — 3.2 GPA, Dean's List Student
Monmouth University, West Long Branch, NJ
* **Internship:** *Night and Day* newspaper, Spring Lake, NJ
  Contributed to the growth of this newspaper by supporting sales staff in expanding its advertising base. Observed staff in conducting high-powered presentations and winning negotiations. Prospected and solicited advertisers throughout Monmouth County. Observed staff forging business partnerships, meeting sales quotas, achieving collection quotas, and working with clients to meet stringent budgetary constraints. Assisted in revising advertising copy and in conceptualizing layouts.

EMPLOYMENT HISTORY

Professional Hair Design, Freehold, NJ (2/06–Present)
Licensed Cosmetologist, Colorist, Hairstylist
* Support a loyal client following and win referrals by applying exceptional skills and providing high-quality customer service.
* Implement service-based customer relationship-management programs to strengthen customer loyalty, including the maintenance of a comprehensive customer file-card system.
* Achieve add-on sales by promoting salon products.
* Train newly hired stylists in coloring and cutting techniques.
* Organize and attend classes to remain abreast of current hairstyles and trends.
* Gained extensive product knowledge of many product lines, including Paul Mitchell, Farouk Systems, Wella, Matrix, and Nexus.

Easy Street, Marlboro, NJ (1/03–3/05)
Achieved fast-track promotion from shampoo girl to hairstylist within a nine-month span by paying attention to detail and learning quickly.

13

Degree: BS, Exercise and Sports Science.
Job Target: An internship in the sports industry.
Strategy: Used a format that will catch attention at job fairs and stand out in a stack of several hundred applications. The left column highlights volunteer experience with some prestigious golf and college organizations.

Allison A. Everett

936 Lincoln • Ames, IA 50014
515-290-2222 • Alverett996@yahoo.com

Education

BS, Iowa State University, Ames, IA (anticipated 2013)
Exercise and Sports Science / Sport Management
- Currently enrolled in Sport Management core classes
- Sport Management Club member

Computer Skills

Microsoft Word, Excel, PowerPoint
(Experience preparing and executing large mail-merges)

Work History

Allianz Championship Golf Tournament, Des Moines, IA
OFFICE STAFF VOLUNTEER (August–September 2011)
- General office assistance; stuffed envelopes for mass mailings and checked ticket orders.

Iowa State University, Athletic Department, Ames, IA
INTERNSHIP (May–August 2011)
- Worked with Varsity Club to increase membership.
- Updated database, typed letters, and prepared mailings.

SPORTS CAMP COUNSELOR (June 2011)
- Supervised 20–40 sports camp participants during two golf camps and one basketball camp. Oversaw dormitory stay; ensured timely arrival at camp and meals.
- Developed solid relationships with coaches and staff, including Julie Manning, Golf Coach.

Hy-Vee Women's Golf Classic, Des Moines, IA
MEDIA RELATIONS RUNNER (May 2011)
- Relayed information from leader board to media continuously throughout tournament.
- Monitored media interviewing schedule with golf personalities.

Professional Property Management, Ames, IA
RENTAL CONSULTANT (February–May 2011)
- Answered phone and booked appointments to show rental apartments; prepared lease contracts and paperwork.

Dr. Tricia J. Johnson, Iowa City, IA
NANNY (July 2010–January 2011)
- Performed daily child-care duties and light housekeeping for two children. Provided transportation to and from school and other activities.

Sports-Related Activities

*National Cyclone Club Tent
Welcoming Host
Fall 2011*

*Allianz Championship
Golf Tournament
Office Staff
Fall 2011*

*ISU Sports Camps
Counselor
Summer 2011*

*Hy-Vee Women's
Golf Classic
Media Relations Runner
May 2011*

*ISU Athletic Department &
National Cyclone Club Intern
May–August 2011*

*Riverbend Golf Course
Jr. Golf League Volunteer
Summer 2010*

*Riverbend Golf Course
Couples' League Co-President
Summer 2010*

*Ballard-Huxley
Community Schools
District Golf Champion 2007*

*Ballard-Huxley
Community Schools
Cross-Country Manager 2007*

14

Degree: BA, Sports Management.
Job Target: A postgraduate sports management internship.
Strategy: Student sought to break into the competitive field of sports management by capturing an internship opportunity. Highlighted extensive athletic involvement and a powerful endorsement.

BRIAN JOHNSON—Internship Applicant

Brianjohnson97@gmail.com
478.837.3774

College Address:
17 College Drive, Campus Box 214, Macon, GA 31211
Home Address:
2984 Magnolia Drive, Atlanta, GA 30303

**SPORTS MANAGEMENT MAJOR – COLLEGIATE TEAM ASSISTANT
PROFESSIONAL SPORT ENTHUSIAST**

College junior preparing to launch a successful sports management career built on a strong academic background, 10 years of experience as a player and team assistant for highly competitive teams, and the business background gained through an internship with a top organization.

Maintain statistical reports, support recruitment efforts, and coordinate video production for collegiate team. Quickly build productive relationships with staff, team members, supporters, and fans. Enthusiastically accept all assignments knowing that every task preformed well contributes to the achievement of organizational goals.

"Brian was a key contributor to our ending the 2011 season ranked 10th in Division II."
Henry Thomas, Head Coach, Albright University Soccer Team
2009, 2011 Division II Southern Region Coach of the Year

EDUCATION

B.A., **Sports Management**, Task School of Business, Albright University, Macon, GA

Graduation:	On-track to graduate in May 2013
Academic Standing:	3.5 GPA
Honors:	Dean's Business Scholarship—University Scholarship
Activities:	University Jazz Band—Member Sigma Phi Epsilon Fraternity
Coursework:	**Accounting—Business Law—Management**

EXPERIENCE

ALBRIGHT UNIVERSITY, Macon, GA   2009–Present
ATHLETIC DEPARTMENT—Soccer Program
Video Coordinator / Team Assistant (2009–Present)
Equipment Manager/Filming Assistant (2009)

Earned recognition for professional-level team support as a volunteer giving up to 40 hours per week to prepare for games, maintain statistics, and videotape practices and games for top-ranked Division II team.

Video Production
- Deliver digital video ready for review 10 minutes after practice and 30 minutes after game.
- Showcased quarterback in edited digital video prepared for San Jose Earthquakes scout.
- Exchanged video with opponents and prepared video for review by coaching staff.

Operational Support
- Calculate and verify statistics for American Soccer Coaches Association for All-American Player nominations.
- Arrive early for home and away games to coordinate team set-up. Connect and test on-field audio equipment, set up video equipment, and coordinate with opposing coaching and video staff.
- Set up practice equipment each day during Fall practice.
- Credited with securing parental support for new recruit's participation.

TECHNICAL / COMPUTER SKILLS

Microsoft Office Suite: Word • Excel • PowerPoint • Publisher • Access
RPEX (Video Editing Software)

AWARDS

Eagle Scout—Boy Scouts of America

15

Degree: BS, Accounting.
Job Target: Accounting co-op position.
Strategy: Emphasized coursework and experience as treasurer of fraternity.

Chang Jan Li

862 Trafalgar Court
Rochester, New York
Phone: (585) 359-2109   E-mail: cjli@yahoo.com

---

objective

A challenging cooperative education assignment with a public accounting firm.

education

May 2013
(Anticipated)

Bachelor of Science, Accounting
Rochester Institute of Technology; Rochester, New York
Dean's List; GPA: 3.25/4.00
Outstanding Transfer Scholarship Winner / Trustee Scholarship Winner

significant courses

— Auditing
— Tax Accounting
— Cost Accounting
— Financial Reporting & Analysis (I, II, III)
— Not-for-Profit/Government Accounting

— Operations Management
— Complex Business Organizations
— Corporate Finance (I & II)
— Management Science
— Statistics

May 2010

Associate of Applied Science, Business Administration
Monroe Community College; Rochester, New York
Dean's List — Three Semesters; GPA: 3.5/4.0

activity

Treasurer, Alpha Beta Gamma Honorary Fraternity
— Collect payments and process disbursements.
— Prepare balance sheets and financial statements.
— Submit financial reports to national headquarters and student government.
— Prepare the annual budget for submission to student government.
— Reconcile bank statements.
— Provide financial information to auditor.

computer literacy

MS Windows, Word, Excel, PowerPoint, and Access; Minitab

experience

Summer 2011

Driveway Sealing Technician, College Guys, Inc.; Henrietta, New York
Applied protective coatings to residential driveways and commercial parking areas.
— Edged driveways and performed other preparation work.
— Interfaced with customers to ensure satisfaction.

Summer 2009
Summer 2008

Assembly Line Operator, Federal Automotive; Rochester, New York
Served as part of 10-member team accountable for assembly of V-6 throttle bodies.
— Met daily production quotas.
— Conducted QC inspections of finished pieces.

2006–2009

Head Waiter, Jade Dynasty; Webster, New York
Oversaw the activities of up to four servers.
— Trained servers in procedures and customer-service skills.
— Assigned workstations and side duties to servers; scheduled breaks.
— Resolved operational problems and customer-satisfaction issues.
— Waited on patrons and attended to their needs.

16

Degree: BS, Management (marketing minor).
Job Target: Construction industry internship in the United States.
Strategy: Emphasized the student's experience in previous internships with a foreign construction company. To overcome potential negative perception of his prior experience with a family-owned business in Brazil, drew out valuable experience from his three internships, one with a large, international theater company. The family-owned status of the construction business became irrelevant.

THOMAS M. GOMEZ

7105 Gulf Breeze Circle, Apt. 12C, Tampa, FL 33602 • (813) 971-5916 • tmgomez@aol.com

---

OBJECTIVE: Complete a marketing or management internship with a U.S. construction firm.

EDUCATION

BS Management, Marketing Minor (Candidate), Southwest Florida College, Tampa, FL   May 2013
Relevant Course Work: Advanced Marketing Research
Collaborated with a team to develop a business plan for an information-technology consulting firm.
- ❖ Researched competitors and products, conducted a survey, and created the marketing plan.
- ❖ Received recognition for completing the best project and for conducting the best presentation.

PROFESSIONAL EXPERIENCE

BERTONE CONSTRUCTION, INC., São Paulo, Brazil   2010, 2011
*(Performed two summer **internships**, totaling seven months, with construction company of 1,800 employees that specializes in residential, road, bridge, and governmental construction.)*
- ❖ Analyzed the results of various surveys on construction quality and customer service; surveys were distributed to current and prospective clients to assist the company in penetrating new geographic markets.
- ❖ Developed and implemented various improvements for the corporate Web site, as follows:
  - ▪ Created a page to display company plans, achievements, recognition, and changes.
  - ▪ Established a toll-free customer service line and added the number to the Web site.
  - ▪ Ensured that the "homes for sale" list was updated weekly to delete "sold" properties.
- ❖ Assisted the Vice President of Human Resources with interviewing internship candidates.
- ❖ Participated in researching product pricing among Bertone's 200 vendors for supplies such as cement, steel, electrical appliances, elevators, computers, and other construction materials.
- ❖ Observed the process for updating headquarters on daily progress at 25 construction sites.

WORLDWIDE THEATER COMPANY, Miami, FL   2009
*(Completed a two-month **internship** with the world's second-largest theater company, which operates theaters throughout the U.S. as well as in Latin America, Europe, and Asia.)*
- ❖ Worked with the directors of the legal, construction, real estate, and marketing departments.
- ❖ Observed contract negotiations with vendors for domestic and international construction.
- ❖ Developed an understanding of legal restrictions governing overseas trade.
- ❖ Trained in writing letters of intent, selecting construction sites, and determining theater size.
- ❖ Attended a meeting of 50 managers from throughout the U.S. to conduct strategic planning toward the goals of increasing service offerings and improving the theaters' seating and architecture.
- ❖ Observed all aspects of selecting movies for specific theaters based on location and audience, and became familiar with film-studio negotiations to rent films for multiple venues.

COMPUTER SKILLS   Proficient in MS Word, Excel, and PowerPoint

LANGUAGES   Fluent in English, Portuguese, and Spanish

AFFILIATION   National Association of Hispanic Accountants

17

Degree: AAS, Construction Management.
Job Target: Construction management internship.
Strategy: Led with a strong summary and included details of extensive hands-on construction experience to show long-time interest in the field.

JOSEPH ADAMS

9776 Sol Rio Drive   707.477.6572
Vacaville, CA 95627   josephadams@northerncareer.edu

INTERNSHIP APPLICANT

Full-time college student prepared to utilize strong academic preparation and more than 10 years of experience in the building trades to successfully complete construction management internship. Excel academically and maintain outstanding attendance record at nationally accredited business college. Gained hands-on experience as a laborer and site supervisor for carpentry, roofing, concrete, and window installation projects.

Dependable, motivated self-starter ready to learn and contribute to a construction company.

EDUCATION

A.A.S., **Construction Management**, Northern Career College, Vacaville, CA

Anticipated graduation: July 2012

Awards: Presidential Awards for 4.0 GPA and perfect attendance
                                          Dean's List—Student of the Quarter

Relevant Courses: ✓ Print Reading   ✓ Codes   ✓ Estimating
                               ✓ Construction   ✓ Materials and Methods   ✓ Surveying
                               ✓ Building Safety   ✓ Project Management   ✓ Microsoft Excel
                               ✓ Planning and Scheduling ✓ Basic Accounting   ✓ Career Success

---

CERTIFICATIONS

Cal. OHSA Forklift Certification (current)—California General Contractors License (inactive)

PROFESSIONAL EXPERIENCE

STATE OF CALIFORNIA, Crescent City, CA   2006–2010
Carpenter
- Trusted to independently complete roofing (Densdeck), concrete form set and finish, rebar installation, framing, and sheetrock installations.
- Commended for being hardworking, task-oriented crew member.

L.M. SMITH CORPORATION, Vacaville, CA   1999–2006
Carpenter
- Assigned projects requiring mastery of rough framing and finish work.
- Met government code and client expectations for all concrete projects.
- Independently completed installations of doors, windows, fixtures, drywall, and roofing.

BEST FENCE & LUMBER, Vacaville, CA   1998–1999
Fence Installer
- Laid out fence lines in residential housing tracts in accordance with survey hubs.
- Supervised fence and gate installations from ordering of supplies to final inspection.
- Complimented by clients for quality of work, minimal impact on landscaping, and post-project cleanup.

CITY BUILDERS, Vacaville, CA   1993–1997
Carpenter/Owner
- Completed projects to code and client specifications: installation of concrete work patios and driveways, post-fire remodeling of a Victorian home, and installation of composition shingle roof.
- Secured jobs and customer loyalty with affordable and timely project estimates.
- Managed all administrative functions including pulling of permits.

18

Degree: BFA, Interior Design.
Job Target: Contract design internship.
Strategy: The objective highlights the value of having both design knowledge and business experience (this individual returned to school after completing her first bachelor's degree and working in marketing for several years). The functional approach maps her relevant skills to her achievements from previous employment, her current studies, and her own initiative to make and sell functional art.

Heather Jones

(212) 980-8424 • 100 East 75ᵗʰ Street #2A, New York, NY 10000 • hjones@yahoo.com

Objective

A **Contract Design Internship** utilizing communication and organizational skills in a team-oriented environment. Qualified by a unique blend of design knowledge and a business administration background.

Education

The Interior Design Institute, New York, NY
Bachelor of Fine Arts, Interior Design—expected May 2013
Dean's List Honors, 3.7 GPA

University of Massachusetts, School of Management, Amherst, MA
Bachelor of Science, Business Administration—2008
Dean's List Honors; Major—Marketing, Minor—Advertising

Related Skills & Career Achievements

Creativity & Design
- Rigorous formal training in color theory, perspective, textiles & finishes, construction documents & drafting, materials & methods of construction, codes, residential design, historical styles, art history, architectural design, design history.
- Designed and sold functional art to local stores.
- Collaborated on the design of advertising and direct-mail pieces.

Project Management
- Organized promotional events for Paramount that increased interest in the films.
- Managed trafficking of insertion orders and creative materials for print publications.

Client & Vendor Relations
- Readily inspired confidence of Small Advertising's clients. Numerous media-placement, public-relations, and graphic-design suggestions were accepted and implemented.
- Increased traffic 23% at the Australian Maritime Museum by conceiving and executing a campaign to educate the local hospitality industry about new, interactive exhibits. Initiated a hands-on art/play area to make the museum more family-oriented.
- Consulted one-on-one with students to resolve financial accounts for housing.

Computer Applications
- Proficient in AutoCAD 2011.
- Highly proficient in Windows and Macintosh applications for word processing, spreadsheets, presentations, database management, and Internet navigation.

Career Chronology

Jr. Media Director, Small Advertising Agency, New York, NY	2009–2011
Paramount College Promotions Representative, Film Advertising, Boston, MA	2008
Student Accounts Assistant, University of Massachusetts Housing Office, Amherst, MA	2007–2008
Marketing Promotions Assistant, Australian Maritime Museum, Perth, Australia	2007

Professional Affiliation

ASID, Student Chapter

19

Degree: BS, Neuroscience.
Job Target: Research internship.
Strategy: Presented a broad range of experiences—a prior internship and other medical-related positions—along with a rich education section showcasing college projects and activities.

❧ SUZETTE FERNANDEZ ❧

3308 Lee Highway • Fairfax, VA 22030 • 703-993-1358 • suzette@gmu.edu

NEUROSCIENCE MAJOR
Up-and-coming professional – a recognized leader committed to performance excellence

❧ PROFILE ❧

- Candidate for B.S. degree in neuroscience in May 2012.
- Promising professional with solid academic foundations as well as multiple research and internship experiences in the neuroscience and public health fields.
- Top-performing student recognized for high level of engagement and enthusiasm for learning.
- Organized self-starter who is effective in balancing the demands of competing projects and flexible in adapting to changing needs.
- Skilled communicator who is able to cultivate warm, comfortable working environments – while building a sense of confidence and trust.

❧ EDUCATION ❧

GEORGE MASON UNIVERSITY, Fairfax, VA
Bachelor of Science Degree in Neuroscience with minor in Public Health (expected May 2012)
GPA: 3.69/4.00; Named to Dean's List 5 semesters.

Research/Class Projects:
- Sought out by professor to assist with research on pediatric asthma. Designed and conducted survey to examine attitudes of Hispanic and non-Hispanic parents toward conventional and alternative treatments. Analyzed results that showed clear preference toward prescription medicines despite concerns. Currently writing paper in anticipation of publication in peer-reviewed journal.
- As part of 5-person market research team (2 professors and 3 students), conducted exploratory research to develop methodologies for assessing implicit (subconscious) attitudes, specifically around brand associations. Learned of and programmed DirectRT to detect hidden responses to products. Read articles on subject and participated in team discussions to find solutions to challenges presented.
- Earned high grade in graduate-level course designed to build skill in initiating research projects. As part of activities, identified topic in the area of neuroscience and pain (chronic pain and its treatment in children) and wrote full-length grant proposal that was hypothetically approved for study.

Leadership & Service:
- As a freshman, co-founded local chapter of Students Helping Honduras, a group formed to raise awareness of humanitarian crisis in Honduras. Currently serve as board member (4th year of service).
- Named as Campus Delegate based on recommendation of professor. Serve as ambassador to prospective students (3rd year of service).
- Serve as member of Colleges Against Cancer, promoting support of Relay for Life and other campus events (4th year of service).
- As supporter of World Vision, maintained long-term sponsorship of Rwandan child in need.

❧ INTERNSHIP EXPERIENCE ❧

OFFICE OF DR. RICHARD GRAVES, Fairfax, VA   May 2011 to present
Technician
Provide comprehensive neuropsychological evaluations for doctor's private practice.
- Working primarily with older patients, capably conduct screening tests for a range of neurological disorders, including dementia, stroke, and head injury. Score tests once done and provide report to physician.
- Build warm, supportive atmosphere to encourage and relax patients during extensive day-long testing.

PAGE 1 OF 2

19 *(continued)*

INOVA HOSPITAL, Fairfax, VA   Jan 2011 to May 2011
Intern – Community Health Department
Met with various groups in hospital, gaining exposure to an array of community health programs.

♦ Gained appreciation of the financial and logistical challenges associated with delivering health services within the community.
♦ Conducted literature reviews for Pediatric Asthma project, work that led to a research study conducted jointly with another student on the treatment preferences of caretakers.

❧ OTHER EXPERIENCE ❧

VICTORY PHARMACEUTICALS, Alexandria, VA   May 2009 to Aug 2010
Intern – Memberships & Chargebacks (5/10 to 8/10)   (summers and breaks only)
Maintained and audited database of contracts during company acquisition.

♦ Excelled in position requiring speed, accuracy, and a keen attention to detail, succeeding despite challenges of highly demanding work environment.

Intern – Talent Acquisition (5/09 to 8/09 & 12/09 to 1/10)
Conducted phone screenings for non-exempt positions and coordinated processes for new hires.

♦ Earned high praise from supervisor for organization skills and ability to take on and master advanced responsibilities.

ARLINGTON MEDICAL ASSOCIATES, Arlington, VA   Jan 2008 to Aug 2008
Intern – Family Practice of Dr. Jacobs
Provided office support to doctor and staff members.

♦ Capably organized and filed patient charts, providing easy retrieval.
♦ Gained reputation for providing top-notch customer service to patients.

LA BONBONNIERE FINE PASTRIES, Alexandria, VA   Jun 2006 to Feb 2007
Sales Associate/Assistant Chef
Assisted chef in kitchen and sold baked goods.

♦ Entrusted with opening and closing responsibilities.
♦ Earned praise for maintaining a clean and organized kitchen and store.

❧ COMPUTER SKILLS ❧

Microsoft Word, Excel, PowerPoint, Access
Lotus Notes, Imany CARS, Oracle, Teleserve
SPSS

20

Degree: BS, Biological Sciences.
Job Target: Clinical laboratory internship.
Strategy: Started with a strong profile and list of applicable skills and knowledge. On page 2, highlighted relevant college activities and volunteer experience.

SAMUEL A. MILLER

721 Carl Ave.   (415) 427-5716
Oakland, CA 94615   samiller@aol.com

CLINICAL LABORATORY TRAINEE APPLICANT— Fall 2012

PROFESSIONAL PROFILE

Hard-working, technically proficient Clinical Laboratory Science graduate with the experience, drive, professional commitment, and academic preparation necessary to complete the UC San Francisco training program. Respected laboratory technician with a record of consistently producing research-quality specimens. Gained a critical understanding of the clinical necessity for rapid and accurate laboratory testing by volunteering for more than 2 years in a hospital emergency room. Willingly accepted leadership roles in professional organizations.

TECHNICAL SKILLS AND KNOWLEDGE

- ✓ Micropipetting, buffer, and serial dilution preparation
- ✓ Conventional and inverted light microscopy
- ✓ Aseptic technique, media preparation, and autoclaving
- ✓ Chromatography and Gel Electrophoresis
- ✓ Eukaryotic and prokaryotic cell culturing
- ✓ Eukaryotic cell counting
- ✓ Preparation and analysis of live-dead eukaryotic cell assays
- ✓ Gram staining
- ✓ ELISA

EDUCATION

B.S., Biological Sciences, California State University, San Francisco, CA   2012
Concentrations: Microbiology and Clinical Laboratory Science
Minor: Chemistry
CSUSF GPA: 3.3
Coursework completed

✓ PATHOGENIC	✓ ANALYTICAL	✓ BODY FLUID	✓ BIOCHEMISTRY
✓ BACTERIOLOGY	CHEMISTRY	ANALYSIS	✓ IMMUNOLOGY
✓ MICROBIOLOGY	✓ MYCOLOGY	✓ HEMATOLOGY	✓ EPIDEMIOLOGY
✓ PARASITOLOGY	✓ VIROLOGY	✓ GENETICS	✓ CELLULAR PHYSIOLOGY

Additional College Coursework
San Francisco Community College District—General Education and **Biological Sciences**
Chabot College (Fall 2006–Summer 2008—3.514 GPA)
Oakland City College (Fall 2008—3.0 GPA)
Solano Community College (Spring 1994–Spring 1995—3.63 GPA)

PROFESSIONAL EXPERIENCE

CALIFORNIA STATE UNIVERSITY, San Francisco, CA   2010–Present
Laboratory Research Assistant
- Apply aseptic technique for colony isolation, identification, and freeze-back preparations.
- Complete media preparation and laboratory clean-up/autoclaving.

CONTINUED

---

20 *(continued)*

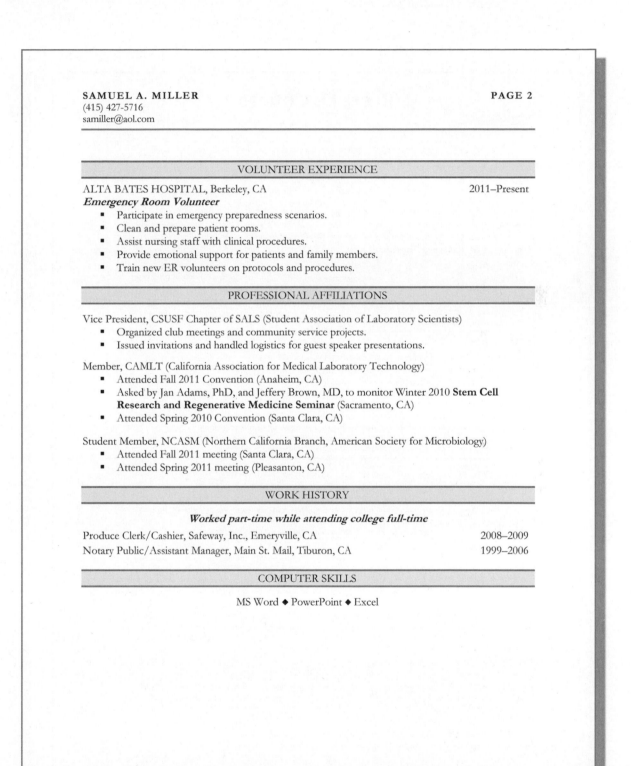

SAMUEL A. MILLER
(415) 427-5716
samiller@aol.com

PAGE 2

VOLUNTEER EXPERIENCE

ALTA BATES HOSPITAL, Berkeley, CA   2011–Present
Emergency Room Volunteer
- Participate in emergency preparedness scenarios.
- Clean and prepare patient rooms.
- Assist nursing staff with clinical procedures.
- Provide emotional support for patients and family members.
- Train new ER volunteers on protocols and procedures.

PROFESSIONAL AFFILIATIONS

Vice President, CSUSF Chapter of SALS (Student Association of Laboratory Scientists)
- Organized club meetings and community service projects.
- Issued invitations and handled logistics for guest speaker presentations.

Member, CAMLT (California Association for Medical Laboratory Technology)
- Attended Fall 2011 Convention (Anaheim, CA)
- Asked by Jan Adams, PhD, and Jeffery Brown, MD, to monitor Winter 2010 **Stem Cell Research and Regenerative Medicine Seminar** (Sacramento, CA)
- Attended Spring 2010 Convention (Santa Clara, CA)

Student Member, NCASM (Northern California Branch, American Society for Microbiology)
- Attended Fall 2011 meeting (Santa Clara, CA)
- Attended Spring 2011 meeting (Pleasanton, CA)

WORK HISTORY

Worked part-time while attending college full-time

Produce Clerk/Cashier, Safeway, Inc., Emeryville, CA   2008–2009
Notary Public/Assistant Manager, Main St. Mail, Tiburon, CA   1999–2006

COMPUTER SKILLS

MS Word ◆ PowerPoint ◆ Excel

21

Degree: BS, Political Science.
Job Target: Congressional internship.
Strategy: Played up political involvement as a student.

Brett D. Covers

2024 Metallic Avenue
Portsmouth, NH 03803

Home: (603) 257-3572
Mobile: (603) 257-7445

*"Politics is the cog that runs our country; it's an extension of education, a constant challenge,
and it's where my heart is."* —Brett D. Covers

Seeking Congressional Internship

Industrious university student with strong work ethic and a lifetime ambition to learn and participate in entire
legislative process. Tactful and diplomatic, easily establish rapport at diverse socioeconomic levels. Possess
excellent problem-solving, research, and time-management skills. Dedicated, trusted, respected team player.
Classified Forest Firefighter I with Haz-Mat and CPR/First Aid Certifications. Attended fund-raising dinner for
42nd District, Republican Party; acquainted with House Republican Organizational Committee.

Areas of Special Ability and Experience:

- Networking
- Campaigns—
  David B. Hunter
  Marta Guevara
  Student Body President,
  Portsmouth High School

- Delegation
- Legal internship
- Research
- Mentoring—
  4th-graders

- PC / Mac computer—
  word processing, database,
  spreadsheet, Internet
- Communication—oral/written
- Firefighting

EDUCATION

B.S., Political Science, University of New Hampshire, Durham, NH   Anticipated 2013

Pi Sigma Alpha Honorary Political Science Association, April 2011

Exterior Liaison (elected position) for Political Science Association, Associated Students Club, 9/2010–present
Perform public speaking, organize campus events, and network with various campus organizations.
Communicate with administrative staff to reserve rooms and ensure proper accommodations
for events. Network off-campus with community leaders. Engage speakers for on-campus events.

Floor Representative (elected position), Nother Hall Dormitory, 9/2009–5/2010
Worked with Residential Director to organize dormitory social events. Collaborated with other
dormitories and residential directors to raise money to fund events.

WORK HISTORY

PART-TIME AND SUMMER EMPLOYMENT WHILE ATTENDING HIGH SCHOOL AND COLLEGE

Sales Associate, Express Men (Clothing Store), Fox Run Mall, Portsmouth, NH   11/2010–present
Organize "floor" to ensure all is clean and orderly and clothing is properly stocked and displayed. Provide
cashiering and quality customer service.
Achieved highest sale per transaction average within two months on the job.

Legal Internship, David C. Founder, Esq., Family Law, Portsmouth, NH   3/2010–6/2010
Researched and gathered evidence for cases; filed pleadings with the court; communicated with judges and lawyers.
Composed letters to clients and other lawyers. Served papers on behalf of plaintiffs and defendants. Worked with a
variety of socioeconomic populations. Analyzed and prepared financial declarations. Performed basic clerical duties
such as answering phones, filing, and word processing. Cooperated with public agencies in collecting and providing
information.

Forest Firefighter, Department of Natural Resources   Summers 2009, 2010, and continuing
Dedicated member of firefighting team with special assignment as sawyer (chain-saw operator) for firefighting
crew. Constantly aware and alert to ensuring the safety of others. Operate engines, pumps, and other heavy
equipment.

Photographer, Sons Photography, Portsmouth, NH   8/2009
Photographed students for elementary and high school yearbooks.

Barista, Cranston's Bagel and Espresso Shop, Strawberry Banke, NH   4/2006–8/2007, Summer 2008
Made and served espresso drinks; cashiered. Opened and closed; balanced till daily. Trained new employees.

AWARDS

Leadership Awards, 2008 and 2009, Portsmouth High School
Senior Essay Award (college scholarship), Portsmouth High School

22

Degree: BA, Political Science.
Job Target: Congressional internship.
Strategy: Used graphic enhancements, including a check box at the top and a photograph at the bottom, to create a visually distinctive resume.

SARAH SMITH

1904 Linda Vista Drive, Stockton, CA 95304
209.566.6020 ♦ sarahsmith@gmail.com

☑ Social Advocate

☑ Consensus Builder

☑ Strategic Planner

☑ Customer Service
Award Recipient

Experienced, energetic, hard-working college graduate ready to begin a career in public service as a **legislative intern**. Grassroots participation in successful implementation of government-legislated renewable energy, transportation, and water management programs. Record of building awareness and empowering peers to advocate for social justice.

Prepared professional eager to provide administrative and technical support for elected officials and legislative staff and utilize excellent verbal and written communications skills to inform and update constituencies.

EDUCATION

BA, **Political Science**, University of California, Santa Cruz, CA   2012
    Minor: Human Development
    • Member, UCSC Inter-Faith Student Association
    • Member, STAND—Genocide Intervention Network

University of California Summer Abroad Program, University of London, England   Summer 2011
    • Studied planned community development.
    • Shadowed local government officials, architects, and city planners.

GOVERNMENT RELATIONS EXPERIENCE

VISIONARY PRODUCTIONS, Watsonville, CA   2005–2006
Production Intern
    • Photographed and videotaped political and community issue forums.
    • Maintained files, booked appointments, and operated office machines.

WORK HISTORY

WORKED WHILE ATTENDING COLLEGE FULL-TIME

UNIVERSITY OF CALIFORNIA, Santa Cruz, CA   2010–2012
ARTS AND RECREATION CENTER
Event Technician
    • Provided technical and aesthetic support for weddings, commencements, and conferences.
    • Greeted and provided information to guests.

WELLS FARGO BANK, Watsonville, CA   2008–2009
Teller
    • Processed and verified accuracy of transactions.
    • **Received Quarterly Awards for excellent customer service.**

BASKIN ROBBINS, Watsonville, CA   2006–2008
Assistant Manager
    • Quickly promoted to assistant manager.
    • Screened applicants and scheduled staff.

TECHNICAL SKILLS

MS Excel ♦ Word ♦ PowerPoint

BRINGING COMMITMENT, UNDERSTANDING, AND PASSION TO THE LEGISLATIVE PROCESS

23

Degree: BA, Criminal Justice.
Job Target: FBI Honors Internship Program.
Strategy: Pulled out the relevant skills and achievements in a separate column on the left for impact. Highlights of Qualifications section sets the stage for the reader to perceive the graduate as an achiever.

MARIA TERESITA GOMEZ

OBJECTIVE: FBI Honors Internship Program

HIGHLIGHTS OF QUALIFICATIONS

- ☑ Self-motivated, disciplined individual with an intense desire to succeed.
- ☑ Able to achieve results independently and as a cooperative team member.
- ☑ Successfully developed and implemented aerobic programs for all athletic levels.
- ☑ Resourceful, creative, and diligent. Noted for consistent professional manner.

LEADERSHIP

- As Freshmen Orientation Leader, addressed groups of incoming freshmen on academic requirements and college life, and assisted them in registration process for 3 orientations.

- In the Marathon Township Police Department Intern Program, entrusted with collecting evidence, such as fingerprints, and accurately cataloguing it in police database. Assisted in speed surveys in the ride-along program.

FITNESS PROGRAM COACH

- Personally instructed and motivated groups in aerobic exercises (3 classes weekly with 30 students) for 2 private fitness centers.

- As Exercise Coach at Dennison College, oriented new members to gym, tailoring the basic program to meet their varying levels and goals. Supervised and evaluated 10 work-study students in gym. Monitored gym members' fitness-level progress and made recommendations for improvement.

PERSONAL ACHIEVEMENTS

- Achieved Dean's List status for 4 years.

- Won title as Dennison Women's Body-Building Champion for 2011.

- Elected President of Police Explorers during high school.

EDUCATION

Bachelor of Arts (B.A.)   May 2012
Criminal Justice and Administration and Planning,
Dennison College of Criminal Justice, New York City

Certifications: Water & Boat Safety, Brown Belt (Karate)

EMPLOYMENT HISTORY

Freshman Orientation Leader   2008–2012
and Exercise Coach
Dennison College, New York City

Intern, Marathon Township Police Dept.   2008
Marathon Township, NJ

Aerobics Instructor   2006–2008
Pump Iron Gym, Hillsborough, NJ
Synergy Spa, Princeton, NJ

COMPUTER SKILLS

Windows and Mac OS
MS Office (Word, Excel, PowerPoint, Outlook)

LANGUAGES

Proficient in Spanish—conversation, reading, and writing.
Knowledge of French and Portuguese.
Currently studying Chinese.

PROFESSIONAL MEMBERSHIPS

Aerobic Association International, member since 2006
International Sports Medicine Assoc., member since 2006

mariagomez@juno.com ▪ **(212) 765-5555**
355 W. 101th Street, New York, NY 10025

24

Degree: BS, Chemical Engineering.
Job Target: Relevant internship or co-op job.
Strategy: Use the Relevant Experience and Skills section to show areas of strength from past employment that are contributing factors to success in the engineering field.

DERRICK S. THOMAS

903 Osage Trail • Manhattan, Kansas 66502 • H: 785-246-3030 • CENGINEER@aol.com

OBJECTIVE

To obtain an internship or co-op position while completing my degree in chemical engineering.

HIGHLIGHTS OF QUALIFICATIONS

- Highly organized and dedicated, with a positive attitude.
- Resourceful; skilled in analyzing and solving problems.
- Good written, verbal, and interpersonal communications.
- Ability to prioritize; complete multiple tasks under stressful situations.
- Proficient in Microsoft Office (Word, PowerPoint, Excel, Access) and Internet resources.
- Fluent in Russian, Serbian, and Croatian.

RELEVANT EXPERIENCE & SKILLS

Research & Analysis

- Trained in interception, transcription, and translation of foreign voice transmissions throughout Germany, Russia, and the United States.
- Experienced in collecting, recording, and distributing secure intelligence information.
- Demonstrated ability to operate intercept receivers to include radio telephones, multichannel systems, and recording equipment.
- Possess a Top Secret Security Clearance granted by the United States Army and the Department of Defense.

Supervision & Training

- Supervised daily activities of personnel, quickly shifting priorities as requested by upper management.
- Provided professional staff training in the areas of new techniques, safety, equipment use, and quality control.

Customer Service & Communications

- Effectively interacted with a wide range of diverse, culturally varied individuals; established and maintained positive interaction with the general public in customer-service capacities.
- Successfully prepared, scheduled, and conducted specialized security training, briefings, and surveys to enhance the security of supported units.

EDUCATION

Bachelor of Science: Chemical Engineering   Expected 2013
Kansas State University, Manhattan, Kansas
Graduate, Defense Language Institute, Monterey, California

WORK HISTORY

Military Linguist and Analyst, United States Army   2004 to 2009

25

Degree: BS, Chemical Engineering.
Job Target: Chemical engineering co-op.
Strategy: Made this young man stand out by using a creative logo and highlighting special skills learned from past three co-ops and leadership in collegiate extracurricular activities. These skills carry over into the workplace and would certainly be emphasized in a cover letter.

WILLIAM ROSS

Permanent Contact
(419) 424-1927
ring215@yahoo.com

Home Address
2009 Churchill Drive
Findlay, OH 45840

Objective: Chemical Engineering Co-Op

PROFILE

A detail-oriented, high-energy individual with keen problem-solving and analytical skills as evidenced by the ability to provide analysis and recommendations to improve plant operations. Strong interpersonal, planning, and organizational skills demonstrated in chemical engineering internships. Qualified by

- Contributing independently, or as part of a team, to coordinate and to manage projects ranging from floor layout designs and thermodynamic calculations to the reproduction of obsolete parts.

- Excellent performance records and personal reviews in three previous co-op positions.

COMPETENCIES

Equipment Functionality Analysis	Capital Project Planning & Management
Equipment Design & Operations	Time Management
Financial Project Analysis	Multidisciplinary Teams
Leadership	Research & Documentation Methods

INTERN EXPERIENCE

BIOTECH ACRYLICS LLC, Hamilton, OH
Maintenance and Engineering Department Co-Op   12/11–3/12
- Researched specifications for a large batch mixer Capital Project and collaborated across business functions to develop engineering operating requirements from startup to installation.
- Facilitated meetings for approval, design, and assembly of new polyfilm applicator. Performed troubleshooting and necessary field changes.
- Collaborated with team members to reengineer bulk powder flow in a hopper of material, improving speed of production process.

Maintenance and Engineering Department Co-Op   6/11–9/11
- Gathered and calculated daily loadings on cooling tower and water chiller to ensure adequate amounts for current usages. Designed backup system for emergency situations.
- Developed layout designs for plant utilities room to house installation of new vacuum system and made improvements to the existing system.
- Compiled information on causes of chemical tote pump failures and developed solutions for reducing breakdown frequency.

Production Department Co-Op   1/11–3/11
- Redesigned plant pigment room layout to accommodate new scales and equipment.
- Worked extensively on updating new plant system P&IDs to "as-built" drawings.
- Modified pump controls to meet operating procedures required by OSHA.

EDUCATION

UNIVERSITY of CINCINNATI, Cincinnati, OH
Bachelor in Chemical Engineering   GPA: 3.44
Major: Chemical Engineering   Anticipated Graduation: December 2012

ACTIVITIES & LEADERSHIP

- University of Cincinnati Chapter Habitat for Humanity, **Treasurer & Collegiate Challenge Coordinator**
  - LeaderShape Institute ▪ Racial Awareness Pilot Program (RAPP) ▪ UC Bookstore Employee

CHAPTER 7

Resumes for Graduates with Bachelor's Degrees

Resume Number	Degree	Job Target
26	BS, Business Administration	Marketing position
27	BA, Business Administration	Human resources/management training position
28	BA, Business Administration	Retail manager
29	BS, Construction Engineering	Sales position
30	BS, Construction Engineering	Construction engineer
31	BA, Communication Sciences and Disorders	Graduate school admission
32	BA, Spanish; BA, German	Lay church leader
33	BA, Visual Art and Art History	Arts management position
34	BS, Finance and Economics	Financial services representative
35	BS, Business Administration/Finance	Finance position
36	BA, Communications	Pharmaceutical salesperson
37	BS, Marketing	Marketing associate
38	BA, Geography	Customer service representative
39	BA (in progress)	Retail salesperson
40	BS, Business Administration/Marketing	Sports-related marketing position
41	BA, Spanish	Communications/public relations/sales/customer service position
42	BS, Communications	Ad copywriter or account executive
43	BFA, Fashion Design and Fashion Merchandising	Fashion coach or stylist
44	BA, Architecture	Architect
45	BA, Interior Design	Interior designer
46	BFA, Photography	Fine-arts museum position
47	BS, Elementary Education	Elementary school teacher
48	BA, Education	High-school history, political science, or geography teacher
49	BA, Health and Exercise Science/Health and Physical Education	Health and physical education teacher
50	BA, Sociology	Social researcher
51	BS, Sociology	Position assisting people with disabilities
52	BA, Psychology	Human service position

Resume Number	Degree	Job Target
53	BA, Gerontology	Geriatric care manager
54	BA, Psychology and Sociology	Criminal justice position
55	BS, Criminal Justice	Victim/witness program coordinator
56	BS, Biological Sciences and BS, Psychology	Crime scene investigator
57	BS, Pathologist's Assistant	Pathologist's assistant
58	BS, Agricultural Studies	Agribusiness position
59	BS, Nursing	Registered Nurse
60	BS, Civil Engineering	Wastewater civil engineer
61	BS, Chemical Engineering	Chemical engineer
62	BS, Management Computer Information Systems	Help desk technician
63	BS, Technology	Automotive mechanical designer
64	BS, Applied Science	Systems analyst
65	BS, Accounting	Accountant
66	Bachelor of Commerce	Corporate accountant
67	BS, Marine Business	Marine business position, investment/ financial analyst, or market researcher
68	BS, Business Management	Management trainee
69	BA, Political Science	Investment banking/financial services position
70	BA, Strategic Communications/ Advertising	Advertising or marketing position
71	BS, Economics	Retail manager
72	BA, Human Resources	Human Resources position
73	BS, Communications	Graduate hall director

Degree: BS, Business Administration.
Job Target: Marketing position.
Strategy: Highlighted coursework and school projects in the Summary of Qualifications section to create a rich profile that supports this graduate's goal of a career in marketing.

Morgan Sorrenson

2245 San Juan Drive • Irvine, CA 92602 • (714) 803-4274
msorrenson235@gmail.com • http://www.linkedin.com/in/morgansorrenson

---

Marketing & Business Management

Outgoing and entrepreneurially driven professional, well rounded by a comprehensive business curriculum and diverse work experience. Excellent sales presentation skills. Track record for achieving results through market research, strategic planning, and rigorous follow-up.

Summary of Qualifications

Marketing & Business Development: Generated new business and increased sales revenue using market analysis, multi-marketing strategies, and professional sales practices. Cultivated leads through networking, direct mail, trade shows, and Internet marketing.

Economic & Financial Analysis: Successfully completed a broad range of business coursework, including Economics I & II, Accounting I & II, Business Statistics, Database Marketing, and Direct/Interactive Marketing. Translated principles into practical application.
—**Marketing News** (Fall 2010)
Performed marketing research for a targeted geographical area. Analyzed data to determine significant trends. Formulated recommendations to improve company's market presence.

Project Planning & Management: Planned and executed business projects.
—**Mugs with Class** (Spring 2011)
Created a business plan for a proposed online enterprise detailing project startup requirements, budget parameters, financing, marketing, and operational activity.

—**Business Student Association Events** (Fall 2010 & Spring 2011)
Led committee planning activities and program oversight for annual recruitment and fundraising. Produced record-breaking results through strong team building and multi-marketing efforts.

Project overviews available upon request.

Education

Bachelor of Science (B.S.) in Business Administration
UNIVERSITY OF CALIFORNIA, IRVINE   2011

Extracurricular Activities
Vice President, Recruitment, Business Student Association (Fall 2010)
Alumni Relations Coordinator, Business Student Association (Fall 2009)

Work Experience

Sales Representative, CELLULAR, SERVICE & MORE, Irvine, CA   2010–Present
Identify customer needs and tailor products to meet their requirements. Disseminate detailed product and service information. Process transactions.
• Consistently exceed sales targets through first-rate service and in-depth product knowledge.
• Utilize a diplomatic, solution-driven approach to resolve complaints and promote customer confidence and loyalty.

Server, HYATT REGENCY, Newport Beach, CA   2008–2010
Subsidized educational expenses working part time in various food service jobs, including food server, room service attendant, and banquet server.
• Managed multiple demands and fluctuating work pace while delivering quality service.

27

Degree: BA, Business Administration.
Job Target: Human resources/management training position.
Strategy: Culled relevant HR experience from five years in retail, and then used side headings to highlight relevant areas of education and experience.

Christopher Dell

29 Highland Avenue
Stoneham, MA 02180
chrisdell@attglobal.net
781-749-2059

GOAL	**Management Training opportunity with emphasis in Human Resources**
SUMMARY OF QUALIFICATIONS	• Bachelor's degree in Business Administration, with concentration in management and additional coursework in organizational behavior. • Track record of advancement based on capabilities, work ethic, and enthusiasm. • Management experience in a fast-paced retail environment. • Training responsibility for all new employees and new managers for 12-store retail district. • Ability to effectively supervise and motivate staff to high performance levels. • Understanding of bottom-line priorities and the importance of customer satisfaction.
EDUCATION *December 2012*	Boston College, Chestnut Hill, MA **Bachelor of Arts in Business Administration** Area of Emphasis: Management

Relevant Coursework

Accounting	*Organizational Management*	*Organizational Behavior*
Economics	*Small Business Management*	*Operations Management*
Finance	*Administrative Personnel Systems*	*First Line Supervisor*
Business Law	*Quantitative Methods for Business*	*Introduction to Computers*
Statistics	*High Performance Teams in Business*	

Accomplishments

• Personally financed 100% of college education through full-time employment; completed bachelor's degree in 4½ years.
• Won Coach's Award as member of track team, freshman year.

EXPERIENCE
2007–Present

BEST BUY—Promoted through 5 levels to current position as second-in-command at the busiest location in the Boston area. Recognized for abilities in training, managing, and motivating staff; providing excellent customer service; and demonstrating initiative and responsibility.

Senior Assistant Manager, Woburn, MA
Train and manage customer service staff and oversee store operations to ensure customer satisfaction, operating efficiency, and compliance with corporate procedures. Handle and resolve customer questions and complaints. Help manage store revenue; handle cash and balance totals. Maintain well-organized inventory and keep customer service staff on track with ongoing operational duties. Manage entire store during manager's absence.

Human Resources and Training

• Assist with interviewing and participate in hiring decisions.
• With store manager, selected as regional training team for a newly launched corporate training program. Personally train all new employees for 12-store North Shore district through week-long program of on-site instruction, observation, and testing; also train new managers in a 3-week program.
• Developed a wide range of training and motivational methods to build on strengths and improve weaknesses of individual employees.

Customer Service

• Communicate customer-service focus to staff, working hard to keep lines short, inventories clean and well stocked, and staff focused on courtesy and helpfulness.
• Developed organizational system for fast, error-free restocking of returned items.

Staff Supervision

• Create effective supervisory relationship with each employee, adapting management style to best motivate individual staff members.

28

Degree: BA, Business Administration.
Job Target: Retail management.
Strategy: For this second resume for the same individual (see Resume 27), reversed order of education and experience because employment was directly related to the career target.

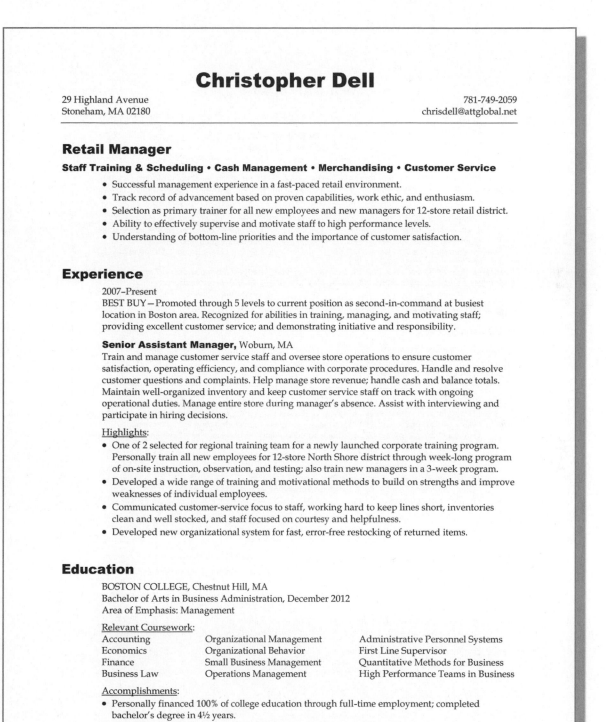

Christopher Dell

29 Highland Avenue
Stoneham, MA 02180

781-749-2059
chrisdell@attglobal.net

Retail Manager
Staff Training & Scheduling • Cash Management • Merchandising • Customer Service

- Successful management experience in a fast-paced retail environment.
- Track record of advancement based on proven capabilities, work ethic, and enthusiasm.
- Selection as primary trainer for all new employees and new managers for 12-store retail district.
- Ability to effectively supervise and motivate staff to high performance levels.
- Understanding of bottom-line priorities and the importance of customer satisfaction.

Experience

2007–Present
BEST BUY—Promoted through 5 levels to current position as second-in-command at busiest location in Boston area. Recognized for abilities in training, managing, and motivating staff; providing excellent customer service; and demonstrating initiative and responsibility.

Senior Assistant Manager, Woburn, MA
Train and manage customer service staff and oversee store operations to ensure customer satisfaction, operating efficiency, and compliance with corporate procedures. Handle and resolve customer questions and complaints. Help manage store revenue; handle cash and balance totals. Maintain well-organized inventory and keep customer service staff on track with ongoing operational duties. Manage entire store during manager's absence. Assist with interviewing and participate in hiring decisions.

Highlights:
- One of 2 selected for regional training team for a newly launched corporate training program. Personally train all new employees for 12-store North Shore district through week-long program of on-site instruction, observation, and testing; also train new managers in a 3-week program.
- Developed a wide range of training and motivational methods to build on strengths and improve weaknesses of individual employees.
- Communicated customer-service focus to staff, working hard to keep lines short, inventories clean and well stocked, and staff focused on courtesy and helpfulness.
- Developed new organizational system for fast, error-free restocking of returned items.

Education

BOSTON COLLEGE, Chestnut Hill, MA
Bachelor of Arts in Business Administration, December 2012
Area of Emphasis: Management

Relevant Coursework:

Accounting	Organizational Management	Administrative Personnel Systems
Economics	Organizational Behavior	First Line Supervisor
Finance	Small Business Management	Quantitative Methods for Business
Business Law	Operations Management	High Performance Teams in Business

Accomplishments:
- Personally financed 100% of college education through full-time employment; completed bachelor's degree in 4½ years.
- Won Coach's Award as member of track team, freshman year.

29

Degree: BS, Construction Engineering.
Job Target: Sales position. (This resume and Resume 30 were written for the same individual seeking two different job targets.)
Strategy: Highlighted entrepreneurial ventures showing measurable sales results; downplayed engineering details of education, projects, and internships.

JORDAN JONES

3834 39TH Street   Home: 806.788.1111
Lubbock, TX 79413   jjones50@aol.com   Mobile: 806.239.1555

QUALIFICATIONS PROFILE
Sales, Business, and Leadership

Talented, resourceful, and dedicated professional offering a unique combination of professional skills. Experienced in developing entrepreneurial businesses and customer relationships. Enthusiastic and detail-oriented. Competitive, decisive, and committed to professional growth and opportunity. Experience includes

- Strategic Planning & Business Development
- Competitive Market Positioning
- Marketing & Sales Development
- Team Building & Leadership

- Business Vision & Strategy
- Customer Development & Relationships
- Special Projects Management
- Numbers Management & Estimating

"Jordan has been successful in both businesses, which he built from the ground up. Jordan is not a stranger to a hard day's work. He will be an asset to any quality organization."
—Kirk Curtis, Director of Marketing, A Group

EDUCATION

Bachelor of Science, Construction Engineering, Texas Tech University, Lubbock, TX, 2012
- Worked throughout college career and earned a 3.1 GPA.
- Recognized on Dean's List, Spring 2011.
- Awarded three scholarships.

Presentations:
- Developed and presented a business and marketing plan for a mobile car wash.
- Planned and presented as a team member a project developed for a local business.
- Researched and presented a project, demonstrating the resolution of a problem for a business.

Specialized Courses:
- Computer Programming
- Contracts & Specifications
- Cost Estimating
- Project Management

- Statistical Methods
- Cost & Profit Analysis
- Professional & Business Communications

Honor graduate, Coronado High School (CHS), Lubbock, Texas • May 2008
- Lettered two years, Varsity Basketball; received All-Academic Athlete Award
- Participant: National Honor Society and Bell Crew Spirit Squad

"Jordan is a winner in every sense of the word."
—Barry Knight, CHS Head Basketball Coach

EXPERIENCE

Owner / Operator
Jordan Jones Mobile Car Care, Lubbock, TX • 2009 to Present
After selling a former business, developed a second entrepreneurial venture, a mobile car wash company.

- Developed more than 25 regular clients.
- Maintain excellent client relationships with a 100% satisfaction rate.
- Drove business to more than $5K in profits annually.

Continued

29 *(continued)*

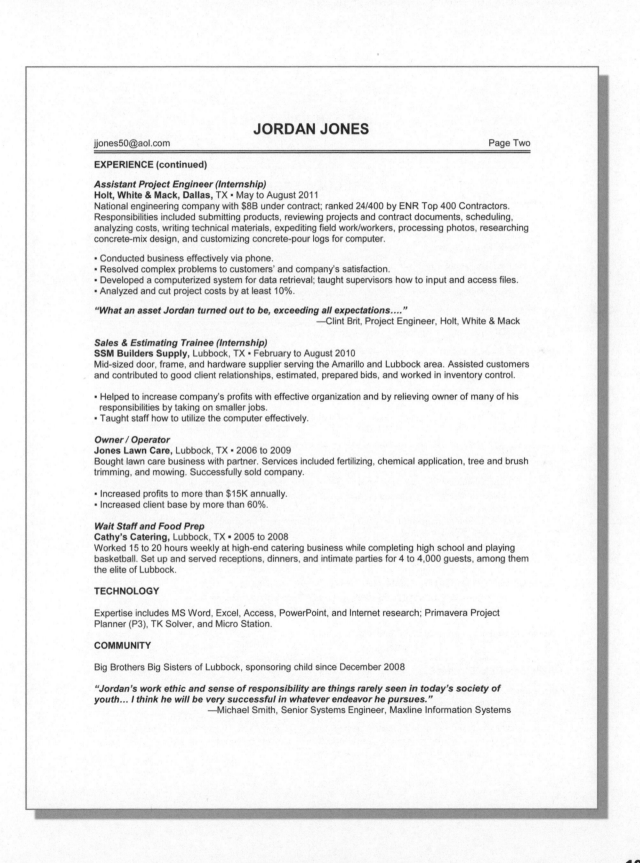

JORDAN JONES

jjones50@aol.com   Page Two

EXPERIENCE (continued)

Assistant Project Engineer (Internship)
Holt, White & Mack, Dallas, TX ▪ May to August 2011
National engineering company with $8B under contract; ranked 24/400 by ENR Top 400 Contractors. Responsibilities included submitting products, reviewing projects and contract documents, scheduling, analyzing costs, writing technical materials, expediting field work/workers, processing photos, researching concrete-mix design, and customizing concrete-pour logs for computer.

▪ Conducted business effectively via phone.
▪ Resolved complex problems to customers' and company's satisfaction.
▪ Developed a computerized system for data retrieval; taught supervisors how to input and access files.
▪ Analyzed and cut project costs by at least 10%.

"What an asset Jordan turned out to be, exceeding all expectations...."
                                                              —Clint Brit, Project Engineer, Holt, White & Mack

Sales & Estimating Trainee (Internship)
SSM Builders Supply, Lubbock, TX ▪ February to August 2010
Mid-sized door, frame, and hardware supplier serving the Amarillo and Lubbock area. Assisted customers and contributed to good client relationships, estimated, prepared bids, and worked in inventory control.

▪ Helped to increase company's profits with effective organization and by relieving owner of many of his responsibilities by taking on smaller jobs.
▪ Taught staff how to utilize the computer effectively.

Owner / Operator
Jones Lawn Care, Lubbock, TX ▪ 2006 to 2009
Bought lawn care business with partner. Services included fertilizing, chemical application, tree and brush trimming, and mowing. Successfully sold company.

▪ Increased profits to more than $15K annually.
▪ Increased client base by more than 60%.

Wait Staff and Food Prep
Cathy's Catering, Lubbock, TX ▪ 2005 to 2008
Worked 15 to 20 hours weekly at high-end catering business while completing high school and playing basketball. Set up and served receptions, dinners, and intimate parties for 4 to 4,000 guests, among them the elite of Lubbock.

TECHNOLOGY

Expertise includes MS Word, Excel, Access, PowerPoint, and Internet research; Primavera Project Planner (P3), TK Solver, and Micro Station.

COMMUNITY

Big Brothers Big Sisters of Lubbock, sponsoring child since December 2008

"Jordan's work ethic and sense of responsibility are things rarely seen in today's society of youth... I think he will be very successful in whatever endeavor he pursues."
                                                              —Michael Smith, Senior Systems Engineer, Maxline Information Systems

30

Degree: BS, Construction Engineering.
Job Target: Construction engineering position (see Resume 29).
Strategy: Highlighted engineering details of education and projects; brought internship experience to the fore and downplayed entrepreneurial ventures.

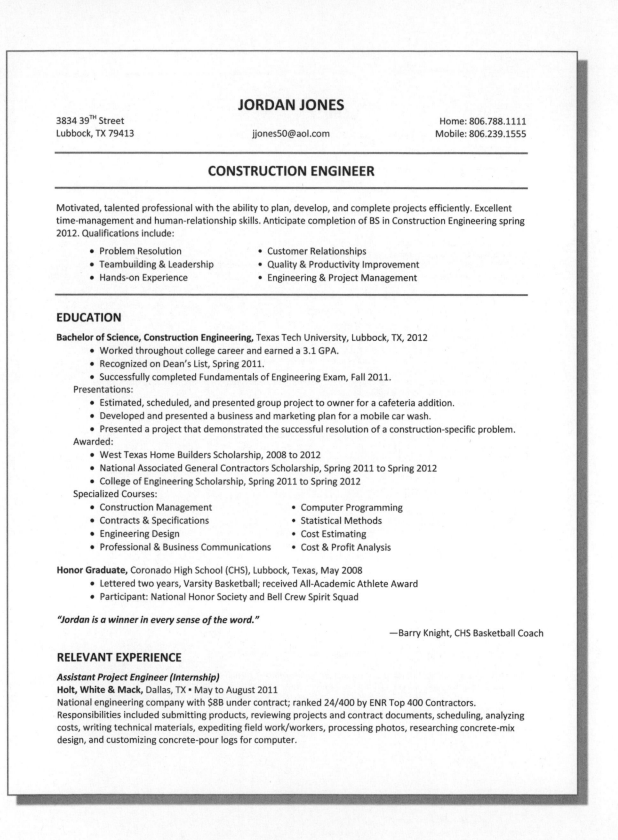

JORDAN JONES

3834 39TH Street
Lubbock, TX 79413

jjones50@aol.com

Home: 806.788.1111
Mobile: 806.239.1555

CONSTRUCTION ENGINEER

Motivated, talented professional with the ability to plan, develop, and complete projects efficiently. Excellent time-management and human-relationship skills. Anticipate completion of BS in Construction Engineering spring 2012. Qualifications include:

- Problem Resolution
- Teambuilding & Leadership
- Hands-on Experience
- Customer Relationships
- Quality & Productivity Improvement
- Engineering & Project Management

EDUCATION

Bachelor of Science, Construction Engineering, Texas Tech University, Lubbock, TX, 2012
- Worked throughout college career and earned a 3.1 GPA.
- Recognized on Dean's List, Spring 2011.
- Successfully completed Fundamentals of Engineering Exam, Fall 2011.

Presentations:
- Estimated, scheduled, and presented group project to owner for a cafeteria addition.
- Developed and presented a business and marketing plan for a mobile car wash.
- Presented a project that demonstrated the successful resolution of a construction-specific problem.

Awarded:
- West Texas Home Builders Scholarship, 2008 to 2012
- National Associated General Contractors Scholarship, Spring 2011 to Spring 2012
- College of Engineering Scholarship, Spring 2011 to Spring 2012

Specialized Courses:
- Construction Management
- Contracts & Specifications
- Engineering Design
- Professional & Business Communications
- Computer Programming
- Statistical Methods
- Cost Estimating
- Cost & Profit Analysis

Honor Graduate, Coronado High School (CHS), Lubbock, Texas, May 2008
- Lettered two years, Varsity Basketball; received All-Academic Athlete Award
- Participant: National Honor Society and Bell Crew Spirit Squad

"Jordan is a winner in every sense of the word."

—Barry Knight, CHS Basketball Coach

RELEVANT EXPERIENCE

Assistant Project Engineer (Internship)
Holt, White & Mack, Dallas, TX • May to August 2011
National engineering company with $8B under contract; ranked 24/400 by ENR Top 400 Contractors. Responsibilities included submitting products, reviewing projects and contract documents, scheduling, analyzing costs, writing technical materials, expediting field work/workers, processing photos, researching concrete-mix design, and customizing concrete-pour logs for computer.

30 *(continued)*

JORDAN JONES

jjones50@aol.com   Page Two

Holt, White & Mack, continued

- Analyzed and cut costs for project by at least 10%.
- Developed computerized system for data retrieval; taught project engineers to input and access files.
- Resolved complex technical problems and conducted business effectively via phone.
- Developed, maintained, and expedited the schedule for a small phase of a large construction project.

"What an asset Jordan turned out to be, exceeding all expectations for a summer intern…."
—Clint Brit, Project Engineer, Holt, White & Mack

Sales & Estimating Trainee (Internship)
SSM Builders Supply, Lubbock, TX • February to August 2010
Estimated, prepared bids, worked in inventory control, assisted customers, and contributed to good client relationships at this mid-sized door, frame, and hardware supplier. Became proficient in material take-off from contract documents, plans, and specifications. Taught staff how to utilize the computer effectively.

- Increased company's ability to take on more work through effective organization and relieving owner of many of his responsibilities.

ADDITIONAL WORK EXPERIENCE

Owner/Operator
Jordan Jones Mobile Car Care, Lubbock, TX • 2009 to Present
Developed a mobile car wash business with more than 25 regular clients and $5K profits annually.

- Selected equipment and assembled car wash trailer.
- Maintain excellent client relationships with a 100% satisfaction rate.

Owner
Jones Lawn Care, Lubbock, TX • 2006 to 2009
Bought and managed lawn care business, providing services that included fertilizing, chemical application, tree and brush trimming, and mowing.

- Increased client base by more than 60%; drove profits to more than $15K yearly.

"Jordan's work ethic and sense of responsibility are things rarely seen in today's society of youth… I think he will be very successful in whatever endeavor he pursues."
—Michael Smith, Senior Systems Engineer, Maxline Information Systems

TECHNOLOGY EXPERTISE

Primavera Project Planner (P3), TK Solver, Micro Station; MS Word, Excel, Access, PowerPoint, Internet research

ASSOCIATIONS / COMMUNITY

Student Member, Association of General Contractors
Member, Society of Engineer Technologists
Participate in Big Brothers Big Sisters of Lubbock, sponsoring the same child since December 2008

"I would highly recommend Jordan Jones to any construction company with which he would seek employment."
—Clint Brit, Project Engineer, Holt, White & Mack

31
Degree: BA, Communication Sciences and Disorders.
Job Target: Entry to graduate school.
Strategy: Created a unique one-page resume using visuals to target field of study (audiology).

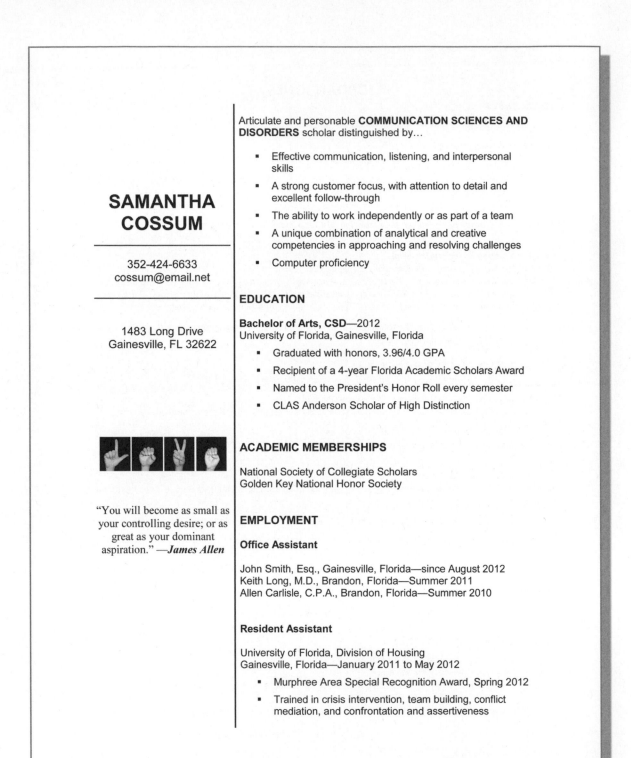

SAMANTHA COSSUM

352-424-6633
cossum@email.net

1483 Long Drive
Gainesville, FL 32622

"You will become as small as
your controlling desire; or as
great as your dominant
aspiration." —*James Allen*

Articulate and personable **COMMUNICATION SCIENCES AND DISORDERS** scholar distinguished by…

- Effective communication, listening, and interpersonal skills
- A strong customer focus, with attention to detail and excellent follow-through
- The ability to work independently or as part of a team
- A unique combination of analytical and creative competencies in approaching and resolving challenges
- Computer proficiency

EDUCATION

Bachelor of Arts, CSD—2012
University of Florida, Gainesville, Florida

- Graduated with honors, 3.96/4.0 GPA
- Recipient of a 4-year Florida Academic Scholars Award
- Named to the President's Honor Roll every semester
- CLAS Anderson Scholar of High Distinction

ACADEMIC MEMBERSHIPS

National Society of Collegiate Scholars
Golden Key National Honor Society

EMPLOYMENT

Office Assistant

John Smith, Esq., Gainesville, Florida—since August 2012
Keith Long, M.D., Brandon, Florida—Summer 2011
Allen Carlisle, C.P.A., Brandon, Florida—Summer 2010

Resident Assistant

University of Florida, Division of Housing
Gainesville, Florida—January 2011 to May 2012

- Murphree Area Special Recognition Award, Spring 2012
- Trained in crisis intervention, team building, conflict mediation, and confrontation and assertiveness

32

Degree: BA, Spanish; BA, German.
Job Target: Position in lay church leadership.
Strategy: Concisely communicated a variety of experiences, both paid and volunteer. Positioned most relevant position, as a Youth Ministry Director, at the top with its own heading.

SHELBY HUTTON

404 S. Franklin St. Apt #2 • St. Louis MO 63101 • srh1234@gmail.com • (347) 282-9653

ENTRY-LEVEL LAY CHURCH LEADERSHIP

Three years of paid work experience as youth ministry director for Rehoboth Baptist Church while attending Amherst College in Massachusetts. Delivered programming, facilitated events, and collaborated with church leadership and parents to create a vibrant, engaging, and highly effective youth ministry for the second-largest Baptist church in Amherst.

Completing a two-year term of service with Teach For America as a Spanish teacher at Sumner High School in St. Louis, with outstanding references from school principal and mentor teacher. Fluent in written and spoken Spanish; proficient in German.

LAY MINISTRY EXPERIENCE

Rehoboth Baptist Church, Amherst, MA   2007–2010
YOUTH MINISTRY DIRECTOR – Increased youth involvement by creating and implementing new programs, facilitating youth events throughout the school year, and collaborating with pastor and deacons to create a youth ministry that meshed with the church's doctrine and the congregation's needs. Taught various Sunday School classes for ages 7–16.

- Created "Bible B.A.B.E.S." (Beautiful, Accepted, Blessed, and Eternally Significant) weekly group for middle- and high-school girls.
- Created a well-attended weekly youth group meeting geared toward nonmembers, with food and activities.
- Retained 100% of students in Sunday School classes.

RELATED EXPERIENCE

Sumner High School, St. Louis, MO   2010–Present
SPANISH TEACHER, TEACH FOR AMERICA – Selected from more than 46,000 applicants. Teach 5 classes of levels 1, 2, and 3 Spanish with approximately 130 students in a high-dropout-rate high school. Prepare daily lesson plans, assess student progress, and meet the stringent learning objectives and assessment measures of Teach For America. Schedule and coordinate periodic student-led, parent-teacher conferences that focus on student achievement while also recognizing areas for improvement.

- Ensured student learning: 100% pass rate on standardized testing; 90% of students earning grade of "B" or above.
- Implemented an aggressive incentive program that increased attendance from 70% to 91% in 1 semester.
- Prepared and presented school's first Spanish play for level 3 students.
- Co-advised Spanish Club; participated in weekly meetings and chaperoned a field trip each semester.

Amherst College, Amherst, MA   2008–2010
EMPLOYER RELATIONS INTERN, CAREER CENTER (2009–2010) – Improved the functionality of the University's employer outreach program by purging existing database and merging other databases into system. Removed duplicates, identified and corrected inaccurate information, and ensured viability of contact information. Sent periodic e-mailings to employers in database to notify them of career fairs and other upcoming events. Assisted Employer Relations Coordinator with research in preparation for visits to companies across the U.S. Coordinated all on-campus recruiting.

- Exceeded goals for employee attendance at career fairs (4% over goal in the fall; 5% over goal in the spring).
- Received consistently positive feedback from employers interacting with the Career Center.

CAREER ASSISTANT, CAREER CENTER (2008–2009) – Critiqued students' resumes and cover letters, provided career and graduate school advice, and assisted students in finding and utilizing career-related resources.

- Chosen for the Center's first Employer Relations internship based on outstanding evaluations; dependability; and exceptional organizational, information management, and communication skills.

EDUCATION

Amherst College, Amherst, MA   2010
BACHELOR OF ARTS IN SPANISH, BACHELOR OF ARTS IN GERMAN   GPA: 3.74/4.0

INTERNATIONAL TRAVEL EXPERIENCE

Costa Rica Summer Program: Significantly improved Spanish skills through 2-month total immersion. Developed knowledge of Central American culture and political system. Earned 12 college credit hours for completion of courses in Latin American culture and society.

German-American Partnership Program: Represented the United States while traveling in Germany and Poland. Increased German language skills and understanding of European governmental and social systems.

33

Degree: BA, Visual Art and Art History.
Job Target: Position in arts management.
Strategy: Create a well-designed resume that clearly communicates this new graduate's deep interest in the arts and commitment to a career in her chosen field of arts management.

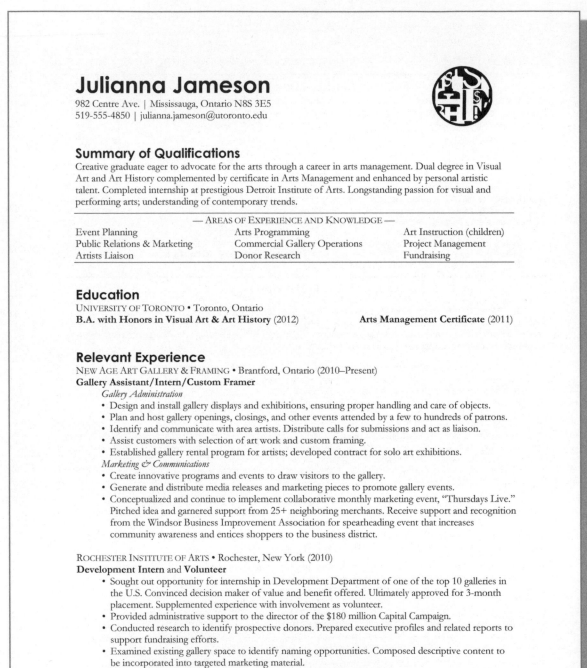

Julianna Jameson

982 Centre Ave. | Mississauga, Ontario N8S 3E5
519-555-4850 | julianna.jameson@utoronto.edu

Summary of Qualifications

Creative graduate eager to advocate for the arts through a career in arts management. Dual degree in Visual Art and Art History complemented by certificate in Arts Management and enhanced by personal artistic talent. Completed internship at prestigious Detroit Institute of Arts. Longstanding passion for visual and performing arts; understanding of contemporary trends.

— AREAS OF EXPERIENCE AND KNOWLEDGE —

Event Planning	Arts Programming	Art Instruction (children)
Public Relations & Marketing	Commercial Gallery Operations	Project Management
Artists Liaison	Donor Research	Fundraising

Education

UNIVERSITY OF TORONTO • Toronto, Ontario
B.A. with Honors in Visual Art & Art History (2012)   **Arts Management Certificate** (2011)

Relevant Experience

NEW AGE ART GALLERY & FRAMING • Brantford, Ontario (2010–Present)
Gallery Assistant/Intern/Custom Framer

Gallery Administration
- Design and install gallery displays and exhibitions, ensuring proper handling and care of objects.
- Plan and host gallery openings, closings, and other events attended by a few to hundreds of patrons.
- Identify and communicate with area artists. Distribute calls for submissions and act as liaison.
- Assist customers with selection of art work and custom framing.
- Established gallery rental program for artists; developed contract for solo art exhibitions.

Marketing & Communications
- Create innovative programs and events to draw visitors to the gallery.
- Generate and distribute media releases and marketing pieces to promote gallery events.
- Conceptualized and continue to implement collaborative monthly marketing event, "Thursdays Live." Pitched idea and garnered support from 25+ neighboring merchants. Receive support and recognition from the Windsor Business Improvement Association for spearheading event that increases community awareness and entices shoppers to the business district.

ROCHESTER INSTITUTE OF ARTS • Rochester, New York (2010)
Development Intern and **Volunteer**
- Sought out opportunity for internship in Development Department of one of the top 10 galleries in the U.S. Convinced decision maker of value and benefit offered. Ultimately approved for 3-month placement. Supplemented experience with involvement as volunteer.
- Provided administrative support to the director of the $180 million Capital Campaign.
- Conducted research to identify prospective donors. Prepared executive profiles and related reports to support fundraising efforts.
- Examined existing gallery space to identify naming opportunities. Composed descriptive content to be incorporated into targeted marketing material.
- Developed spreadsheets to the specifications of the Campaign Director.

Continued

33 *(continued)*

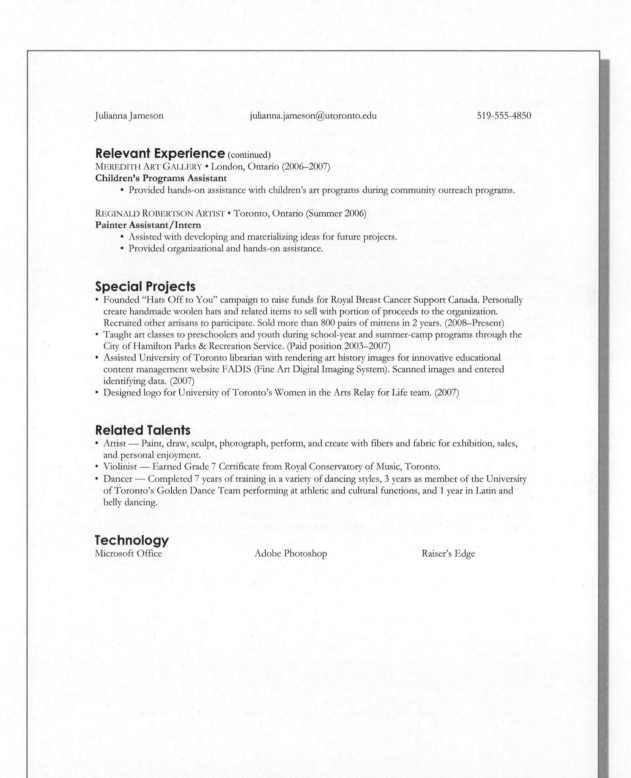

Julianna Jameson   julianna.jameson@utoronto.edu   519-555-4850

Relevant Experience (continued)
MEREDITH ART GALLERY • London, Ontario (2006–2007)
Children's Programs Assistant
  • Provided hands-on assistance with children's art programs during community outreach programs.

REGINALD ROBERTSON ARTIST • Toronto, Ontario (Summer 2006)
Painter Assistant/Intern
  • Assisted with developing and materializing ideas for future projects.
  • Provided organizational and hands-on assistance.

Special Projects
• Founded "Hats Off to You" campaign to raise funds for Royal Breast Cancer Support Canada. Personally create handmade woolen hats and related items to sell with portion of proceeds to the organization. Recruited other artisans to participate. Sold more than 800 pairs of mittens in 2 years. (2008–Present)
• Taught art classes to preschoolers and youth during school-year and summer-camp programs through the City of Hamilton Parks & Recreation Service. (Paid position 2003–2007)
• Assisted University of Toronto librarian with rendering art history images for innovative educational content management website FADIS (Fine Art Digital Imaging System). Scanned images and entered identifying data. (2007)
• Designed logo for University of Toronto's Women in the Arts Relay for Life team. (2007)

Related Talents
• Artist — Paint, draw, sculpt, photograph, perform, and create with fibers and fabric for exhibition, sales, and personal enjoyment.
• Violinist — Earned Grade 7 Certificate from Royal Conservatory of Music, Toronto.
• Dancer — Completed 7 years of training in a variety of dancing styles, 3 years as member of the University of Toronto's Golden Dance Team performing at athletic and cultural functions, and 1 year in Latin and belly dancing.

Technology
Microsoft Office   Adobe Photoshop   Raiser's Edge

34

Degree: BS, Finance and Economics.
Job Target: Financial services representative.
Strategy: Highlighted a wide range of employment experiences and college activities to paint the picture of a highly valued associate.

Jessica Levitz   215 New Street, Apartment D | Columbus, GA 31801
                                          229.341.7704 | jmlevitz@hotmail.com

ENTRY-LEVEL FINANCIAL SERVICES REPRESENTATIVE

✓ **Outstanding analytical abilities** honed through finance degree and additional coursework in marketing, management, and actuarial science.
✓ **Strong work ethic** developed through extensive experience in diverse environments that include retail, telemarketing, food service, and administration.
✓ **Excellent communication, multitasking, adaptability, and time management skills** sharpened through multiple customer service positions.

SKILLS & QUALIFICATIONS

Financial Management: Crystal Ball Software | Excel | Financial Statements | DuPont Analysis Governmental Accounting Regulations (SEC, GAAP) | IFRS Guidelines | Hoover's | MSN Money.com Balance Sheets | Income Statements | Microeconomics | Macroeconomics

Customer Service: Cash-Handling Procedures | Customer Complaint Resolution | Phone Etiquette Shift-Closing Procedures | Active Listening | Communication with Managers and Team Members Patron Safety during Emergencies | Special Assistance for Customers with Specific Needs

EDUCATION

Columbus State University, Columbus, GA   May 2012
Bachelor of Science, Finance and Economics
GPA 3.25/4.0 | University Scholarship (2008–2009) | Honors College (2009–2010)

EXPERIENCE

FITTERS, Columbus, GA   August 2010–Present
Waitress
Perform full scale of customer service functions in a fast-paced bar/restaurant. Take orders, respond to customer requests and complaints, serve food, and stock and clean kitchen.

   ✓ Work 20–25 hours per week during school year, including most Friday and Saturday nights.
   ✓ Informally given the title of head waitress; play significant role in training new staff.

PREFERRED FAMILY HEALTHCARE, Albany, GA   May–August 2010
Secretary
Completed numerous office administration tasks, including sorting and filing confidential client information, faxing client information to other facilities, and preparing handouts and instructional materials for weekend classes for DUI and MIP offenders.

   ✓ Worked 40 hours per week.
   ✓ Received a raise within three months of employment.

PANHELLENIC HALL, Columbus, GA   December 2009–May 2010
Office Assistant
Monitored and assisted 500 building residents by providing directions, giving advice, and sorting and filing mail. Implemented security measures such as securing doors and notifying authorities in case of fire, tornado, or intruder. Received emergency training.

   ✓ Worked four days per week 3:00 a.m.–7:00 a.m.
   ✓ Frequently worked immediately prior to and after breaks, allowing other workers to spend more time at home with their families.

Page One

---

34 *(continued)*

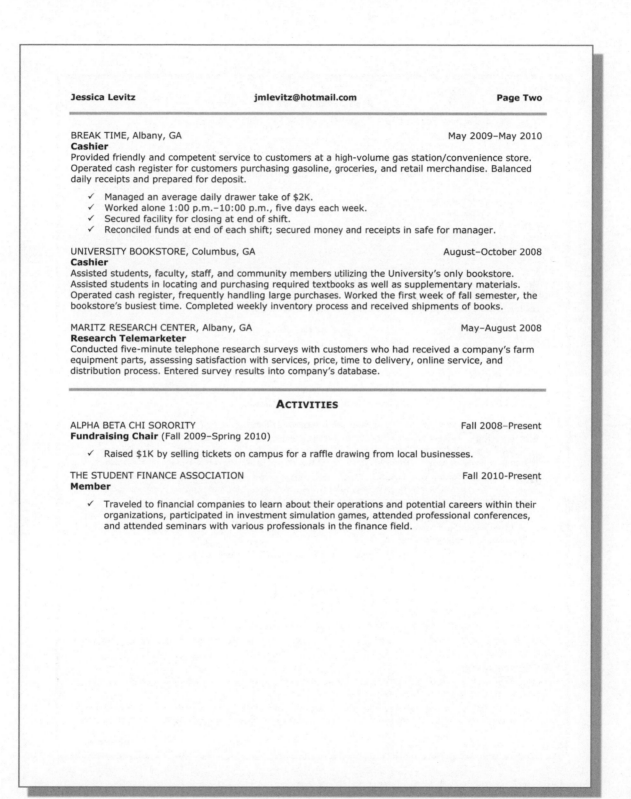

Jessica Levitz   jmlevitz@hotmail.com   **Page Two**

BREAK TIME, Albany, GA   May 2009–May 2010
Cashier
Provided friendly and competent service to customers at a high-volume gas station/convenience store.
Operated cash register for customers purchasing gasoline, groceries, and retail merchandise. Balanced
daily receipts and prepared for deposit.

- ✓ Managed an average daily drawer take of $2K.
- ✓ Worked alone 1:00 p.m.–10:00 p.m., five days each week.
- ✓ Secured facility for closing at end of shift.
- ✓ Reconciled funds at end of each shift; secured money and receipts in safe for manager.

UNIVERSITY BOOKSTORE, Columbus, GA   August–October 2008
Cashier
Assisted students, faculty, staff, and community members utilizing the University's only bookstore.
Assisted students in locating and purchasing required textbooks as well as supplementary materials.
Operated cash register, frequently handling large purchases. Worked the first week of fall semester, the
bookstore's busiest time. Completed weekly inventory process and received shipments of books.

MARITZ RESEARCH CENTER, Albany, GA   May–August 2008
Research Telemarketer
Conducted five-minute telephone research surveys with customers who had received a company's farm
equipment parts, assessing satisfaction with services, price, time to delivery, online service, and
distribution process. Entered survey results into company's database.

ACTIVITIES

ALPHA BETA CHI SORORITY   Fall 2008–Present
Fundraising Chair (Fall 2009–Spring 2010)

- ✓ Raised $1K by selling tickets on campus for a raffle drawing from local businesses.

THE STUDENT FINANCE ASSOCIATION   Fall 2010-Present
Member

- ✓ Traveled to financial companies to learn about their operations and potential careers within their
  organizations, participated in investment simulation games, attended professional conferences,
  and attended seminars with various professionals in the finance field.

Degree: BS, Business Administration.
Job Target: Career in finance.
Strategy: Explained college projects and activities in depth and used interesting sports background as an added differentiator.

ANTHONY VITI

822 Husky Trail ◆ Seattle, WA 98195 ◆ 206-543-8898 ◆ tonyviti@gmail.com

ASPIRING FINANCE PROFESSIONAL

Market Research ~ Investment Analysis ~ Client Relations

High-performing recent graduate with BBA in Finance. Promising finance professional with strong research and analysis skills and budding interest in investment analysis. Take-charge individual with solid work record; a recognized leader who is disciplined in approach and highly committed to achieving goals. Ready learner who is quick to pick up new things. Adaptable team player who works effectively with people from diverse cultures.

EDUCATION

UNIVERSITY OF WASHINGTON, Seattle, WA
Bachelor of Science in Business Administration/Finance, 12/2011

Academic Highlights

- Graduated *magna cum laude*; GPA: 3.88/4.00.
- Earned dual minors in **General Business Administration** and **Economics.**
- Completed 1-semester study abroad program at University of Auckland, New Zealand, Fall 2009.
- Participated in university honors program for all 4 years.
- Inducted into Beta Gamma Sigma Honor Society as top 10% of class.

Coursework & Activities Highlights

- Completed 2 semesters of experiential investment management class, serving as part of small team charged with managing $500,000 fund by researching and recommending stocks under direction of CFA. As team, raised fund by $50,000. Successfully made case for 2 stocks, each achieving above-average performance.
- Earned top grade for stock and market analysis conducted as part of Investment Analysis and Portfolio Management course. Completed 3-tier top-down analysis of company, industry, and economic outlook, presenting sound evaluation that was extremely well received by professor.
- Completed mind-opening study abroad program in New Zealand university with 7000 international students. Developed multicultural appreciation while mastering how to address thought-provoking questions in comprehensive essays and papers.
- While in New Zealand, competed in University Games in Auckland as member of golf team.

EXPERIENCE

JACKSON COUNTRY CLUB, Seattle, WA   2007 to 2011
Pro Shop Associate/Starter/Snack Shop Assistant/Cart Cleaner
Took on roles of increasing responsibility at Washington's oldest and largest golf resort offering top-rated facilities and services.

Key Contributions:

- Earning promotion to coveted pro shop associate position (1 of only 4 resortwide), often ran shop during evening hours and directed activities of as many as 5 employees.
- As starter, welcomed and reviewed rules with golfers while overseeing course activities to ensure pleasant golfing experience for all. Effectively managed conflicts, defusing situations by remaining calm and professional.

continued...

35 *(continued)*

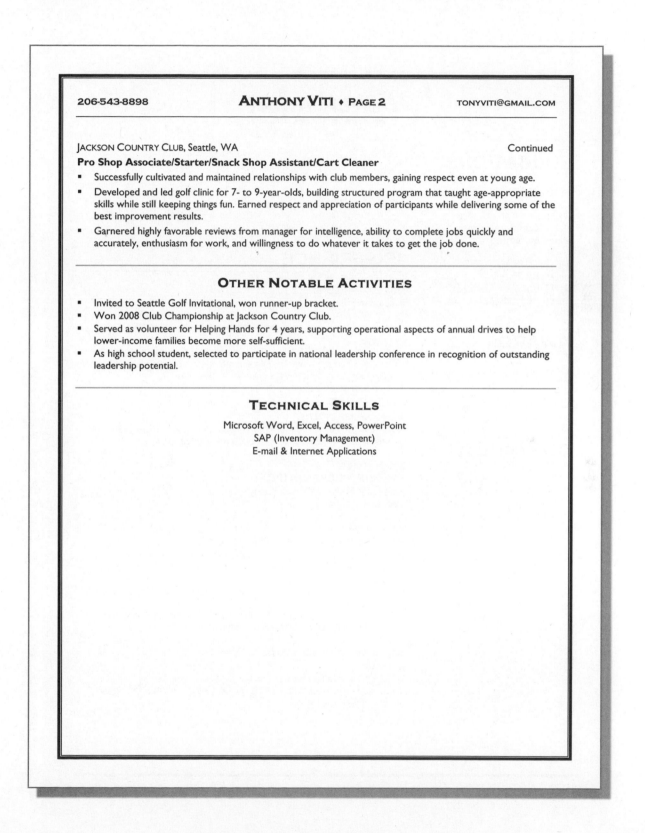

206-543-8898   **ANTHONY VITI ♦ PAGE 2**   TONYVITI@GMAIL.COM

JACKSON COUNTRY CLUB, Seattle, WA   Continued
Pro Shop Associate/Starter/Snack Shop Assistant/Cart Cleaner
- Successfully cultivated and maintained relationships with club members, gaining respect even at young age.
- Developed and led golf clinic for 7- to 9-year-olds, building structured program that taught age-appropriate skills while still keeping things fun. Earned respect and appreciation of participants while delivering some of the best improvement results.
- Garnered highly favorable reviews from manager for intelligence, ability to complete jobs quickly and accurately, enthusiasm for work, and willingness to do whatever it takes to get the job done.

OTHER NOTABLE ACTIVITIES

- Invited to Seattle Golf Invitational, won runner-up bracket.
- Won 2008 Club Championship at Jackson Country Club.
- Served as volunteer for Helping Hands for 4 years, supporting operational aspects of annual drives to help lower-income families become more self-sufficient.
- As high school student, selected to participate in national leadership conference in recognition of outstanding leadership potential.

TECHNICAL SKILLS

Microsoft Word, Excel, Access, PowerPoint
SAP (Inventory Management)
E-mail & Internet Applications

Degree: BA, Communications.
Job Target: Pharmaceutical sales.
Strategy: Created an attention-getting resume for a new grad seeking a position in a very competitive field. Focused on education as well as sales experience and accomplishments, obtained in internships and work experience.

OLIVER TRENT

555 Fifth Avenue
Duluth, Minnesota 55777
(218) 879-5555
olivertrent@yahoo.com

EDUCATION

UNIVERSITY OF
MINNESOTA, Duluth
Bachelor of Arts—2010
Major: **Communications**
Minor: **Marketing**

NOTTINGHAM TRENT
UNIVERSITY,
NOTTINGHAM, ENGLAND
Study Abroad—Summer
2009

AWARDS

- Mayo Clinic Scholarship
- Arrowhead Award:
  Outstanding Student in
  a student organization,
  MN Board of Regents

COMMUNITY

- Habitat for Humanity,
  assisted in building a
  house.
- Channel One Food
  Shelf, stock shelves.
- Blanket Duluth.

*"Committed on a
personal and
professional level to
achieve and set
higher goals."*

EXPERIENCE

May 2010–Present
ACCOUNT EXECUTIVE
Mount Rose Publishing
*Sell advertising for the University of Minnesota, Duluth, telephone
directory.*
- Service existing accounts. Contact potential customers by telephone
  and arrange appointments. Negotiate contracts, occasionally bartering
  services. Upsell advertising whenever possible.
- Arrange graphic designs manually.
- Handle billing.

ACCOMPLISHMENTS
*Contact potential clients more than once, often resulting in a sale that
otherwise would not be made, through persuasive selling.*

2009–Present
SALES REPRESENTATIVE
No Limitz Snowboard Company
Sell snowboards.

2007–Present
(Certified Professional) SKI INSTRUCTOR
Ghost Mountain Ski Resort, Duluth, MN
- Part of hiring process of new ski instructors. Train new hires and
  evaluate their performance.
- Teach advanced-level classes. Persuade students to continue their
  ski lessons.
- Receive additional instruction from Ski Instructors of America.
- Provide information and sell products at pro shop.

September–November 2010
INTERN
UMD University Relations
Wrote and edited magazine articles, bi-weekly newsletter, telephone
directory, and news releases.

CONTINUED

36 *(continued)*

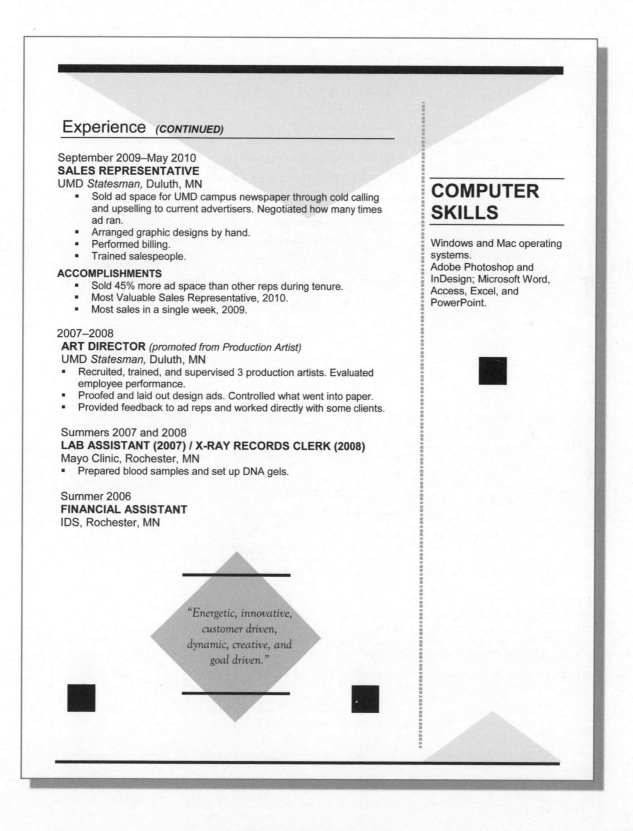

Experience *(CONTINUED)*

September 2009–May 2010
SALES REPRESENTATIVE
UMD *Statesman,* Duluth, MN
- Sold ad space for UMD campus newspaper through cold calling and upselling to current advertisers. Negotiated how many times ad ran.
- Arranged graphic designs by hand.
- Performed billing.
- Trained salespeople.

ACCOMPLISHMENTS
- Sold 45% more ad space than other reps during tenure.
- Most Valuable Sales Representative, 2010.
- Most sales in a single week, 2009.

2007–2008
ART DIRECTOR *(promoted from Production Artist)*
UMD *Statesman,* Duluth, MN
- Recruited, trained, and supervised 3 production artists. Evaluated employee performance.
- Proofed and laid out design ads. Controlled what went into paper.
- Provided feedback to ad reps and worked directly with some clients.

Summers 2007 and 2008
LAB ASSISTANT (2007) / X-RAY RECORDS CLERK (2008)
Mayo Clinic, Rochester, MN
- Prepared blood samples and set up DNA gels.

Summer 2006
FINANCIAL ASSISTANT
IDS, Rochester, MN

COMPUTER SKILLS

Windows and Mac operating systems.
Adobe Photoshop and InDesign; Microsoft Word, Access, Excel, and PowerPoint.

"Energetic, innovative, customer driven, dynamic, creative, and goal driven."

37

Degree: BS, Marketing.
Job Target: Entry-level marketing associate.
Strategy: Used academic projects and independent experience of starting an Internet-based business to position this new graduate as someone with the knowledge and experience to be successful.

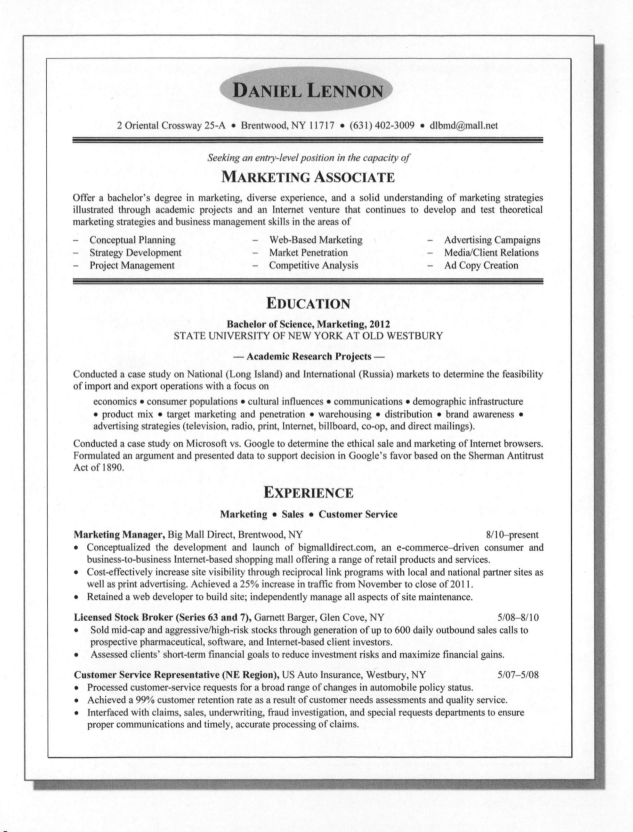

DANIEL LENNON

2 Oriental Crossway 25-A • Brentwood, NY 11717 • (631) 402-3009 • dlbmd@mall.net

Seeking an entry-level position in the capacity of

MARKETING ASSOCIATE

Offer a bachelor's degree in marketing, diverse experience, and a solid understanding of marketing strategies illustrated through academic projects and an Internet venture that continues to develop and test theoretical marketing strategies and business management skills in the areas of

– Conceptual Planning	– Web-Based Marketing	– Advertising Campaigns
– Strategy Development	– Market Penetration	– Media/Client Relations
– Project Management	– Competitive Analysis	– Ad Copy Creation

EDUCATION

Bachelor of Science, Marketing, 2012
STATE UNIVERSITY OF NEW YORK AT OLD WESTBURY

— **Academic Research Projects** —

Conducted a case study on National (Long Island) and International (Russia) markets to determine the feasibility of import and export operations with a focus on

economics • consumer populations • cultural influences • communications • demographic infrastructure • product mix • target marketing and penetration • warehousing • distribution • brand awareness • advertising strategies (television, radio, print, Internet, billboard, co-op, and direct mailings).

Conducted a case study on Microsoft vs. Google to determine the ethical sale and marketing of Internet browsers. Formulated an argument and presented data to support decision in Google's favor based on the Sherman Antitrust Act of 1890.

EXPERIENCE

Marketing • Sales • Customer Service

Marketing Manager, Big Mall Direct, Brentwood, NY   8/10–present
- Conceptualized the development and launch of bigmalldirect.com, an e-commerce–driven consumer and business-to-business Internet-based shopping mall offering a range of retail products and services.
- Cost-effectively increase site visibility through reciprocal link programs with local and national partner sites as well as print advertising. Achieved a 25% increase in traffic from November to close of 2011.
- Retained a web developer to build site; independently manage all aspects of site maintenance.

Licensed Stock Broker (Series 63 and 7), Garnett Barger, Glen Cove, NY   5/08–8/10
- Sold mid-cap and aggressive/high-risk stocks through generation of up to 600 daily outbound sales calls to prospective pharmaceutical, software, and Internet-based client investors.
- Assessed clients' short-term financial goals to reduce investment risks and maximize financial gains.

Customer Service Representative (NE Region), US Auto Insurance, Westbury, NY   5/07–5/08
- Processed customer-service requests for a broad range of changes in automobile policy status.
- Achieved a 99% customer retention rate as a result of customer needs assessments and quality service.
- Interfaced with claims, sales, underwriting, fraud investigation, and special requests departments to ensure proper communications and timely, accurate processing of claims.

38

Degree: BA, Geography.
Job Target: Customer service representative.
Strategy: Included diverse life experiences along with employment background as key qualifications. Created a profile that clearly emphasized interpersonal skills and positive personality, both keys to success in customer service.

ALEXANDER REYES

areyes@gmail.com • (cell) 919.351.5022
6820 Beldan Ave #52 • Durham, NC 27701

Objective: Entry-level, customer-facing position that leverages my ability to make authentic connections with people of all backgrounds in order to advance the company's goals

PROFILE

Self-motivated; thrive in challenging environments through a distinctive blend of problem-solving abilities, interpersonal skills, and humor.

Strong work ethic, warm personality, and ability to set priorities and meet deadlines. Adapt easily to diversity, change, and new responsibilities. Enjoy teaching and coaching others to achieve goals.

AREAS OF PROVEN STRENGTH

- Team Leadership & Motivation
- Verbal & Written Communication
- Analysis & Planning
- Public Speaking
- Relationship Building
- Cross-Cultural Understanding

EXPERIENCE

UNIVERSITY OF NORTH CAROLINA – HEALTH SCIENCES LIBRARY   Chapel Hill, NC • 2009—Present

ID Check
Apply proficiency for problem-solving to enrich the experience of library patrons. Regulate entry to facility.

- **Acquired reputation for dependability and helpfulness** by staff and students for rapidly locating library materials and answering inquiries regarding circulations.

DEAN SMITH BASKETBALL CAMP   Chapel Hill, NC • Summer 2010

Counselor • Basketball Coach
Channeled a passion for basketball into successful coaching of students from grades 1–9 in the fundamentals of the sport. Supported UNC coaches with daily camp operations.

- **Transformed the Father-Son Camp into an enjoyable experience** by helping all the campers improve their skills; secured the trust of parents and gained credibility as a trusted coach.

UNIVERSITY OF NORTH CAROLINA HOUSING & FOOD SERVICE   Chapel Hill, NC • Summer 2009

Food Service Team Member
Prepared and served food for student clientele, maintaining health, safety, and cleanliness standards. Operated cash register with accuracy. Engaged in catering University functions.

STATE FARM INSURANCE – AGENT BILL CANNA   Raleigh, NC • Summer 2007

Office Assistant
Supported agent's business by performing clerical duties, including updating and filing customer documents.

QUALIFICATIONS

EDUCATION

Bachelor of Arts in Geography – UNIVERSITY OF NORTH CAROLINA   Chapel Hill, NC • 2012

INTERNATIONAL EXPERIENCE

Lived for 3 years in Brazil. Attended international high school that attracted students from around the world, providing an intensive cross-cultural experience that strengthened my ability to communicate and collaborate with people across all borders. Basic Portuguese language skills.

39

Degree: BA (in progress).
Job Target: Retail salesperson (while going to school).
Strategy: Immediately established that she is experienced in retail sales, with an outstanding performance record; an achiever who pushes the envelope, whether competing for retail sales or being awarded a foreign exchange student slot (the only one chosen out of 50 applicants). Used Outward Bound experience to show high stamina, energy, and ability to handle changing situations.

KATALINA SANDERS

OBJECTIVE	**Sales Associate—Retail Sales**
PROFILE	☑ College student with more than 4 years of retail sales experience. ☑ Professional and approachable manner. Talent for identifying customers' needs and presenting solutions that drive purchases. ☑ Highly motivated team player—willing to take on added responsibilities. ☑ Proven skills in problem solving and customer relations. Fluent Spanish.
COMPUTER	Mac and Windows OS, MS Word, retail sales databases, Internet, e-mail
WORK HISTORY	**SENTIMENTS,** Randallstown Center, Randallstown, MD 2011–present **Sales Associate** Provide sales, merchandising, and customer service to upscale clientele in 700-square-foot card and stationery retail store. ▪ Successfully interact with more than 50 customers daily, achieving $300 to $500 in sales per day. Upsell and cross-sell products, ensuring customer satisfaction. Assigned managerial authority for opening store. ▪ Cultivate cooperative, team-oriented relationships with 10 co-workers and managers, assisting with custom orders and demanding customers. **CENTER STORE,** Magnolia Mall, Magnolia Heights, MD 2008–2011 **Senior Sales Associate** (Children's and Electronics Departments) Conducted inventory, merchandising, pricing, sales, and customer service of children's clothing, video games, and toys in 3,000-square-foot department. Worked in teams of 2–3 sales associates/managers, as well as alone. ▪ Promoted to Senior Sales Associate. Given open and close authority for store. Assisted in quarterly inventory-assessment program. ▪ Sold $1,000 in merchandise daily, serving 50–80 customers per day. Proofed cash drawer (including credit card sales) with low error rate. ▪ Developed loyal clientele and increased sales through personal attention to customers' needs. Resolved customer complaints diplomatically.
EDUCATION	Bachelor of Arts (in progress), Baltimore State University, Baltimore, MD Diploma, Magnolia Heights High School, Magnolia Heights, MD 2008
ACTIVITIES	Foreign Student Exchange Program—Seville, Spain Summer 2008 Chosen from 50 candidates; traveled throughout Spain. Outward Bound, The Appalachian Trail (Maryland) October 2006 Participated in weeklong wilderness experience in a group of 10 students.

14 Magnolia Lane, Baltimore, MD 12345 ▪ (410) 825-5555 ▪ ksanders@mail.com

---

Degree: BS, Business Administration/Marketing.
Job Target: Marketing position with a pro sports team.
Strategy: Capitalized on an internship with a financial services company, as well as his coaching and athletics experience.

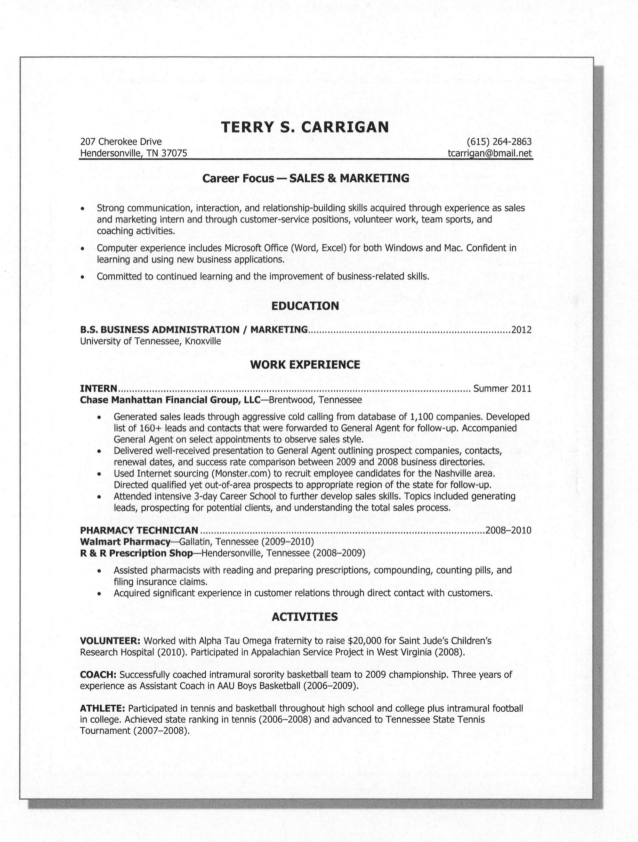

TERRY S. CARRIGAN

207 Cherokee Drive
Hendersonville, TN 37075

(615) 264-2863
tcarrigan@bmail.net

Career Focus — SALES & MARKETING

- Strong communication, interaction, and relationship-building skills acquired through experience as sales and marketing intern and through customer-service positions, volunteer work, team sports, and coaching activities.

- Computer experience includes Microsoft Office (Word, Excel) for both Windows and Mac. Confident in learning and using new business applications.

- Committed to continued learning and the improvement of business-related skills.

EDUCATION

B.S. BUSINESS ADMINISTRATION / MARKETING..2012
University of Tennessee, Knoxville

WORK EXPERIENCE

INTERN.. Summer 2011
Chase Manhattan Financial Group, LLC—Brentwood, Tennessee

- Generated sales leads through aggressive cold calling from database of 1,100 companies. Developed list of 160+ leads and contacts that were forwarded to General Agent for follow-up. Accompanied General Agent on select appointments to observe sales style.
- Delivered well-received presentation to General Agent outlining prospect companies, contacts, renewal dates, and success rate comparison between 2009 and 2008 business directories.
- Used Internet sourcing (Monster.com) to recruit employee candidates for the Nashville area. Directed qualified yet out-of-area prospects to appropriate region of the state for follow-up.
- Attended intensive 3-day Career School to further develop sales skills. Topics included generating leads, prospecting for potential clients, and understanding the total sales process.

PHARMACY TECHNICIAN 2008–2010
Walmart Pharmacy—Gallatin, Tennessee (2009–2010)
R & R Prescription Shop—Hendersonville, Tennessee (2008–2009)

- Assisted pharmacists with reading and preparing prescriptions, compounding, counting pills, and filing insurance claims.
- Acquired significant experience in customer relations through direct contact with customers.

ACTIVITIES

VOLUNTEER: Worked with Alpha Tau Omega fraternity to raise $20,000 for Saint Jude's Children's Research Hospital (2010). Participated in Appalachian Service Project in West Virginia (2008).

COACH: Successfully coached intramural sorority basketball team to 2009 championship. Three years of experience as Assistant Coach in AAU Boys Basketball (2006–2009).

ATHLETE: Participated in tennis and basketball throughout high school and college plus intramural football in college. Achieved state ranking in tennis (2006–2008) and advanced to Tennessee State Tennis Tournament (2007–2008).

41

Degree: BA, Spanish.
Job Target: Communications/public relations/sales/customer service.
Strategy: Used testimonials from instructors and employers demonstrating work ethic, enthusiasm, and ability to communicate and motivate others to action, with the goal of overcoming somewhat "unrelated" college degree and work history (she had no previous sales training or experience).

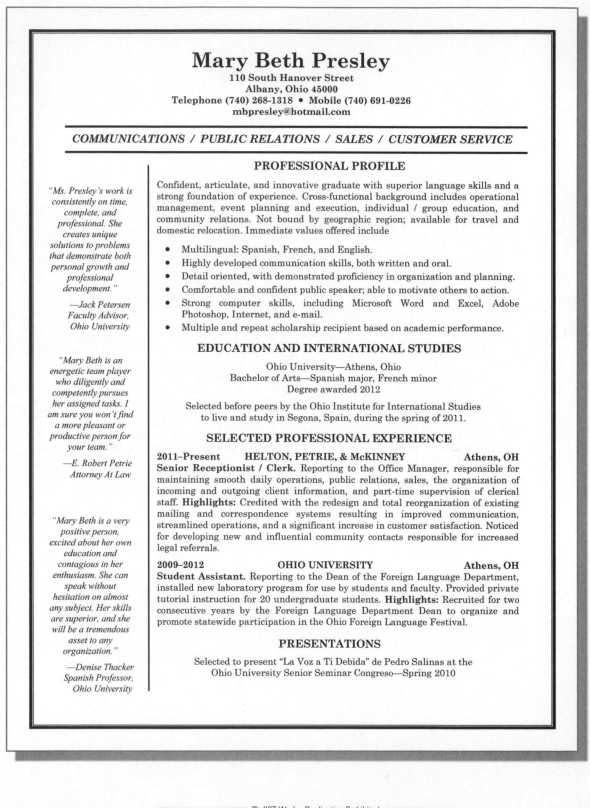

Mary Beth Presley

110 South Hanover Street
Albany, Ohio 45000
Telephone (740) 268-1318 • Mobile (740) 691-0226
mbpresley@hotmail.com

COMMUNICATIONS / PUBLIC RELATIONS / SALES / CUSTOMER SERVICE

PROFESSIONAL PROFILE

"Ms. Presley's work is consistently on time, complete, and professional. She creates unique solutions to problems that demonstrate both personal growth and professional development."

—Jack Petersen
Faculty Advisor,
Ohio University

Confident, articulate, and innovative graduate with superior language skills and a strong foundation of experience. Cross-functional background includes operational management, event planning and execution, individual / group education, and community relations. Not bound by geographic region; available for travel and domestic relocation. Immediate values offered include

- Multilingual: Spanish, French, and English.
- Highly developed communication skills, both written and oral.
- Detail oriented, with demonstrated proficiency in organization and planning.
- Comfortable and confident public speaker; able to motivate others to action.
- Strong computer skills, including Microsoft Word and Excel, Adobe Photoshop, Internet, and e-mail.
- Multiple and repeat scholarship recipient based on academic performance.

EDUCATION AND INTERNATIONAL STUDIES

"Mary Beth is an energetic team player who diligently and competently pursues her assigned tasks. I am sure you won't find a more pleasant or productive person for your team."

—E. Robert Petrie
Attorney At Law

Ohio University—Athens, Ohio
Bachelor of Arts—Spanish major, French minor
Degree awarded 2012

Selected before peers by the Ohio Institute for International Studies to live and study in Segona, Spain, during the spring of 2011.

SELECTED PROFESSIONAL EXPERIENCE

2011–Present   HELTON, PETRIE, & McKINNEY   Athens, OH
Senior Receptionist / Clerk. Reporting to the Office Manager, responsible for maintaining smooth daily operations, public relations, sales, the organization of incoming and outgoing client information, and part-time supervision of clerical staff. **Highlights:** Credited with the redesign and total reorganization of existing mailing and correspondence systems resulting in improved communication, streamlined operations, and a significant increase in customer satisfaction. Noticed for developing new and influential community contacts responsible for increased legal referrals.

"Mary Beth is a very positive person, excited about her own education and contagious in her enthusiasm. She can speak without hesitation on almost any subject. Her skills are superior, and she will be a tremendous asset to any organization."

—Denise Thacker
Spanish Professor,
Ohio University

2009–2012   OHIO UNIVERSITY   Athens, OH
Student Assistant. Reporting to the Dean of the Foreign Language Department, installed new laboratory program for use by students and faculty. Provided private tutorial instruction for 20 undergraduate students. **Highlights:** Recruited for two consecutive years by the Foreign Language Department Dean to organize and promote statewide participation in the Ohio Foreign Language Festival.

PRESENTATIONS

Selected to present "La Voz a Ti Debida" de Pedro Salinas at the Ohio University Senior Seminar Congreso—Spring 2010

42

Degree: BS, Communications.
Job Target: Ad copywriter, account executive, or related entry-level position in an advertising/public relations firm or radio/TV station.
Strategy: Highlighted two internships and related college experience in a strong functional skills section.

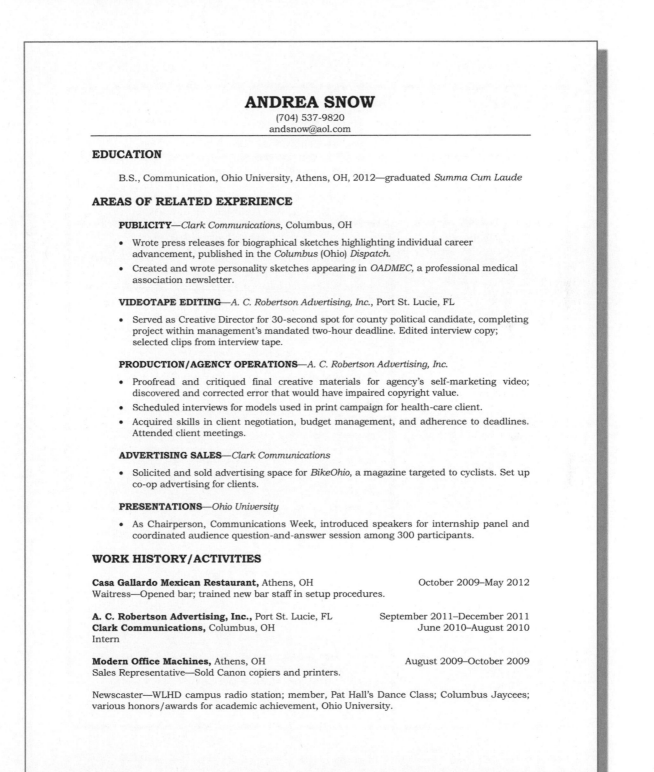

ANDREA SNOW
(704) 537-9820
andsnow@aol.com

EDUCATION

B.S., Communication, Ohio University, Athens, OH, 2012—graduated *Summa Cum Laude*

AREAS OF RELATED EXPERIENCE

PUBLICITY—*Clark Communications*, Columbus, OH

- Wrote press releases for biographical sketches highlighting individual career advancement, published in the *Columbus* (Ohio) *Dispatch*.
- Created and wrote personality sketches appearing in *OADMEC*, a professional medical association newsletter.

VIDEOTAPE EDITING—*A. C. Robertson Advertising, Inc.*, Port St. Lucie, FL

- Served as Creative Director for 30-second spot for county political candidate, completing project within management's mandated two-hour deadline. Edited interview copy; selected clips from interview tape.

PRODUCTION/AGENCY OPERATIONS—*A. C. Robertson Advertising, Inc.*

- Proofread and critiqued final creative materials for agency's self-marketing video; discovered and corrected error that would have impaired copyright value.
- Scheduled interviews for models used in print campaign for health-care client.
- Acquired skills in client negotiation, budget management, and adherence to deadlines. Attended client meetings.

ADVERTISING SALES—*Clark Communications*

- Solicited and sold advertising space for *BikeOhio*, a magazine targeted to cyclists. Set up co-op advertising for clients.

PRESENTATIONS—*Ohio University*

- As Chairperson, Communications Week, introduced speakers for internship panel and coordinated audience question-and-answer session among 300 participants.

WORK HISTORY/ACTIVITIES

Casa Gallardo Mexican Restaurant, Athens, OH   October 2009–May 2012
Waitress—Opened bar; trained new bar staff in setup procedures.

A. C. Robertson Advertising, Inc., Port St. Lucie, FL   September 2011–December 2011
Clark Communications, Columbus, OH   June 2010–August 2010
Intern

Modern Office Machines, Athens, OH   August 2009–October 2009
Sales Representative—Sold Canon copiers and printers.

Newscaster—WLHD campus radio station; member, Pat Hall's Dance Class; Columbus Jaycees; various honors/awards for academic achievement, Ohio University.

43

Degree: BFA, Fashion Design and Fashion Merchandising.
Job Target: Fashion coach or stylist.
Strategy: Emphasized unique activities and notable recognition to create the image of a fashion professional who is already a success.

BILLIE JONES

Email: billiejones@ymail.com • **Cell:** 763-353-9399

Permanent Address: 5151 Sunshine Street, Minneapolis, MN 55443

University Address (through May 30, 2012): 635 8th Mile Road, Detroit, MI 48235

FOCUS: FASHION COACH • STYLIST

Seeking an entry-level consultant position where I can utilize my fashion experience, diverse business knowledge, and strong leadership skills to deliver breathtaking runway events.

PROFESSIONAL ENDORSEMENTS

- "Billie has a reputation for turning ordinary runway shows into extravagant New York events."

- "Billie has established herself as the go-to student designer who delivers eloquent results time after time."

EDUCATION

International Academy of Design and Technology, Detroit, MI

Candidate for Bachelor of Fine Arts Dual Majors in Fashion Design and Fashion Merchandising (May 2012)

ACADEMIC HONORS
- Current GPA: 3.84
- Dean's List every semester

LANGUAGES

Conversational Spanish and German

ACADEMIC PROFILE

- Consumer Trends and Behavior
- Fashion Show Production
- Human Anatomy
- Color, Proportions, and Textiles
- Business Fundamentals
- Team Work and Collaboration
- Broadcasting Ads
- Consumer Market Segments
- Clothing Merchandise
- Electronic Marketing
- Retail Management
- Event Planning
- Apparel Design

PROFESSIONAL INTERNSHIP

Student Intern, Powers Modeling Agency   June–August 2009
Detroit, MI

Handpicked out of five interns to shadow president. Made suggestions that were implemented by the agency. Exposed to top fashion gurus throughout the U.S.

- **Coordinated** and single-handedly implemented a two-day talent scout advertisement that attracted more than 300 models. Selected 50 for local jobs.
- **Designed** a five-week modeling boot camp to teach local teens about runway presence, latest walks, and appropriate accessories.
- **Translated** Spanish and German for agents and models during international fashion events.

Student Intern, Jays' Fashion Production   June–September 2010
Minneapolis, MN

Choreographed more than 20 fashion shows for Minnesota Fashion Week and Rip the Runway events. Turned average outfits into fashionable designs through coordination of style and fabric, accessories, and body types. Taught fashion segments for St. Paul Middle School students to educate them on proper techniques to compete for the Junior Achievement Fashion Show.

- **Received** citywide recognition for the best fashion premiere hosted by a college student.
- **Handpicked** by six modeling agencies for the lead stylist position during Fall Fashion Week.
- **Named** "Student Fashion ICON" for 2010.

EMPLOYMENT EXPERIENCE

Lead, Angie's Hair Salon   June–August 2008
Minneapolis, MN

Promoted to assistant manager within 30 days on the job. Trained hair stylists on customer service and conflict resolution skills.

- **Hired and trained** more than 15 new employees within 30 days to support high-volume season.
- **Resolved** customer concerns in the absence of manager—earned reputation as an "office coach."
- **Organized** a Friends and Family Day to increase clientele and profits.

44

Degree: BA, Architecture.
Job Target: Architect in a large city.
Strategy: Captured key skills using a sleek presentation unlike any others: The resume, along with an outstanding portfolio of Web designs and more, was stored on a CD-ROM and sent in a classy folder with a cover letter.

BRIAN KITTS

Permanent Address:
3226 Lexington Drive
Findlay, OH 45840
(419) 423-1952

Campus Address:
5262 Brown Road, Apt. #18
Kent, OH 44240
(330) 461-3040
kittsba@yahoo.com

Seeking position as … Architectural Designer

✶ **Digital-Based Architectural Media Development & Design** ✶
A Team Player with Excellent Interpersonal Skills

PROFILE

A detail-oriented, high-energy individual with strong creative and technical skills as evidenced by the ability to provide innovative practical design solutions utilizing …

Photo Realistic Rendering & Animation	Architectural Design
Photo Manipulation	Graphics Design/Layout
3D Virtual & Physical Modeling	Project Management
Multimedia Presentation Development	Computer IT Services

EDUCATION

KENT STATE UNIVERSITY, Kent, OH   2012
Bachelor of Arts, School of Architecture   GPA: 3.7

DESIGN/MEDIA EXPERIENCE & INTERNSHIPS

KENT STATE UNIVERSITY ARCHITECTURE LAB, *Lab Consultant,* Kent, OH   2010–PRESENT
- Instruct and implement computing resources for students.
- Monitor usage of computer lab and maintain facilities.

DIGITAL i LTD., *Independent Contracting Intern,* Kent, OH   SUMMER 2011
- Performed three-dimensional modeling for Apollo Homes Corporation.
- Generated three-dimensional animations/virtual walkthroughs for Kelly Corporation.

PERSONAL PHOTO SERVICE, INC., *Digital Photography Assistant,* Kent, OH   SUMMER 2011
- Constructed, operated, and maintained high-end workstations.
- Performed image manipulation and graphic-design consulting.

MARATHON/ASHLAND, LLC, *Graphics Department Intern,* Findlay, OH   SUMMER 2010
- Created national corporate advertisements.
- Performed image manipulation, document cropping, and file exportation.

ACTIVITIES & AFFILIATIONS

Architectural Mentoring Program
Kent State University Architectural Advisory Council,
   Student Representative
Kent State University Steel Drum Band

> "Brian has the ability to perform at a high level within a team environment and to maintain his sense of individuality and personal drive."
> Larry Williams
> Supervisor, Digital i Ltd.

COMPUTER TECHNOLOGIES

Environments:	Microsoft Windows, Macintosh OSX
Languages:	BASIC, Visual C++, Pascal
PC Software:	3dsMAX, Form_Z Modeling, AutoCAD
	Adobe Photoshop, InDesign, Flash, Dreamweaver
	Microsoft Office: Word, Excel, PowerPoint

45

Degree: BA, Interior Design.
Job Target: Designer with a home design trend leader.
Strategy: Created a visually compelling resume to attract attention from a highly desired employer in a competitive industry.

Jacqueline P. Jones

459 Pine Valley Circle ❏ Idaho Falls, Idaho 83406 ❏ (208) 528-0770 ❏ (208) 521-0945 Cell ❏ E-mail: dezynr@email.com

CAREER OBJECTIVE
Residential, Showroom, and Office Interior Design

PROFESSIONAL SUMMARY
- More than six years of experience in family-owned interior design business.
- Successful in selling a variety of interior design products by establishing good rapport with clients, determining their needs, and making recommendations on products based on competent knowledge.
- Have established clientele including contractors, businesses, and private individuals.
- Won Best Decorated Home—Builder's Show 2010.
- Organized, scheduled, and marketed events and shows for automobiles and RVs.
- Decorated campers, trailers, and motor homes for trade shows.
- Redesigned a 30,000-square-foot showroom and won Second Place in Display Competition.

PROFESSIONAL SKILLS
- Expertise in coordinating wallpaper, window treatments, floor coverings, tile, accessories, and overall design.
- Highly motivated, resourceful, and can get the job done.
- Excellent customer service and public relations.
- Prompt, reliable, dependable, and willing to learn.
- General office skills including answering multi-line telephone system and operating copy, facsimile, and other office machines.
- Computer literate—experience in Word, Excel, DesignCAD, AutoCAD, Illustrator, Quark, Photoshop, Visio, Internet, and e-mail.

WORK EXPERIENCE
INTERIORS BY DESIGN, Idaho Falls, Idaho. May 2007–Present (Part-time). Family-owned business.
Designer Trainee. 2011–Present. Produce floor plans and designs for homes, offices, and commercial space. Work with clients to determine color schemes, lighting, window treatments, accessories, wallpaper, and overall design.

Salesperson. 2008–2011. Sold a variety of wallpaper, carpet, linoleum, furniture, and accessories. Made office visits and in-home visits to assess customer needs. Placed orders and tracked sales.

Inventory Stocker/Receptionist/Cashier. 2007–2008. Answered multi-line phone system, directed calls, balanced cash drawer, and made bank deposits. Regrouped and organized wallpaper and accessories to make them easier to locate.

EDUCATION
Idaho State University, Pocatello, Idaho
Bachelor of Arts in Interior Design, 2012

Degree: BFA, Photography.
Job Target: A position in a fine-arts museum with future growth to director level.
Strategy: Emphasized valuable and highly relevant internships; created interesting visual design. Note the reference to the online portfolio at the end.

Margo L. Kramer

2520 Main Street • Townsville, MA 01583 • (508) 355-1034 • pixperfect@cs.com

Objective

To apply photography education along with freelance and internship experience in a studio or fine-arts institution.

Education

Bachelor of Fine Arts, May 2012   The Art Institute of Boston, Boston, MA
   Photography major
   Portfolio scholarship award for "Rails" Series, 2009

Internships

The Image Maker, Boston, MA   A non-profit photography gallery
   Assistant to Director during auction and member selection for exhibits. Independently built and maintained an accurate mailing list.

The Art of Life, Inc., Boston, MA   A custom black-and-white photofinishing, matting, and framing studio
   Applied photography techniques to assist with retouching/spotting of finished fine-art photographs for gallery inventory and professional darkroom clients. Acquired experience and became proficient in matting and framing fine-art photographs. Utilizing computer skills, scanned photographs and entered pertinent data relative to individual photographs into database, creating a foundation for the existing photographic database.

Exhibits

   Gallery 601, "Behind the Scenes Portfolio"
   Equinox Grille, "Mixed Media"
   Water Street Café, "Thanksgiving Parade"
   Kougeaus Gallery, "Waiting" (from "Rails" series; selected photography)
   First Impression Gallery, "Student Exhibit"

Publications

   Old House Interiors ....Stylist/Photo Assistant, "Bates Mansion 2012"
   Gallery Guide ....Advertisement for Kougeaus Gallery Exhibition
   Art Institute of Boston...Awards Brochure, "Connections"

Additional

   Experienced with medium-format photography and digital photography for portraits, documentaries, and special events, including weddings, birthdays, and anniversaries. Additional experience includes extensive knowledge of textures and patterns for visual display.

   Funded education working in local restaurant and as freelance photographer, stylist, and garden planner.

Portfolio available   www.margosart.com/portfolio

47

Degree: BS, Elementary Education.
Job Target: Elementary school teacher.
Strategy: Used appropriate fonts and graphics to help this new teacher's resume stand out. Created clever "A-B-C-D-E" profile. Detailed student-teaching experience to effectively convey teaching abilities.

 ANNE C. ELLIS

360-445-1256 • acellis@gmail.com
210 Candlewood Court • Lacey, Washington 98509

OBJECTIVE

A position as an **Elementary School Teacher** that will utilize strong teaching abilities to create a nurturing, motivational, and stimulating learning environment to help children achieve their potential.

PROFILE

A highly motivated, enthusiastic, and dedicated educator who wants all children to be successful learners.
"**Believe** in the impossible"; continually research educational programs and procedures to benefit students.
Committed to creating a classroom atmosphere that is stimulating and encouraging to students.
Demonstrated ability to consistently individualize instruction, based on students' needs and interests.
Exceptional ability to establish cooperative, professional relationships with parents, staff, and administration.

EDUCATION

B.S. in Elementary Education, Troy State University, Dothan, Alabama   May 2012
• Summa Cum Laude • President's Honor List • Kappa Delta Phi
• National Collegiate Education Award Winner
• Who's Who Among Students in American Universities and Colleges
• Participated in the Test for Teaching Knowledge field project, 2011
A.A. in Arts and Sciences, Pierce College, Tacoma, Washington   2008

CREDENTIALS

Elementary Education   Washington License (K–8)—Alabama License (K–6)

STUDENT TEACHING

Student Teacher—Grade 1, Harrand Creek Elementary School, Enterprise, Alabama   Fall 2011
Completed 200 hours of hands-on teaching in a first-grade classroom. Utilized children's literature to teach and reinforce reading, writing, grammar, and phonics. Coordinated and taught math lessons and activities. Collaborated with teacher in planning, preparing, and organizing thematic units. Observed the use of teaching techniques to meet the needs of visual, kinesthetic, and auditory learners for all subject areas. Assisted in the quarterly grading.

STUDENT INTERN EXPERIENCE (60 hours)

2nd Grade, Reading, Clover Park Elementary School, Dothan, Alabama
4th Grade, Reading, Science & Social Studies, Headland Elementary School, Dothan, Alabama
4th Grade, Math, EastGate Elementary School, Dothan, Alabama
5th Grade, Art & Social Studies, EastGate Middle School, Ozark, Alabama
1st Grade, Reading Tutor for student at-risk program, Troy State University, Alabama

RELATED EXPERIENCE

Director, Kinder-Care Learning Centers, Lacey, Washington   2003 to 2005
Oversaw day-to-day operations of child care center for 65 children. Ensured all local, state, and federal rules and regulations were adhered to.

AFFILIATIONS

Member, National Council for Exceptional Children
Leader, Girl Scouts of America

48

Degree: BA, Education.
Job Target: High-school history, political science, or geography teacher.
Strategy: Combined all relevant teaching positions (even though they were unpaid) in one section to demonstrate substantive teaching experience despite new-grad status.

EDUARDO DIAZ

2104 E. 12th St. #7 | Fremont, NE 68025 | (402) 464-8460 | eduardo@uno.edu

EDUCATION

University of Nebraska at Omaha   2012
☑ Bachelor of Arts in Education — Social Science 7–12 Field Endorsement
☑ Cumulative GPA: 3.97/4.0 — Dean's List 7 consecutive semesters from 2008–2011

CORE COMPETENCIES

Teaching and training experience both in schools and in business. Competent, results-oriented instructor able to motivate students of differing abilities to achieve their potential.
☑ Certified to Teach: History, Political Science, Geography, Economics, Sociology, Psychology
☑ Strengths: Integrated Curriculum, Multicultural, Service Learning, Special-Needs Students
☑ Classroom Media: PowerPoint, Internet Research, Microsoft Word

TEACHING EXPERIENCE

Student Teacher, Grades: 7–12   Auburn Public Schools, Auburn, NE   2012
☑ Taught World History, American History, American Government, and Sociology to 100 students.
☑ Instructed students on how to research political parties, develop platforms, and debate ideas.

Student Practicum, Grades: 7–8   Hildreth Middle School, Fremont, NE   2011
☑ Created and taught unit on Louisiana Purchase to 20 students.
☑ Planned and implemented service-learning project to increase awareness of economically disadvantaged persons.

Master-Level Tutor, Undergraduates   University of Nebraska at Omaha   2010–2011
☑ Certified by International College Reading and Learning Association.
☑ Tutored students in History, Political Science, Sociology, and Geography.
☑ Trained new tutors at workshops.

Student Mentor, Grade: 8   Central Catholic High School, Fremont, NE   2009–2010
☑ Tutored student with AD/HD in English, Math, Science, and History.
☑ Implemented creative learning techniques that resulted in student passing exams.

WORK EXPERIENCE

Shift Manager/Crew Member   Mexican Fiesta, Fremont, NE   2007–present
☑ Managed up to five employees, including hiring, training, and scheduling.
☑ Balanced daily receipts and deposited cash at bank.

PROFESSIONAL ACTIVITIES

Presented *Atlantic Conflict* paper at Phi Alpha Theta National Conference in San Antonio   2011
Phi Alpha Theta (History Honor Society): Vice President, 1 year   2009–present
History Club: President, 2 years   2009–present
History Department liaison to incoming freshmen   2011
Phi Eta Sigma (Freshman Honor Society)   2008–2009

CREDENTIALS ON FILE

Office of Career Services, University of Nebraska at Omaha, Omaha, NE 68182 | (402) 554-8501

49

Degree: BA, Health and Exercise Science/Health and Physical Education K–12.
Job Target: Health and physical education teacher.
Strategy: Employed powerful quotes as part of the summary section to immediately establish the fact that she has excellent experience and recommendations as a teacher.

PAMELA GRATZ

233 Oakland Drive ▪ Freehold, NJ 07728 ▪ 732-555-5987 ▪ gratz233@email.com

TEACHER / SECONDARY EDUCATION
HEALTH AND PHYSICAL EDUCATION

"Ms. Gratz is exceptionally skilled in keeping the students motivated and focused through innovative exercise programs that she developed to increase confidence, teamwork, and physical fitness." (Ronald Fox, Phys. Ed Teacher, Chester Township Middle School)

Dedicated professional with demonstrated ability in **creating innovative lesson plans and interactive games and exercises for the physical and mental development of mainstream and special education students.** Experienced with skill assessments, one-on-one instruction with disabled students, and teaching strategies that create student enthusiasm for learning. **Fluent in Spanish.**

"...Pamela organized and promoted the entire agenda for Fitness Awareness Week. Her energy and dedication to the success of this event went beyond all expectations. She is an exceptional leader... motivating students to participate and learn." (Janet Frye, Assistant Principal, Wilton Elementary School)

EDUCATION

Rowan University, Glassboro, NJ
B.A. – Health and Exercise Science / Health and Physical Education K-12 (2012)
NJ Teacher's Certification (expected July 2012)

Computer: Microsoft Word, Excel, PowerPoint, Outlook; Adobe Dreamweaver, Photoshop
Personal Activities: Certified Yoga Instructor, Women's Field Hockey and Softball

WORK EXPERIENCE

STUDENT TEACHING (Spring 2012)

WILTON ELEMENTARY SCHOOL, Vineland, NJ
Taught yoga to K–4th grade students, integrating curriculum to meet the needs of 3 inclusion students.
- **Developed and organized Fitness Awareness Week for the entire school.** Contacted and **secured 2 guest speakers from the NFL.** Set up guidelines and prize donations for a student poster contest and spelling bee. **Created Fitness Express, an interactive assembly that quizzed students on their health and fitness knowledge.** Coordinated the activities of students, teachers, and parent volunteers.

HARDING HIGH SCHOOL, Millville, NJ
Coached the girls' volleyball team and assisted coach with boys' varsity baseball.
- Increased awareness of the horrible consequences of drugs and drunk driving. Secured a guest speaker from The Center on Addiction and Substance Abuse (CASA) for juniors and seniors before prom season.

PRACTICUM (Fall 2011)

CRESTVIEW ELEMENTARY SCHOOL, Westmont, NJ
Taught physical education and health to 4th and 5th grade students. Created a lesson plan that included activities focused on learning the different bones and muscles in the body.
- **Assisted 2nd grade students in the preparation of the NJ ASK assessment.** Provided guidance in developing writing and spelling skills through student journals.

CHESTER TOWNSHIP MIDDLE SCHOOL, Pittsgrove, NJ
Assisted the physical education teacher with 6th and 8th grade girls, organizing competitive sports and team building games. Introduced new exercises to increase flexibility and enhance warm-up activities.
- **Taught adaptive physical education class that involved one-on-one instruction for disabled students.** Activities were customized to meet the needs of each student. Techniques included coordination exercises, disability research, and creative games centered on increasing individual focus.

PART-TIME ACTIVITIES COORDINATOR (Summers 2009, 2010)

CHILD'S PLAY, Freehold, NJ
Created and organized educational games, themed parties, and special theatrical events for children ages 3–10.
- **Developed a fitness-themed party that increased bookings 20% in summer 2010.**

50

Degree: BA, Sociology.
Job Target: Social researcher.
Strategy: Highlighted common threads in this all-over-the-board experience from internships, the Peace Corps, and post-college assignment to position her as having the social, analytical, and multilingual skills needed to do social research—even though she had never performed this job.

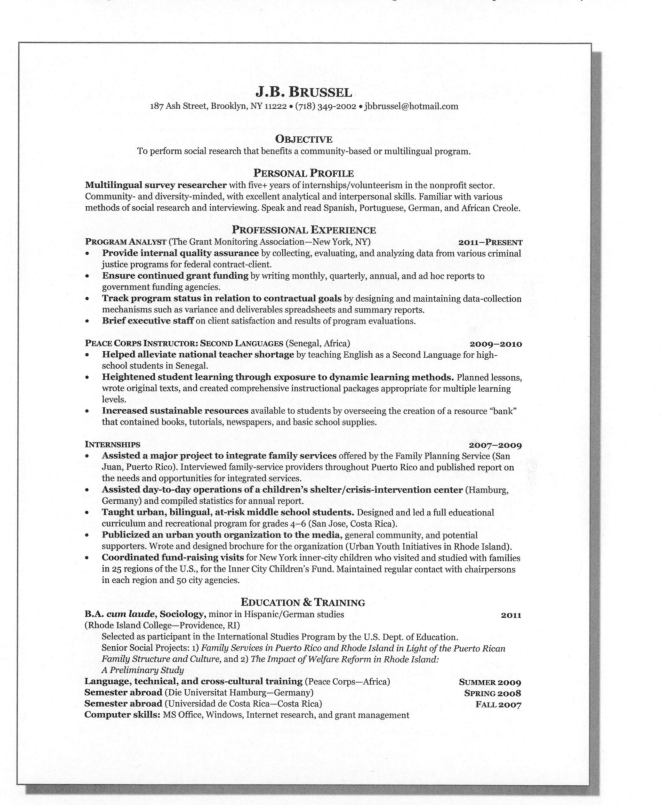

J.B. BRUSSEL
187 Ash Street, Brooklyn, NY 11222 • (718) 349-2002 • jbbrussel@hotmail.com

OBJECTIVE
To perform social research that benefits a community-based or multilingual program.

PERSONAL PROFILE
Multilingual survey researcher with five+ years of internships/volunteerism in the nonprofit sector. Community- and diversity-minded, with excellent analytical and interpersonal skills. Familiar with various methods of social research and interviewing. Speak and read Spanish, Portuguese, German, and African Creole.

PROFESSIONAL EXPERIENCE
PROGRAM ANALYST (The Grant Monitoring Association—New York, NY)   **2011–PRESENT**
- **Provide internal quality assurance** by collecting, evaluating, and analyzing data from various criminal justice programs for federal contract-client.
- **Ensure continued grant funding** by writing monthly, quarterly, annual, and ad hoc reports to government funding agencies.
- **Track program status in relation to contractual goals** by designing and maintaining data-collection mechanisms such as variance and deliverables spreadsheets and summary reports.
- **Brief executive staff** on client satisfaction and results of program evaluations.

PEACE CORPS INSTRUCTOR: SECOND LANGUAGES (Senegal, Africa)   **2009–2010**
- **Helped alleviate national teacher shortage** by teaching English as a Second Language for high-school students in Senegal.
- **Heightened student learning through exposure to dynamic learning methods.** Planned lessons, wrote original texts, and created comprehensive instructional packages appropriate for multiple learning levels.
- **Increased sustainable resources** available to students by overseeing the creation of a resource "bank" that contained books, tutorials, newspapers, and basic school supplies.

INTERNSHIPS   **2007–2009**
- **Assisted a major project to integrate family services** offered by the Family Planning Service (San Juan, Puerto Rico). Interviewed family-service providers throughout Puerto Rico and published report on the needs and opportunities for integrated services.
- **Assisted day-to-day operations of a children's shelter/crisis-intervention center** (Hamburg, Germany) and compiled statistics for annual report.
- **Taught urban, bilingual, at-risk middle school students.** Designed and led a full educational curriculum and recreational program for grades 4–6 (San Jose, Costa Rica).
- **Publicized an urban youth organization to the media,** general community, and potential supporters. Wrote and designed brochure for the organization (Urban Youth Initiatives in Rhode Island).
- **Coordinated fund-raising visits** for New York inner-city children who visited and studied with families in 25 regions of the U.S., for the Inner City Children's Fund. Maintained regular contact with chairpersons in each region and 50 city agencies.

EDUCATION & TRAINING
B.A. *cum laude,* **Sociology,** minor in Hispanic/German studies   **2011**
(Rhode Island College—Providence, RI)
    Selected as participant in the International Studies Program by the U.S. Dept. of Education.
    Senior Social Projects: 1) *Family Services in Puerto Rico and Rhode Island in Light of the Puerto Rican Family Structure and Culture,* and 2) *The Impact of Welfare Reform in Rhode Island: A Preliminary Study*
Language, technical, and cross-cultural training (Peace Corps—Africa)   **SUMMER 2009**
Semester abroad (Die Universitat Hamburg—Germany)   **SPRING 2008**
Semester abroad (Universidad de Costa Rica—Costa Rica)   **FALL 2007**
Computer skills: MS Office, Windows, Internet research, and grant management

51

Degree: BS, Sociology.
Job Target: A position assisting people with disabilities.
Strategy: Highlighted diverse experiences that show a common theme and support this new graduate's career goal.

Monica Salazar

8812 Delmar Boulevard • San Diego, CA 92101
Cell: 619.986.2122 • monica.salazar@msn.com

Assisting People with Disabilities

- Special Needs Programming
- Presentation Skills
- Communication Skills
- Event Planning
- Fluent in Spanish

- Tutoring
- Needs Assessment
- Supervising Children
- Diversity Programming
- Special Olympics

EDUCATION

San Diego State University   2012
BACHELOR OF SCIENCE, SOCIOLOGY
Minor in Psychology   GPA: 3.8

PROFESSIONAL EXPERIENCE

San Diego Families   2010-2012
TUTOR - Coordinated and taught weekly tutoring sessions in English for Spanish-speaking San Diego families.

- Tutored 3 Hispanic students in English on an on-going basis, logging more than 200 tutoring hours.
- Organized opportunities for Spanish-speaking adults to interact with English-speaking adults to improve their oral competency while also increasing their language confidence.

Multicultural Affairs, San Diego State University   2009-2011
OFFICE ASSISTANT - Networked, conducted programs, and collaborated throughout campus and San Diego to enhance appreciation of diversity. Developed campus support system for underrepresented students.

- Conducted 16 programs in first year and 21 programs in second year addressing diversity with student organizations, classes, and special events.
- Organized and managed evening tutoring program, consisting of 27 tutors and more than 75 tutees.

Camp Wonderland, Rocky Mount, MO   Summer 2011
INTERN, ACTIVITIES AND SPECIAL EVENTS - Conceptualized, developed, and delivered structured activities and programs geared toward specific population of campers each week.

- Developed and implemented tie-dyed t-shirt competition for children with Down Syndrome.
- Instituted a karaoke competition and water-balloon game for children with cerebral palsy.
- Conducted a swim relay competition each week modeled after Special Olympics, including medals for winners and certificates of participation for all competitors.

Summer Camp Program, San Diego Family YMCA   Summer 2010
CAMP COUNSELOR - Mentored campers; provided structured activities that emphasized YMCA's core principles.

- Supervised 40-50 campers daily on-site and on field trips with 5-member team of counselors.

ACTIVITIES

Residential Hall Association   2009-2011
VICE PRESIDENT, COMMUNITY ENGAGEMENT CHAIR

- Planned numerous social events including *All Hall Ball* and *Dog Days* for 2,000 on-campus residents.
- Implemented a service requirement for all residents by creating a friendly competition with a pizza party for winning team.

Student Council for Exceptional Children, San Diego, CA   2007-2011

- Collaborated with other Council members to organize annual San Diego Special Olympics.
- Volunteered 25 hours in special education class at Ray Miller Elementary.

52

Degree: BA, Psychology.
Job Target: Employment in human service field while working on postgraduate degree.
Strategy: Created a strong profile to sum up qualifications and strengths; emphasized diverse employment while pursuing a degree to communicate work ethic.

PILAR A. JERASIMO
■ Human Service / Psychology Professional

4922 Church Street, Apt. 24
Nashville, Tennessee 37203

615.255.6223 cell ▪ pilar@yahoo.com

■ PROFILE

Ambitious professional with strong work ethic; substantial knowledge of behavioral and emotional disorders among men, women, and children; and treatment plan design experience.

Hands-on leader, driven by eagerness to help others, and able to assess complex situations and formulate solutions. Motivated and effective communicator who learns quickly, develops expertise, and produces immediate contributions to people, teams, and organizations.

■ EDUCATION

Bachelor of Arts, Psychology (Magna Cum Laude)   2012 Graduate
VANDERBILT UNIVERSITY; Nashville, Tennessee
Coursework included Childhood Psychopathology, Abnormal Psychology, Psychology of Women, Multicultural Communications, Racial and Ethnic Diversity, and numerous other Human Service courses.

■ CAREER EXPERIENCE

Volunteer Aide   2006 to Present
LINCOLN MEMORIAL ELEMENTARY SCHOOL; Hendersonville, Tennessee
Work one-on-one with first and second graders in classroom setting providing guidance with projects and math, spelling, and reading skills; several students suffer from various behavioral and emotional problems, including ADD, ADHD, and ODD.

Intern   2011 to 2012
THE CHILDREN'S SANCTUARY; Nashville, Tennessee
Co-led group-therapy sessions, tutored and assisted residents with homework assignments, reviewed daily journals and logs, wrote words of encouragement in journals, and participated in weekly treatment-team meetings.
▪   Earned perfect job evaluation.

Volunteer   2006 to 2010
ST. MARY HOSPITAL EMERGENCY ROOM; Nashville, Tennessee
Assisted nurses and staff; communicated with and consoled patients and their families; transported blood to and from lab for nurses and doctors.

■ EMPLOYMENT WHILE FINANCING EDUCATION

Dance Instructor   2003 to Present
NEW YORK DANCE STUDIO; Hendersonville, Tennessee
Lead students through various levels of training, coordinate rehearsals and performances for national competitions, encourage and motivate students to discover strengths and talents, and meet with parents regarding their children's well being.

Office Manager   2008 to 2009
HENDERSONVILLE FAMILY HEALTHCARE CLINIC; Hendersonville, Tennessee
Evaluated patient charts and recorded various diagnoses under direction of doctor, participated in resolving patient medical and financial issues, mediated interactions between dentist and patients, and counseled high-anxiety child and adult patients.

Cruise Staff Member / Featured Dancer   2007 to 2008
NORWEGIAN CRUISE LINES; Miami, Florida
Guided guests through excursions, assisted physically challenged guests embarking and debarking ship, and reduced and resolved guest complaints.

53

Degree: BA, Gerontology.
Job Target: Geriatric care/management.
Strategy: Started with a strong profile of qualifications and devoted most of the space on the page to three meaningful internships.

KATHRYN R. REDPATH

1350 Edgewood Drive
Tampa, FL 37906

813-727-0671
kredpath@yahoo.com

GERIATRIC CARE PROFESSIONAL

- ❑ Compassionate and professional—dedicated to providing quality care to the aging.
- ❑ Successful in leadership roles and equally effective as member of a team.
- ❑ Highly organized—able to accomplish multiple objectives.
- ❑ Knowledgeable in proven techniques and latest advances in field of gerontology from recent education and extensive hands-on experience.

EDUCATION

B.A., Gerontology, 2012—University of South Florida, Tampa, FL
Major GPA 4.0; cumulative GPA 3.87

Honors:
Dean's List of Scholars, Sigma Phi Omega Gerontological Honor Society,
National Society of Collegiate Scholars, Golden Key National Honor Society

Selected course work:

Geriatric Case Management	Business Management in an Aging Society
Physical Changes in Later Life	Disability and Society
Death and Dying	Gerontological Counseling

INTERNSHIPS

Case Manager Intern, Fall 2011
Providence Senior Services, Tampa, FL
- ❑ Developed care plans focused on keeping client in home and as self sufficient as possible.
- ❑ Coordinated in-home services with appropriate agencies.
- ❑ Conducted initial assessments and quarterly and annual reviews.
- ❑ Worked with specialty programs including Home Care for the Elderly (HCE), Alzheimer's Diseases Initiative (ADI), and Assisted Living Waiver.

Eldercare Program Intern, Fall 2010
Catholic Charities, Tampa, FL
- ❑ Created, organized, and supervised activities for an Alzheimer's respite program designed to give caregivers personal time while providing meaningful activities for patients.
- ❑ Developed and implemented a special volunteer-education program to train volunteers in the care of and interaction with Alzheimer's patients.
- ❑ Facilitated Alzheimer's support group for client caregivers.

Assistant to Geriatric Care Manager, Summer 2010
Lifespan Services, Inc., Tampa, FL
- ❑ Selected to supervise in-home visits of family members with Alzheimer's patient (mother) with aim to educate them on the disease and how it has affected the patient.
- ❑ Provided detailed written progress reports to case manager.

ADDITIONAL EXPERIENCE

Worked 25–30 hours per week during college career:
Server, Chili's Restaurant, Tampa, FL
Data processor, H.D. Osborne & Associates

Degree: BA, Psychology and Sociology, minor in Criminology.
Job Target: A position in the criminal justice field.
Strategy: Made the most of education, relevant coursework, and general knowledge of criminal justice; highlighted relevant volunteer experience.

AMANDA CARTER

307 Oglesby Court   Home: (615) 824-5629
Hendersonville, TN 37075   Email: carter_ac@yahoo.com

Career Focus—CRIMINAL JUSTICE

Position in Criminal Justice where education, initiative, and a desire to serve
will be of value in administering and safeguarding criminal and judicial processes.

Qualifications Summary

- Recent college graduate with career interest in criminal justice. Familiar with the concepts of justice, due process, criminal behavior, and criminal rehabilitation.
- Strong communication, interaction, and relationship-building skills acquired through work experience and volunteer activities.
- Computer experience with Windows-based software (Word, Excel) and online Internet research. Confident in learning and using new technology and computer applications.

Education

UNIVERSITY OF KENTUCKY—Lexington

| **BACHELOR OF ARTS** | Dual Major—Psychology and Sociology |
| May 2012 | Minor—Criminology |

| Coursework | Criminology—Criminal Law—Penology |
| Highlights: | Juvenile Delinquency—Deviant Behavior |

Work Experience

TEACHER .... 2011 to Present
Children's World, Inc.—Hendersonville, TN

- Provide daily child care for toddlers ages 18 to 24 months in an active learning environment.
- Supervise children during playtime. Interact with parents delivering and picking up children.

KID'S COACH... 2009 to 2010
Discovery Zone—Goodlettsville, TN

- Coordinated and supervised age-appropriate games and activities for children's birthday parties and other special events.
- Kept events running smoothly through effective problem-solving and good decision-making.

SECRETARY / OFFICE ASSISTANT .... Summers 2006 to 2008
Regent Manufacturing Co., Inc.—Portland, TN

- Provided general office support, including answering phones, filing, and accepting deliveries.

Volunteer Activities

- Observed behavior and interaction of children at Kentucky Safe Adoption agency. Reviewed case files and sat in on parenting classes.
- Traveled to Mexico and Costa Rica on youth mission trips. Coordinated VBS activities and helped with construction of new church facility.
- Provided office assistance to Hendersonville Chamber of Commerce (2011).

55

Degree: BS, Criminal Justice (degree pending).
Job Target: Victim/witness program coordinator.
Strategy: Emphasized internships, work experience, and bilingual skills.

Mary Short

1247 Sands Drive
Columbia, MD 21045

410.239.0987
Mshort@yahoo.com

Victim/Witness Program Specialist

PROFILE

Highly skilled coordinator offering the following expertise, competencies, and technical proficiencies:

· Legal Issues	· Case Management	· Problem Solving Abilities
· Legal Research	· Program Coordination	· Superior Organizational Skills
· Constitutional Rights	· Administration Management	· Excellent Interpersonal Skills
· Depositions	· Official Liaison	· Quality Customer Service
· QuickBooks	· Adaptable	· Sensitive to Critical Deadlines
· MS Word, Excel, PowerPoint	· Dependable	· Bilingual (Spanish)

- Two years of direct experience as an advocate and coordinator for Victim/Witness programs. Assist individuals in understanding their rights and entitlements. Represent the division and respond to general and specific inquiries regarding varied types of hearings.

- Work with complex laws governing Grand Theft and Victim/Witness programs and carefully analyze, explain, and apply appropriate laws when guiding or assisting clients. Respond directly to inquiries, demonstrating excellent oral and written communications skills.

- Collect documentary evidence to present to attorneys; ensure victims and witnesses are available for pre-file meetings; process and maintain detailed records and case files.

- Absorb, retain, and recall large amounts of data and information.

PROFESSIONAL EXPERIENCE

Internship. Part time during the school year, full time in summers.
Felony Screening Paralegal/Victim-Witness Coordinator   2009 to 2012
State Attorney's Office, MD

- Conduct telephone interviews of victims who did not witness a crime or do not know the defendant. These crimes involve burglary into a dwelling, structure, or vehicles or a crime dealing with forgery, uttering, or theft of personal documents or property.

- Victim/Witness Advocate Coordinator: Impart strong legal and administrative support to Assistant State Attorneys managing a caseload for victims and witnesses. Coordinate felony cases that are pending trial. Apply a working knowledge of the complete cycle that a victim or witness must complete to resolve cases.

- Coordinate and maintain detailed and accurate calendars for three Assistant State Attorneys, including meetings, victim and witness conferences held at the office, and court dates.

- Maintain accurate client files and assure the availability of victims, witnesses, and law enforcement agents for meetings, pretrial conferences, and court appearances.

(continued)

55 *(continued)*

Mary Short, page two   410.239.0987 ▪ mshort@yahoo.com

Professional Experience, Continued…

- Coordinate depositions. Schedule court reporters and interpreters for state witnesses and victims for the defense attorney assigned to each felony case. Refer victims and witnesses to other services as required, including the Attorney General Crimes Compensation Program for such services as funeral expenses, counseling, emergency monetary assistance, and more.

- Work closely with victims and witnesses, keeping them apprised of the progress of their case or of upcoming hearing dates. Assist individuals in understanding their rights and entitlement to receive special benefits or protection due to their victim/witness status.

- Coordinated legal support requirements for various other hearings and specialized felony cases: Adversary Preliminary Hearings, Arthur Hearings, and Probation Violation Hearings; Homicide Cases, Domestic Violence Cases, and Career Criminal Cases. Guide and assist victims and witnesses, offering compassionate sensitivity to ensure their cooperation on Career Criminal Cases, as they are very reluctant to come forward because the subjects are facing mandatory life sentences.

- On a daily basis, issue subpoenas, provide victim data information on appeal sent from the Attorney General's Office, and update civilian data information on the case file discovery. Maintain a working knowledge of the county database for marriage licenses, real estate, voter registration, Sala and Bressers, and PID Umbrella for investigative research.

- Conduct liaison and build strong working relationships with public resources including Safe Space, Shelter for the Homeless, Elderly Services, Department of Children's and Family Crimes Compensation program, and Department of Corrections and Probation.

- Conduct investigative searches on missing state witnesses and speak with law enforcement officials, witnesses, victims, and medical professionals to obtain information. Contact other civilian resources or the head detectives for any leads on missing witnesses.

- Work efficiently in a fast-paced and pressured environment. Meet or exceed all deadlines.

EDUCATION

- University of Maryland, College Park, MD
  Criminal Justice Major (BS degree), anticipated completion: December 2012
- AA in Business, Howard Community College, MD, 2010

PROFESSIONAL DEVELOPMENT/SEMINARS

- Emergency Response Team Member, 2012, 16 hours
- Domestic Training Seminar, 2012, 40 hours
- Leadership and Effective Communications Skills, 2012, 24 hours

LANGUAGES

- Fluent Spanish (speaking and writing)

56

Degree: BS, Biological Sciences and BS, Psychology.
Job Target: Crime scene investigator/field investigator.
Strategy: Showcased dual qualifications in biological science techniques and psychology knowledge, both desirable for her job target. Listed specific coursework to detail knowledge in scientific techniques and psychology.

Maggie Sarkoff

888 Mantle Drive, Kansas City, MO 64114
Phone: (816) 724-5785
Email: msarkoff@pcbell.net

CRIME SCENE INVESTIGATOR/FIELD INVESTIGATOR

EDUCATION

University of Kansas-Lawrence
B.S., BIOLOGICAL SCIENCES, December 2012
B.S., PSYCHOLOGY, May 2012
Cumulative GPA: 3.5

BIOLOGICAL SCIENCES

- <u>BIOLOGY</u> – Microbiology, Human Anatomy, Cellular Biology, Genetics, Immunology, Virology, Zoology, Botany, and Ecology.

- <u>ORGANIC CHEMISTRY</u> – Focused on nomenclature, reactions, and properties of alkanes, alkenes, alkynes, aromatic compounds, alcohols, ethers, aldehydes, ketones, carboxylic acids, and their derivatives. Utilized thin-layer chromatography, distillation, filtration, NMR, IR, and mass spectroscopy in simple and multistep syntheses for purification and identification.

- <u>QUANTITATIVE CHEMICAL ANALYSIS</u> – Application of gravimetric, volumetric, colorimetric, and electroanalytical determinations.

- <u>OBSERVED AND STUDIED</u> – Electron microscopy, scanning electron microscopy, fluorescence microscopy, Western blot, Northern blot, Southern blot, PCR, gel electrophoresis, ELISA, SDS-PAGE, spectrophotometer, mass spec, and culturing of microorganisms for identification and purification. Highly proficient in light microscopy.

- <u>ENGINEERING PHYSICS</u> – Developed a fundamental understanding of mechanics, with an emphasis on kinematics, dynamics, and statics. Acquired working knowledge of the properties of electricity, magnetism, and light.

PSYCHOLOGY

- <u>ABNORMAL AND CLINICAL PSYCHOLOGY</u> – Anxiety disorders, depression, schizophrenia, bipolar personality disorders, and gender and sexuality disorders. Used DSM-IV as tool to diagnose disorders. Demonstrated the uses and limitations of intelligence testing.

- <u>NEUROSCIENCE AND COGNITIVE NEUROSCIENCE</u> – Anatomy of the brain and its relationship to speech, visual development, spatial acuity, neural plasticity, smell, taste, perception, basic life functions, left brain vs. right brain, and clinical disorders and diseases.

Page 1 of 2

56 *(continued)*

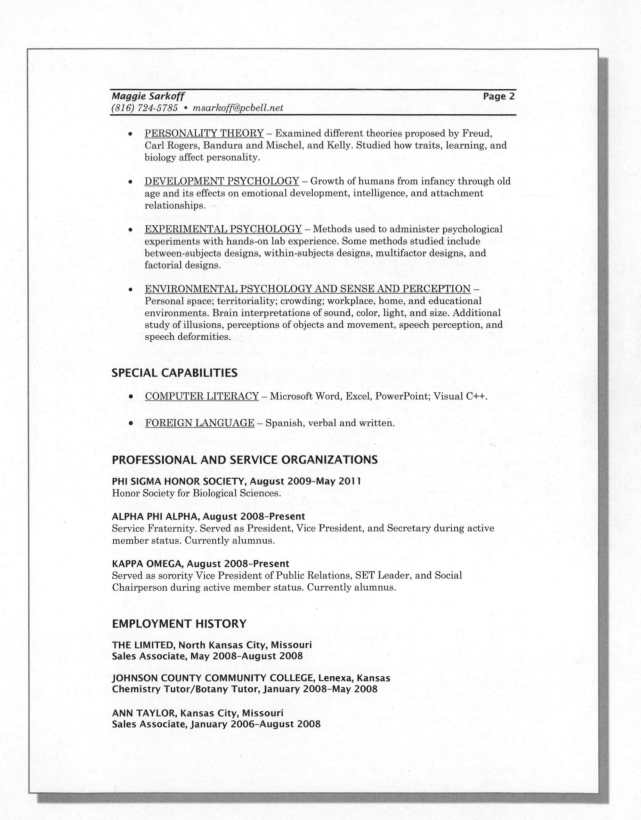

- PERSONALITY THEORY – Examined different theories proposed by Freud, Carl Rogers, Bandura and Mischel, and Kelly. Studied how traits, learning, and biology affect personality.

- DEVELOPMENT PSYCHOLOGY – Growth of humans from infancy through old age and its effects on emotional development, intelligence, and attachment relationships.

- EXPERIMENTAL PSYCHOLOGY – Methods used to administer psychological experiments with hands-on lab experience. Some methods studied include between-subjects designs, within-subjects designs, multifactor designs, and factorial designs.

- ENVIRONMENTAL PSYCHOLOGY AND SENSE AND PERCEPTION – Personal space; territoriality; crowding; workplace, home, and educational environments. Brain interpretations of sound, color, light, and size. Additional study of illusions, perceptions of objects and movement, speech perception, and speech deformities.

SPECIAL CAPABILITIES

- COMPUTER LITERACY – Microsoft Word, Excel, PowerPoint; Visual C++.

- FOREIGN LANGUAGE – Spanish, verbal and written.

PROFESSIONAL AND SERVICE ORGANIZATIONS

PHI SIGMA HONOR SOCIETY, August 2009–May 2011
Honor Society for Biological Sciences.

ALPHA PHI ALPHA, August 2008–Present
Service Fraternity. Served as President, Vice President, and Secretary during active member status. Currently alumnus.

KAPPA OMEGA, August 2008–Present
Served as sorority Vice President of Public Relations, SET Leader, and Social Chairperson during active member status. Currently alumnus.

EMPLOYMENT HISTORY

THE LIMITED, North Kansas City, Missouri
Sales Associate, May 2008–August 2008

JOHNSON COUNTY COMMUNITY COLLEGE, Lenexa, Kansas
Chemistry Tutor/Botany Tutor, January 2008–May 2008

ANN TAYLOR, Kansas City, Missouri
Sales Associate, January 2006–August 2008

Degree: BS, Pathologist's Assistant.
Job Target: Pathologist's assistant.
Strategy: Emphasized impressive experience gained through volunteer work—showing initiative and helping her stand out from other applicants.

JENNIFER J. JAMES

1010 Schreier Road • Rossford, Ohio 43460
419-666-4518 • E-mail: Jjames@juno.com

PATHOLOGIST ASSISTANT

Candidate for Bachelor of Science in Pathologist's Assistant program combined with numerous hours volunteering in career-related positions. Organized, detail oriented, resourceful, and responsible, with exceptional follow-through abilities. Excellent communicator capable of working effectively with a diverse group of individuals from all levels, maintaining an excellent rapport with peers and interdisciplinary staff. Perform extremely well under pressure; enjoy tackling new challenges and learning new concepts. Honest, confident, and hardworking with keen judgement and record of integrity and dependability. Adhere to high ethical and professional standards.

Bachelor of Science in Pathologist's Assistant—Scheduled graduation December 2012
Wayne State University, Detroit, Michigan
Scheduled for Fellowship Examination in February 2013

Clinical rotations: Sinai Grace, Huron Valley Hospital, Histopathology Associations, Hutzel Hospital, Harper Hospital, Botsford Hospital, and Wayne County Medical Examiner's Office

Member of the American Association of Pathologists' Assistants • 2011–Present

WORK EXPERIENCE AND VOLUNTEER PROFILE

WAYNE STATE UNIVERSITY ATHLETIC OFFICE—Ticket Sales / Hostess / Monitor	2008–Present
TENNIS & GOLF COMPANY, Southfield, MI—Sales Cashier	2009
CROY'S RESTAURANT, Dearborn, MI—Waitress	2007
MANOR HOUSE NURSING HOME, Novi, MI—Activities Coordinator	2006
BELMONT HEALTH CARE CENTER, Farmington Hills, MI—Business Office Assistant	2006

HENRY FORD HOSPITAL—PATHOLOGY DEPARTMENT, Detroit, MI   2008–2010
Lab Assistant—STAT Core Lab

Recorded 300 hours as a volunteer working in the STAT Core Lab. Offered paid part-time lab assistant's position handling the receiving and ordering of tests for specimens and delivering STAT and routine specimens per physician's orders. Prepared blood slides and filed specimen tags.

DR. GONZALES, WAYNE STATE UNIVERSITY BIOENGINEERING CENTER, Detroit, MI   2009–2010
Volunteer—150 hours

Observed bioengineering tests performed on cadavers and assisted in the removal of biohazardous waste. Entered cadaver measurements into database. Maintained inventory, processed orders, and contained costs through cost analysis that enabled efficient procurement of supplies.

JOHN HELTON, CERTIFIED PATHOLOGIST'S ASSISTANT, Detroit, MI   2008–2010
Volunteer—80 hours

Gained valuable experience working closely with this certified Pathologist's Assistant observing grossing and dictating as well as autopsies. Processed specimen information.

OBSERVATIONS   2005–2007
Arranged for visitations to gain hands-on experience in the role of a Pathologist's Assistant.

* Wood County Medical Examiner's Office—observed autopsies.
* Pathologist—Medical College of Ohio—grossing and dictating.
* Pathologist—The Toledo Hospital & Children's Hospital—mini-internship observing first autopsy; noted appropriate measurements and witnessed microscopic analysis of slides.

58

Degree: BS, Agricultural Studies.
Job Target: A position in agribusiness.
Strategy: Created an interesting format to grab attention at college job fairs.

James L. Rasmusson

301 North 8th Street #1
Boone, IA 50010
Home: (515) 233-3333
Cell: (515) 231-3333
jrasmuss@aol.com

Profile

Lifelong interest in agriculture showcased by education, internships, and work experience in ag-related environments in crop management, production sales, customer relations, and systems technology.

Strong work ethic, dependability, and ability to perform independently or as part of a team.

Education

BS, Iowa State University
Ames, IA (May 2012)
AGRICULTURAL STUDIES

TEAM PROJECTS:
Nutrient Management

Fly-Ash Environmental Soil Management

AAS, Des Moines Area Community College
Ankeny, IA (2009)
AGRICULTURAL BUSINESS

Computer Skills

Microsoft Office
(Word, Excel, Access, PowerPoint)

GIS / ArcView

Work History

Ag Leader Technology, Inc., Boone, IA
SHIPPING AND RECEIVING (6/11–PRESENT)

- Member of four-person shipping and receiving team for global leader of precision farming electronics. Work with efficiency and timeliness to meet customers' needs during critical seasonal periods.

- Enter received parts and equipment into computer-inventory system for warehousing. Manage shipping duties for customer orders of 10 major products that support precision farming practices, including electronic yield monitors, global positioning satellite systems (GPS), and other precision equipment.

- Record returned parts, GPS, and electronic monitors into computer database for tracking repairs and maintaining customer accounts. Ship repaired products back to customer.

Ames Youth Sports Complex, Ames, IA
GROUNDSKEEPER (6/11–8/11)

- Spread fertilizer, applied chemicals, and prepared irrigation on soccer, baseball, and softball fields. Chalked and dragged softball and baseball diamonds, and painted lines on soccer fields as preparation for activities.

- Aerated, mowed, and seeded grass when needed throughout season to keep complex looking respectable for public use. Cleaned up trash, operated trimmer, and graded driveways.

TJ Ag Service, Inc., Cambridge, IA
Heart of Iowa Co-op, Roland, McCallsburg, IA
INTERNSHIPS—TRUCK DRIVER (4/10–6/10) / LABORER (4/08–6/08)

- Managed chemical building for TJ during post-chemical-application season. Prepared chemical and dry fertilizer orders for customer and company use; filled, weighed, and calibrated chemical bulk tanks; filled trucks with water or liquid nitrogen.

- Drove liquid- and dry-fertilizer tender truck during both internships; filled anhydrous ammonia tanks and delivered to customers; set up unloading process for liquid nitrogen and dry fertilizer from railroad car to company storage.

- Performed maintenance on equipment and buildings for storage and display. Used excellent customer-service skills while delivering seed and filling customers' orders from warehouse.

Degree: BS, Nursing.
Job Target: Registered Nurse.
Strategy: Described internships in some detail because they provide hands-on nursing experience to supplement her classroom education.

FE MANALO, R.N.

815 Mott Way ◆ Long Valley, NJ 07853 ◆ 973-971-3856 Cell ◆ femanalo@aol.com

REGISTERED NURSE
Meticulous, knowledgeable nurse with a demonstrated passion for delivering the best in patient care

SUMMARY OF QUALIFICATIONS

- Licensed Registered Nurse with recent BSN degree from NLNAC–accredited program.
- Driven healthcare professional with solid academic foundations and highly favorable evaluations for performance during 682 hours of clinical experience across 5 rotations.
- Dedicated caregiver known for patient-first style; a committed patient advocate who leverages critical-thinking skills to seek out the best for patients to deliver the best in patient care.
- Effective multitasker who thrives in demanding, fast-paced environments. A meticulous, detail-oriented professional who effectively manages workloads to get the job done–and done right.
- Skilled communicator who is effective in building rapport with patients from diverse backgrounds, easily establishing sense of confidence and trust.

EDUCATION

COLLEGE OF ST. ELIZABETH, Morristown, NJ
Bachelor of Science Degree in Nursing (BSN), 2011
   ▷ Graduated *cum laude*, GPA: 3.5/4.0.
   ▷ Inducted into Sigma Theta Tau, the international nursing honor society, October 2010.

CLINICAL EXPERIENCE

MORRISTOWN HOSPITAL, Morristown, NJ
Nursing Intern
Completed 550 hours of clinical practice with rotations in medical/surgical (375 hours), PICU (135 hours), and pediatrics (40 hours). With minimal supervision, provided total patient care in each unit for as many as 4 patients at a time. Monitored patients, charted progress, addressed patient needs, and handled necessary procedures.

- Gained very positive feedback from patients for level of care delivered and dedication to needs.
- Earned high marks from instructors for ability to meet and manage job demands, capably keeping up with charting while providing excellent care to patients.
- Completed voluntary "passions" class, working one-on-one with preceptor for 135 hours to build clinical mastery. Impressed preceptor with knowledge, skills, and development, earning high praise for performance.
- Working in pediatrics, effectively interacted with parents, building a strong sense of confidence and trust in caring for their children.

GREYROCK MENTAL HEALTH HOSPITAL, Morris Plains, NJ
Nursing Intern
Completed 60 hours of clinical experience in locked adolescent unit in psychiatric hospital. Observed caregivers and interacted with patients (children aged 11 to 18).

- From nurses working in difficult situations, learned methods to de-escalate tensions and restore calm.

HOLY CROSS MEDICAL CENTER, Somerville, NJ
Nursing Intern
Completed 72 hours of clinical experience in labor/delivery and postpartum nursery unit.

- Observed delivery of services to moms and provided nursery care to newborns.

PROFESSIONAL CREDENTIALS

Licensed Registered Nurse, 2011; **BLS for Health Care Provider** Card Holder

---

60

Degree: BS, Civil Engineering.
Job Target: Wastewater civil engineer.
Strategy: Emphasized problems solved in class because he hadn't been able to obtain a summer job or an apprenticeship in engineering.

Charles W. Morgan

861 Lem Morrison Drive Auburn, Alabama 36830 ✦ cwmorgan@wahoo.com ✦ [334] 555-5555

What I bring to the Wastewater Department as an Entry-Level Civil Engineer:

✦ **Drive** to solve difficult problems — for the fun of doing it.

✦ **Discipline** to handle complex challenges well.

✦ Natural **aptitude** for advanced mathematics.

Education:

✦ B.S., **Civil Engineering,** Auburn University, Auburn, Alabama — 2012

Worked up to 20 hours a week for six semesters while carrying 15 credit hours. Athlete of the year every year from 2008 to 2011.

Selected coursework:

✦ Pipe and channel flow

✦ Soils engineering

✦ AutoCAD

✦ Wastewater treatment

✦ Open channel flow

✦ Statistics

✦ Water treatment

✦ Stormwater drainage design

✦ Environmental design

✦ Engineering materials

✦ Technical and blueprint drawing

Selected Examples of Problems Solved in Civil-Engineering Classes:

✦ Helped design town's entire drinking and wastewater plant. Contributed to 30-page report. Presented oral report before civil engineer with years of on-the-job experience. Got good grade — even though I hadn't taken a prerequisite course.

✦ Did extensive work to find the best site for a county landfill. Factored in major variables from elevation to soil type to climate. My written report well received.

✦ Reviewed hundreds of pages of stringent regulations to help design airport. Laid out three runways that met tough operational requirements.

✦ Analyzed three major engineering projects, parts of Denver International Airport. Demonstrated understanding of how engineering disciplines are integrated in the most challenging situations.

Basic Computer Literacy:

✦ AutoCAD; MS Windows, Excel, Word, and PowerPoint; Internet search tools

Relevant Work Experience:

✦ Summer jobs, including work as a **construction assistant** for W.K. Charning Construction, Montgomery, Alabama

61

Degree: BS, Chemical Engineering.
Job Target: Entry-level chemical engineering position.
Strategy: Highlighted numerous technical skills and experiences, including engineering class projects, as well as technical employment and internship. Included relevant keywords in course titles as well as work experiences.

SIMON R. PEREZ
2523 Pioneer Road, Hillsborough, NJ 08844
908-281-5555 Home ▪ srperez@juno.com

OBJECTIVE

Entry-level Chemical Engineering position utilizing my experience and knowledge in process improvement as well as technical support.

PROFILE

- ☑ Recent college graduate with proven technical and analytical abilities.
- ☑ Demonstrated track record of achieving goals in a team environment.
- ☑ **Computer Skills:** MS Windows, Word, Excel, and PowerPoint; RS3Excel; ChemDraw; Hysys; ProII; Visio.
- ☑ **Technical Equipment and Skills:** Instron tensile tester, Brabender torque rheometer, Brookfield viscomenter, and particle size analysis.

EDUCATION

Bachelor of Science, Chemical Engineering (GPA 3.0)   May 2012
Rutgers State University, New Brunswick, NJ
Specific coursework topics included Process Control, Chemical Plant Design, Polymer Processing, and Engineering Materials.

Engineering Class Projects (one per semester):
- ✓ Electrodialysis Membrane: Participated in 3-person team that increased the efficiency of a precious-metals refinery operation (Diamond Corporation) by introducing ionic separation of components to the refinery process.

- ✓ Biomedical Research: Conducted experiments in chemical engineering of the human body, particularly kidney dialysis and IV drug dosage.

- ✓ Thermal Crosslinking of Kevlar Fiber: Team project to perform tensile testing on heated Kevlar fiber and statistical data analysis.

EMPLOYMENT

Technical Assistant   November 2011–May 2012
Johnson Chemicals Research, Chemistry Division—Skillman, NJ

- Edited confidential documentation for 60 clinical trial projects in preparation for the development of drug-simulation software by an outside company. Assured accuracy of technical content, and eliminated and/or disguised proprietary information.

- Contributed to quality control of pharmaceutical research database, increasing the efficiency of data queries by editing data for uniformity. Utilized RS3Excel to extract research data in editing process.

Chemical Engineering Internship   May 2010–August 2010
Chemical Resins, Inc., Technical Service Division—Princeton, NJ

- Tested properties of Polyvinyl Chloride (PVC) resin (particle size, heat stability, and viscosity testing) for this specialty chemicals manufacturer.

- Provided technical support to three staff chemists in participatory team approach to testing and development of new PVC resin types.

ACTIVITIES

American Institute of Chemical Engineers, College Chapter   2008–2012
- ✓ Charter Member and Newsletter Editor (4 years)

Habitat for Humanity, Mountain Park Clean-up, Princeton, NJ   2006
- ✓ Volunteer

Willing to relocate within the tri-state area.

62

Degree: BS, Management Computer Information Systems.
Job Target: Help desk position.
Strategy: Showed intern and work-study experience combined with education to demonstrate employability for this individual, who is a quadriplegic and has no paid experience.

MICHAEL R. PATEL

94 Dover Parkway   Albany, New York 12211   (518) 682-8810   mpatel94@hotmail.com

OBJECTIVE:	Position utilizing training and hands-on experience in MIS, help-desk services, technical support, and customer service.
SUMMARY:	■ Provide technical assistance and training to computer users in diverse software including Microsoft Office Suite, Adobe Photoshop, and WordPress.
	■ Assist users in Windows and Mac operating system upgrades.
	■ Direct students and staff members in the operation of peripheral equipment.
	■ Help PC users to improve ease of use, increase productivity, access Internet resources, utilize e-mail, and enhance efficiency.
	■ Utilize strong communication and interpersonal skills to assist students from diverse backgrounds and with varied knowledge base.
COMPUTERS:	**Operating Systems:** Windows and Mac OS
	Software: Microsoft Office Suite (Word, Access, Excel, PowerPoint), Adobe Photoshop, WordPress
	Hardware: PCs, printers
EDUCATION:	Siena College, Richard R. Smith School of Business, Loudonville, New York
	Bachelor of Science—Management Computer Information Systems, 12/12
	<u>Relevant Courses</u>: Program Concepts for Business I and II (C++), Database Management Systems, Data Communications and Network, Business Computing Environment, Systems Analysis and Design

EXPERIENCE:

Siena College, Loudonville, New York   9/10–11/12
<u>**ITS Computer Consultant**</u>
Offered technical assistance to the 4,000 students and faculty using the systems and programs in the computer labs.
■ Fielded questions about Microsoft Office productivity software, e-mail applications, and Internet browsers.
■ Aided students and faculty in using peripheral equipment, such as scanners and printers.

NationsBanc Mortgage Corp., Albany, New York   5/10–8/10
<u>**Programming Intern**</u>
Created documentation for various system applications, including macros used to manipulate loan information. Utilized Visual Basic.

Phillips, Lytle, Hitchcock, Blaine & Huber, Albany, New York   6/09–8/09
<u>**MIS Intern**</u>
Collaborated with the law firm's Information Services staff in troubleshooting, diagnosing, and resolving a wide variety of technology problems.
■ Installed software upgrades.
■ Performed troubleshooting of network card problems on individual systems and identified solutions.
■ Installed and upgraded Windows operating system.
■ Synchronized desktop computers with smart phones and troubleshot connectivity problems.

63

Degree: BS, Technology, major in Mechanical Design Technology.

Job Target: Mechanical design in the automotive industry.

Strategy: Presented a well-rounded and prepared professional-to-be by showcasing internship experience at a major automotive corporation and background as captain of her high school golf team.

Jenna L. Sweeney

JLSengineer@yahoo.com

8405 Meadowbrook Lane • Novi, Michigan 48377 • 248.555.6101

CAREER FOCUS

Mechanical Design in the Automotive Industry

EDUCATION & TRAINING

ARIZONA STATE UNIVERSITY—WEST; Phoenix, AZ
Bachelor of Science in Technology, May 2012
Major: Mechanical Design Technology (GPA in Major: 3.7)
Recipient of Society of Manufacturing Engineering (SME) Scholarship—2011
Recipient of Educational Association Merit Scholarship—2008

Technical Skills:
Manual Drafting, AutoCAD, Mechanical Desktop, Unigraphics

Computer Applications:
Microsoft Word, PowerPoint, and Excel; Adobe Photoshop

RELATED EXPERIENCE

DAIMLERCHRYSLER CORPORATION, Fuel Delivery Systems (2009–2011)
PAD Room Intern—Technical Center; Auburn Hills, MI; Summer 2011
Member of Product Assembly Drawings team to explode and analyze assemblies of fuel lines. Attended slow-build production processes at other plants.

- Assisted with developing design drawings and specifications for the diesel high-pressure pump; drafted multiple views of assemblies.
- Participated in Design for Manufacturing meetings and biweekly mockup and design review meetings for information sharing and collaboration.
- Presented a PowerPoint presentation of overall accomplishments at conclusion of Internship.

Design Room Intern—Brighton Engineering Center; Brighton, MI; Summer 2010
Developed technical skills that benefited overall performance and expanded knowledge of detail and accuracy. Attended meetings to update group members on projects and programs.

- Modified drawings of air control values and production actuators.
- Created retainer application specifications.

Design Room Intern—Brighton Engineering Center; Brighton, MI; Summer 2009
Created detailed spreadsheets for parts included in fuel system projects. Developed technical skills as well as teamwork and communication skills while focusing on details and accuracy.

- Adapted existing drawings of in-tank reservoirs, single-phase torque motor to support a throttle body, and development of high-temperature actuators.
- Produced engineering work order for electromechanical fuel alternatives.
- Presented a PowerPoint presentation of overall accomplishments.

---

63 *(continued)*

OTHER EXPERIENCE

ARIZONA STATE RECREATION CENTER; Phoenix, AZ
Certified Aerobic Instructor, 2010–present
Teach all levels of aerobic sports at the university recreation center.

THE GAP; Bloomfield, MI & Scottsdale, AZ
Sales Representative, Summers/Part-time; 2006–2010
Provided customer assistance with merchandise selection and returns. Handled financial transactions (charge/credit and currency); worked on the computerized register. Worked with customers to identify and resolve problems.

PRECISION METAL INDUSTRIES; Trenton, MI
Lab Technician, 2006
Tested aluminum oxide and steel to ensure quality-control specifications were met. Worked independently toward problem identification and resolution.

ORGANIZATIONS & ACTIVITIES

College Of Technology Organization (COTO)—Chair, 2011–present

Society of Manufacturing Engineers (SME)—Chair, Student Chapter, 2010–present

Beta Mu Chapter of Delta Gamma Fraternity—Director of Activities, 2011–present; VP of New Member Education, 2010; Social Chair, 2009

HIGH SCHOOL
Senior Captain of Varsity Golf Team—Earned All-Area and All-Conference Honors

First female in the history of the high school to complete Computer-Aided Design Education Program.

Jenna L. Sweeney
JLSengineer@yahoo.com
8405 Meadowbrook Lane • Novi, Michigan 48377 • 248.555.6101

Degree: BS, Applied Science.
Job Target: Systems analyst.
Strategy: Dressed up a no-frills presentation with a unique logo and plenty of black-and-white facts that support his job target.

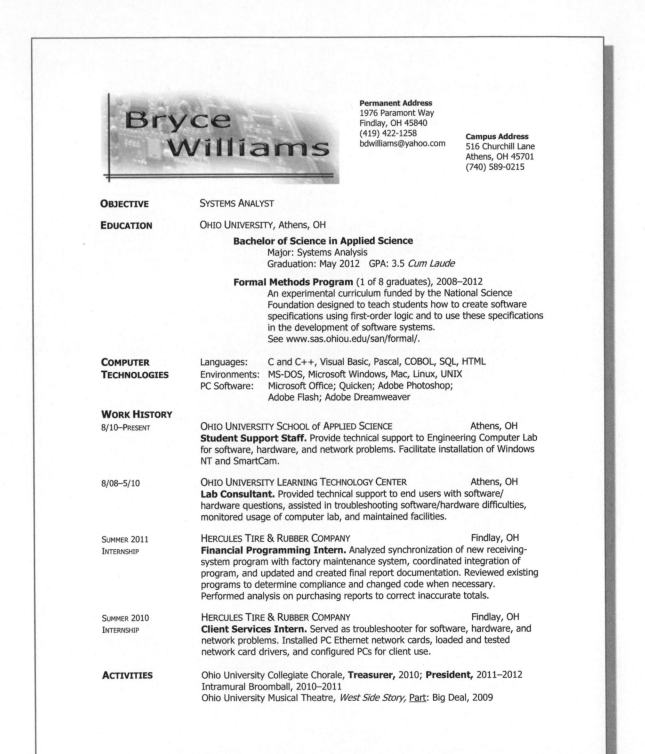

Bryce Williams

Permanent Address
1976 Paramont Way
Findlay, OH 45840
(419) 422-1258
bdwilliams@yahoo.com

Campus Address
516 Churchill Lane
Athens, OH 45701
(740) 589-0215

OBJECTIVE	SYSTEMS ANALYST
EDUCATION	OHIO UNIVERSITY, Athens, OH

Bachelor of Science in Applied Science
Major: Systems Analysis
Graduation: May 2012   GPA: 3.5 *Cum Laude*

Formal Methods Program (1 of 8 graduates), 2008–2012
An experimental curriculum funded by the National Science Foundation designed to teach students how to create software specifications using first-order logic and to use these specifications in the development of software systems.
See www.sas.ohiou.edu/san/formal/.

COMPUTER TECHNOLOGIES
Languages: C and C++, Visual Basic, Pascal, COBOL, SQL, HTML
Environments: MS-DOS, Microsoft Windows, Mac, Linux, UNIX
PC Software: Microsoft Office; Quicken; Adobe Photoshop; Adobe Flash; Adobe Dreamweaver

WORK HISTORY

8/10–PRESENT
OHIO UNIVERSITY SCHOOL of APPLIED SCIENCE   Athens, OH
Student Support Staff. Provide technical support to Engineering Computer Lab for software, hardware, and network problems. Facilitate installation of Windows NT and SmartCam.

8/08–5/10
OHIO UNIVERSITY LEARNING TECHNOLOGY CENTER   Athens, OH
Lab Consultant. Provided technical support to end users with software/ hardware questions, assisted in troubleshooting software/hardware difficulties, monitored usage of computer lab, and maintained facilities.

SUMMER 2011
INTERNSHIP
HERCULES TIRE & RUBBER COMPANY   Findlay, OH
Financial Programming Intern. Analyzed synchronization of new receiving-system program with factory maintenance system, coordinated integration of program, and updated and created final report documentation. Reviewed existing programs to determine compliance and changed code when necessary. Performed analysis on purchasing reports to correct inaccurate totals.

SUMMER 2010
INTERNSHIP
HERCULES TIRE & RUBBER COMPANY   Findlay, OH
Client Services Intern. Served as troubleshooter for software, hardware, and network problems. Installed PC Ethernet network cards, loaded and tested network card drivers, and configured PCs for client use.

ACTIVITIES
Ohio University Collegiate Chorale, **Treasurer,** 2010; **President,** 2011–2012
Intramural Broomball, 2010–2011
Ohio University Musical Theatre, *West Side Story,* Part: Big Deal, 2009

65

Degree: BS, Accounting.
Job Target: Entry-level accounting position.
Strategy: Equally emphasized strong education, activity, and employment experiences to present the picture of a multitalented, well-balanced individual.

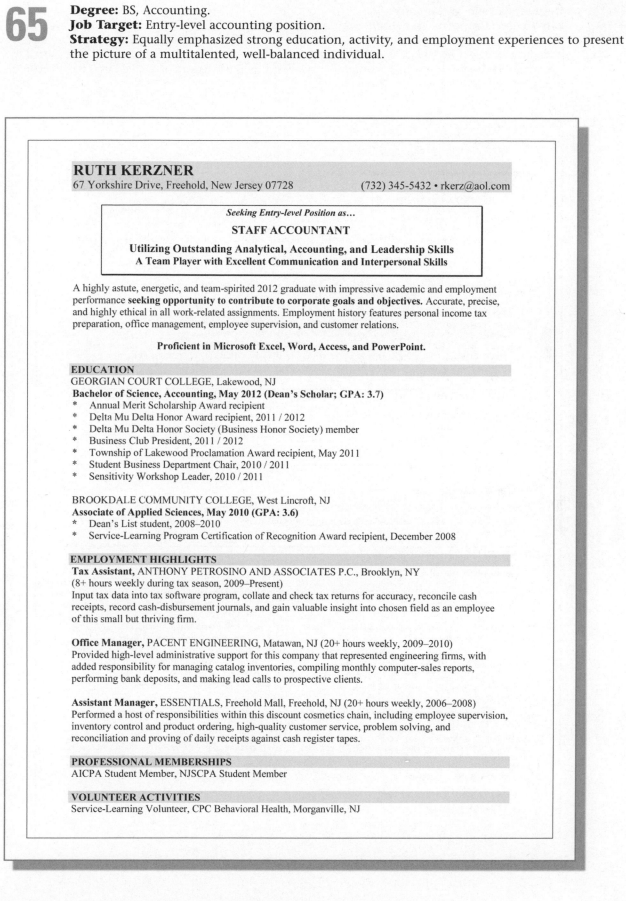

RUTH KERZNER
67 Yorkshire Drive, Freehold, New Jersey 07728   (732) 345-5432 • rkerz@aol.com

Seeking Entry-level Position as…
STAFF ACCOUNTANT
Utilizing Outstanding Analytical, Accounting, and Leadership Skills
A Team Player with Excellent Communication and Interpersonal Skills

A highly astute, energetic, and team-spirited 2012 graduate with impressive academic and employment performance **seeking opportunity to contribute to corporate goals and objectives.** Accurate, precise, and highly ethical in all work-related assignments. Employment history features personal income tax preparation, office management, employee supervision, and customer relations.

Proficient in Microsoft Excel, Word, Access, and PowerPoint.

EDUCATION
GEORGIAN COURT COLLEGE, Lakewood, NJ
Bachelor of Science, Accounting, May 2012 (Dean's Scholar; GPA: 3.7)
* Annual Merit Scholarship Award recipient
* Delta Mu Delta Honor Award recipient, 2011 / 2012
* Delta Mu Delta Honor Society (Business Honor Society) member
* Business Club President, 2011 / 2012
* Township of Lakewood Proclamation Award recipient, May 2011
* Student Business Department Chair, 2010 / 2011
* Sensitivity Workshop Leader, 2010 / 2011

BROOKDALE COMMUNITY COLLEGE, West Lincroft, NJ
Associate of Applied Sciences, May 2010 (GPA: 3.6)
* Dean's List student, 2008–2010
* Service-Learning Program Certification of Recognition Award recipient, December 2008

EMPLOYMENT HIGHLIGHTS
Tax Assistant, ANTHONY PETROSINO AND ASSOCIATES P.C., Brooklyn, NY
(8+ hours weekly during tax season, 2009–Present)
Input tax data into tax software program, collate and check tax returns for accuracy, reconcile cash receipts, record cash-disbursement journals, and gain valuable insight into chosen field as an employee of this small but thriving firm.

Office Manager, PACENT ENGINEERING, Matawan, NJ (20+ hours weekly, 2009–2010)
Provided high-level administrative support for this company that represented engineering firms, with added responsibility for managing catalog inventories, compiling monthly computer-sales reports, performing bank deposits, and making lead calls to prospective clients.

Assistant Manager, ESSENTIALS, Freehold Mall, Freehold, NJ (20+ hours weekly, 2006–2008)
Performed a host of responsibilities within this discount cosmetics chain, including employee supervision, inventory control and product ordering, high-quality customer service, problem solving, and reconciliation and proving of daily receipts against cash register tapes.

PROFESSIONAL MEMBERSHIPS
AICPA Student Member, NJSCPA Student Member

VOLUNTEER ACTIVITIES
Service-Learning Volunteer, CPC Behavioral Health, Morganville, NJ

66

Degree: Bachelor of Commerce.

Job Target: Corporate accounting position.

Strategy: For this individual with no paid work experience, played up academic strengths and ended on a high note with a significant academic project. Note in the summary of professional expertise, the qualifying words "comprehensively trained in" instead of "skilled in," which would imply real-world experience.

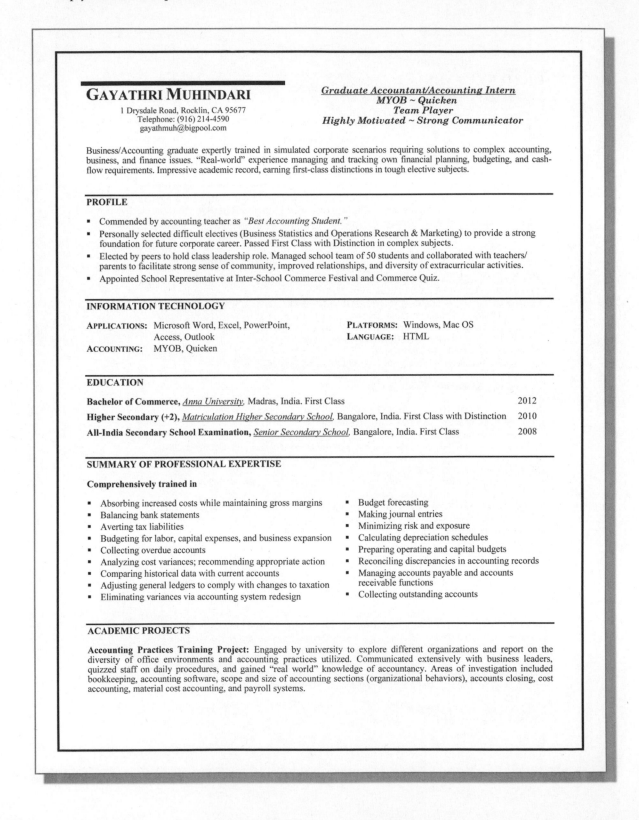

GAYATHRI MUHINDARI

1 Drysdale Road, Rocklin, CA 95677
Telephone: (916) 214-4590
gayathmuh@bigpool.com

Graduate Accountant/Accounting Intern
MYOB ~ Quicken
Team Player
Highly Motivated ~ Strong Communicator

Business/Accounting graduate expertly trained in simulated corporate scenarios requiring solutions to complex accounting, business, and finance issues. "Real-world" experience managing and tracking own financial planning, budgeting, and cash-flow requirements. Impressive academic record, earning first-class distinctions in tough elective subjects.

PROFILE

- Commended by accounting teacher as *"Best Accounting Student."*
- Personally selected difficult electives (Business Statistics and Operations Research & Marketing) to provide a strong foundation for future corporate career. Passed First Class with Distinction in complex subjects.
- Elected by peers to hold class leadership role. Managed school team of 50 students and collaborated with teachers/parents to facilitate strong sense of community, improved relationships, and diversity of extracurricular activities.
- Appointed School Representative at Inter-School Commerce Festival and Commerce Quiz.

INFORMATION TECHNOLOGY

APPLICATIONS: Microsoft Word, Excel, PowerPoint, Access, Outlook	**PLATFORMS:** Windows, Mac OS
ACCOUNTING: MYOB, Quicken	**LANGUAGE:** HTML

EDUCATION

Bachelor of Commerce, *Anna University*, Madras, India. First Class	2012
Higher Secondary (+2), *Matriculation Higher Secondary School*, Bangalore, India. First Class with Distinction	2010
All-India Secondary School Examination, *Senior Secondary School*, Bangalore, India. First Class	2008

SUMMARY OF PROFESSIONAL EXPERTISE

Comprehensively trained in

- Absorbing increased costs while maintaining gross margins
- Balancing bank statements
- Averting tax liabilities
- Budgeting for labor, capital expenses, and business expansion
- Collecting overdue accounts
- Analyzing cost variances; recommending appropriate action
- Comparing historical data with current accounts
- Adjusting general ledgers to comply with changes to taxation
- Eliminating variances via accounting system redesign

- Budget forecasting
- Making journal entries
- Minimizing risk and exposure
- Calculating depreciation schedules
- Preparing operating and capital budgets
- Reconciling discrepancies in accounting records
- Managing accounts payable and accounts receivable functions
- Collecting outstanding accounts

ACADEMIC PROJECTS

Accounting Practices Training Project: Engaged by university to explore different organizations and report on the diversity of office environments and accounting practices utilized. Communicated extensively with business leaders, quizzed staff on daily procedures, and gained "real world" knowledge of accountancy. Areas of investigation included bookkeeping, accounting software, scope and size of accounting sections (organizational behaviors), accounts closing, cost accounting, material cost accounting, and payroll systems.

67

Degree: BS, Marine Business.

Job Target: Primarily marine business, but also interested in investment/financial analysis or market research.

Strategy: Because the graduate's experience in chosen field was nonexistent, emphasized courses relevant to his career interests as well as skills he applied and contributions he made as an employee and intern.

JOHN DENNISON

Email: jden45@aol.com   56 Main Street • Newport Beach, CA 89970   (978) 466-8866

PROFILE

Marine Business ... Investment/Financial Analysis ... Market Research

Talented professional with a solid academic foundation and cross-functional training in **business and marine management.** Demonstrated analytical, research, quantitative, and problem-solving skills. Excellent communications, detail/follow-through, and organizational skills; excel in fast-paced, demanding environments. Customer-service and team oriented. Recognized for productivity and dependability. Advanced computer skills; adept in quickly learning new technologies and applications. Fluent in Spanish and German.

Computer Capabilities—Operating Systems: Windows and Mac. **Applications:** Microsoft Word, Excel, Access, and PowerPoint; Adobe Photoshop and Dreamweaver; CPAS; and various financial applications. **Programming:** Knowledge of JavaScript, HTML, Visual Basic, and website design/maintenance.

EDUCATION

UNIVERSITY OF CALIFORNIA, Irvine, CA, May 2012
Bachelor of Science in **Marine Business** with minor in **Resource Economics**
- Magna cum laude, 3.9 GPA.
- Financed college tuition and expenses through various employment.

Relevant courses: Personal Finance Applications, Shipping & Port Management, Marine Resource Management, Human Use & Management, Economics of Resource Management, Economics & Politics, International Trade in Economics.

Activities: One of only 4 students chosen out of 230 applicants by the Alumni Relations Council to attend the Leadership Academy Training Program, a weeklong seminar held at Purdue University.

EXPERIENCE

Market Research Intern—PETERSON TECHNOLOGIES, Orange, CA (6/10–12/11)

Acquired market-research experience and contributed to business-development efforts at one of the nation's top 15 Internet technology consulting firms. Researched and generated sales lead contacts, as well as company and industry data. Updated and maintained an extensive client database. *Accomplishments:*
- Established more than 2,000 new client leads, boosting sales during the summer months.
- Co-authored training manual for new interns using both print and multimedia applications.

Administrative Support—UNIVERSITY OF CALIFORNIA—ALUMNI RELATIONS, Irvine, CA (9/09–5/10)

Initially hired as part of work-study program in Alumni Relations Office and quickly offered salaried position based on demonstrated skill set. Performed general office and technical support assignments, including creating several new databases that streamlined and enhanced information access.

Dock Manager—NEWPORT MARINA, Newport Beach, CA (9/07–9/09)

Promoted within first month of employment to co-manage dock area, seafood market, and lobster pound at one of the busiest marinas on the West Coast serving recreational and commercial fishing fleets. Key role in managing major fishing tournaments with nationwide competitors. Liaison between commercial fishermen and area fish brokers. *Accomplishments:*
- Achieved record sales, resulting in one of the most financially successful years to date.
- Instilled teamwork; supervised and trained 8 employees in all aspects of marina operations.

Additional: Established seasonal landscaping service and grew business to 50 accounts with 50% repeat/referral clientele based on consistent service quality and excellent customer relations (6/06–9/08).

Degree: BS, Business Management.
Job Target: A management trainee position in finance.
Strategy: Concentrated on solid academics, including leadership training and a broad range of business courses. Highlighted skills and potential.

BRIAN ROBERTS

505 Buffalo Avenue, #128   (216) 515-1408
Cleveland, Ohio 44115   brian505@hotmail.com

BUSINESS GRADUATE
Management Trainee / Financial Services / Investing

Professional Profile:

Proactive business graduate with training and hands-on experience in stock analysis, customer service, marketing, and account development. Extensive training in economics, statistics, and business management. Hands-on experience includes work in business services, individual investment, tutoring, and sales.

Core Skills:
Financial Research … Customer Interface … Solicitation / Marketing … Written / Oral Communication … Internet and Microsoft Office … Marketplace Analysis … Consumer Satisfaction … Statistics

Indicators of Potential:
➤ Demonstrated versatility by successfully handling varied and diverse work experiences, including customer service, research, office administration, and sales / marketing activities.
➤ Performed damage control and problem avoidance by interacting extensively with all parties to gather information, solicit feedback, and listen carefully to concerns and suggestions.
➤ Energized by challenges and described as "intellectually curious and critical with an inner strength and discipline."
➤ Planned and presented lectures, seminars, and presentations, utilizing superior organizational, communication, and interpersonal skills.

Education:

John Carroll University, University Heights, Ohio
Bachelor of Science — Business Management   May 2012
GPA 3.2, Dean's List, Outstanding Student Award

Courses included

Applied Statistics	Business Ethics	International Business
Decision Making	Organizational Behavior	Business Law I and II
Supervision / Management	Communication in Organizations	Human Resources Management
Entrepreneurship	Management Information Systems	Microeconomics
Macroeconomics	Advanced French	Financial Management
PCs for Managers	Business Policy	Principles of Marketing

John Carroll University, Leadership Development Institute, University Heights, Ohio
Completed 8-week Leadership Training Program   2011

Topics included

Team Building	Effective Communication	Conflict Resolution
Proactive Problem Solving	Diversity Education	Organizational Development

Computer:

Microsoft Word, Excel, and PowerPoint

(continued)

---

68 *(continued)*

BRIAN ROBERTS   **Page Two**
(216) 515-1408 • brian505@hotmail.com

Experience:

<u>Career Services Center, John Carroll University</u>, University Heights, Ohio   2009–Present
Student Assistant
Assist students with job search and placement activities.
- Answer telephones, schedule appointments, and research job search resources.
- Prepare brochures, workshop flyers, and campus literature for bulk mailings.

<u>Portfolio Management</u>, Cleveland, Ohio   2008–Present
Individual Investor
Develop and manage a portfolio of six stocks with a 4% average rate of return.
- Research and analyze individual company performance with a focused interest in positive marketplace events.
- Analyze long-range growth and performance and invest with long-term goals in mind.
- Utilize such investment tools as *Wall Street Journal*, *Barron's*, *Morningstar*, Sharebuilder.com, ChaseMellon.com, and NBR.com.

<u>Better Business Bureau</u>, Cleveland, Ohio   Summer 2011
Business Intern
Handled consumer complaints and assisted with agency marketing.
- Processed complaints and forwarded them to companies.
- Documented companies' responses for internal records.
- Compiled business profiles for the general public.
- Revised consumer pamphlets and condensed contents into a more concise format.
- Filed consumer complaints, answered telephones, and prepared bulk mailings.

<u>American Red Cross</u>, Cleveland, Ohio   Summer 2011
Telerecruiter
Performed a variety of marketing and administrative tasks.
- Solicited donors by telephone.
- Managed donor files and updated database.

<u>Total Relaxed Learning Day Camp, John Carroll University</u>, University Heights, Ohio   Summer 2011
Counselor
Taught study skills to college students at academic risk.
- Utilized study techniques such as Pegging, Venn Diagram, Chunking, and Mind Maps.
- Supervised, encouraged, and disciplined program participants.
- Engaged in regular planning and strategy sessions with instructors.

Volunteer:

John Carroll University Residence Council
Multicultural Affairs Coalition

Interests:

Jazz, reading, and foreign films

69

Degree: BA, Political Science.
Job Target: Investment banking/financial services.
Strategy: As this graduate's major, political science, wasn't exactly on target with his career goal, highlighted his significant coursework in economics and an internship with a Wall Street firm. Included impressive information about study abroad in England and extracurricular activities.

TOBIAS JACOBS

E-mail: TobiasJay@gmail.com

42 East 65th Street, Apartment G • New York, New York 10019

212-307-9476

OBJECTIVE

An entry-level position in investment banking or financial services that will capitalize on education, strong interpersonal skills, and excellent organizational capabilities.

EDUCATION

Notre Dame University, Notre Dame, Indiana
Bachelor of Arts, Political Science, 2012
Concentration in International Politics & Economics / Minor in Economics
GPA: 3.3/4.0 (in major); Dean's List; Scholarship Athlete – Division I Lacrosse

Significant Coursework

International Relations	Micro Economics
International Conflict & Solutions	Macro Economics
International Politics & Economics in Developing Areas	Money & Banking

Cambridge University, Cambridge, England
Lord Rothemore Scholar, Summer 2011 – *Selected through competitive application.*
Studied Modern British Social & Economic Policies under Cambridge University professor.

EXTRACURRICULAR ACTIVITIES

Phi Delta Upsilon Fraternity
Served as Director of Campus Affairs and Sergeant-at-Arms. Coordinated campus-wide events, including faculty programming, social events, and charity fund-raisers.

Digger Phelps Celebrity Auction & Fund-Raiser
Played a key role in organizing this charity event that raised more than $140,000 for cancer research at South Bend Medical Center Hospital.

WORK EXPERIENCE

Marketing Consultant, MatTran, Inc.; Penfield, New York   **Feb. 2011–May 2011**
Assisted this manufacturer and distributor of industrial materials-handling equipment to develop and refine Web site.
- Evaluated existing website to identify potential improvements.
- Made recommendations to improve site navigation and increase repeat traffic.
- Worked closely with web developer to create interactive features for online parts ordering, online quoting, and real-time interaction with engineers and customer service.
- Doubled size of website and included information on various case studies, which enhanced firm's credibility with prospective customers.

Intern, Wall Street Investments; New York, New York   **Summer 2010**
- Gained knowledge of equity trading as it relates to hedge funds.
- Observed NYSE trading practices and procedures at J & K Securities and on Merrill Lynch trading floor.
- Assisted stock analyst with various research activities and special projects.

Camp Counselor / Coach, College Lacrosse Camps   **Summer 2009**
- Taught basic lacrosse skills at camps held at Nazareth College, Notre Dame, and Hobart College.
- Worked with middle-school and high-school students to develop leadership and teamwork skills.

COMPUTER SKILLS

Microsoft Word, Excel, Outlook; HTML/XML programming

70

Degree: BA, Strategic Communications/Advertising.
Job Target: A position in advertising or marketing.
Strategy: Detailed a relevant study abroad experience. Immediately established focus with a large, clear headline.

Sarah Williams

329 Chandler Street, Charlottesville, VA 22074 ● sarah.williams@gmail.com ● 703-555-5555

Advertising & Marketing Professional

PROFILE:
Outgoing, energetic professional with a successful record of embracing new challenges and a passion for the art of promotion. **Driven** to establish and achieve business objectives. Excellent listening skills and a positive demeanor. **Resourceful** team member, skilled in identifying project needs and creatively solving problems. Conversational German.

KEY SKILLS:
Branding, Communications, Product Development, Launches, Project Planning, Relationship Building, Market Analysis, Trend Tracking, Organization, Planning, Follow-Through

EDUCATION:
Bachelor of Arts in Strategic Communications, Advertising Major
University of Virginia – Charlottesville, VA, 2012

►**Study Abroad – Fashion Center Rome,** Summer 2011

One of only 14 students selected for study in Rome. Coursework: *Made in Italy – Marketing the Distinct Italian Brand* and Italian Culture, History, and Ethics.

— Engaged with local entrepreneurs and corporate marketing professionals to gain insight into their marketing and advertising strategies for global brands.

— Participated on 4-member team whose 6-week project entailed **creating, marketing, and launching a "Made in Italy" natural skincare product line.**

    o Derived 4-product line from white figs of Cambria renowned for their mythological significance and age-defying, regenerative powers.

    o Conducted market research to determine target demographics, branded the product, and wrote advertising communications and press releases.

    o Developed launch budget and coordinated logistics of a New York "launch party" in cooperation with large fitness center and restaurant.

    o In addition to course requirements, created book on product line derivation, marketing and advertising, advertising budget planning, bottling identification, and packaging design.

►Highlights of additional coursework:

— Market research and ad campaign with a new angle for the **Maybelline** brand.

— Ad campaign for new **Williams Sonoma** gourmet salad dressing.

►Homecoming Alumni Tour Volunteer, 2011
►National Student Advertising Competition, 2010
►Campus Outreach, 2008–2010

SKILLS:
Windows & Macintosh OS   Adobe Photoshop, InDesign, Illustrator
MS Office Suite   Internet Explorer, Mozilla Firefox, Safari

EXPERIENCE:
MACY'S – New York, NY: Sales Associate (Women's & Men's Accessories), 2009–2010
Part-time summer and holiday: Set store record for $8000+ sales in one day.

CON CORPORATION – Apple, VA: Inventory Specialist/Secretary, 2007–2009
Full-time summer and holiday position with global manufacturer/supplier of paper products.

UNIVERSITY OF VIRGINIA MEDICAL CENTER – Patient Records/Secretary: 2008–2009
Part-time clerical position that included creating 16-page patient brochure.

71

Degree: BS, Economics.
Job Target: Retail management.
Strategy: Highlighted his eagerness to seize opportunities to learn more about his product and serve the customer better, in addition to his exposure to various areas of retail operations.

Joseph Plumb

378 196th St.
Chicago, IL 60429

(780) 326-5214
joe445@yahoo.com

Profile

College senior possessing professional management internship and multiple retail work experiences seeking an opportunity in retail management. Prepared to "hit the ground running," drawing on customer service strengths, a desire to work with the public, and keen awareness of business-management principles. Bilingual in English and Spanish.

Education

Bachelor of Science, June 2012
Saint Joseph's College, Rensselaer, IN
Major: Economics **Minor:** Spanish

Experience

- Mozart's Music; Indianapolis, Indiana—August 2011–December 2011
  Management Intern; cross-trained in sales, credit, inventory management, repair department, and account management; learned key management aspects of operating a customer-focused business; offered an opportunity to return in a full-time position.

- Saint Joseph's College; Rensselaer, Indiana—August 2010–December 2011
  Resident Assistant; maintained a comfortable and safe student environment, organizing multifaceted activities and providing peer counseling for 60 residents.

- Olive Garden; Calumet City, Illinois—Summer 2010
  Customer Host; specifically trained for host-stand position after demonstrating superior customer-service skills; proved ability to handle multiple tasks and maintain composure during peak business.

- Kohl's Department Store; Calumet City, Illinois—Summer 2010
  Receiving associate; readily pitched in where needed to provide a seamless backroom operation for storefront efficiency; completed inventory-organization project.

- Home Depot; Glendale Heights, Illinois—Summer 2009
  Sales associate; took initiative in working with vendors to gain product knowledge in order to provide helpful information toward customer purchase decisions; maintained a clean and organized department in an effort to provide convenience to the customer.

- Chicago YMCA; Chicago, Illinois—Summer 2009
  Lifeguard; chosen to administer youth and adult aquatic instruction; CPR and first aid certified; maintained chlorine/ Ph balance of pools and provided security service; forklift trained and tested.

Extracurricular

Symphonic/Jazz/Concert Bands
Minority Student Union Board
Percussion Instructor—Kankakee, Beech Grove, Eastwood High Schools
NCAA Division II Basketball
Selected for Marine Officer Candidate School
Tutored peers in major and minor areas

72

Degree: BA, Human Resources.
Job Target: HR position.
Strategy: Focused on great background as an intern at NBC Studios.

Jeannie M. Adamson

Current Address   E-mail: jadamson@juno.com   *Permanent Address*
MS 222, 4381 S. Benton St.   546 Kouburn St.
Baltimore, MD 21210   Elmira, NY 14904
Phone: (410) 555-4009   Phone: (607) 712-7733

*Enthusiastic college graduate with outstanding work history
and experience in Human Resources.*

Education

LOYOLA COLLEGE, Baltimore, MD, 2012
Bachelor of Arts, Human Resources

Related Professional Experience

NATIONAL BROADCAST COMPANY (NBC), New York, NY   Summer 2011
Human Resources Intern
- Researched and developed plan for first comprehensive intern program.
- Designed, planned, and facilitated business workshops and seminars for more than 120 summer interns.
- Researched MSNBC and CNBC intern programs; compiled binder materials for intern orientation.
- Screened 273 applicant resumes, conducted 82 preliminary interviews, and made recommendations for the Fall 2011 internship placement.
- Drafted NBC Intern community service proposal for Summer 2012 implementation.
- Created intern flyers and presentations after extensive Internet research.
- Developed an evaluation instrument that assessed intern needs.

LOYOLA COLLEGE, Baltimore, MD   2010-present
Student Coordinator
- Recruit and select students to participate in weekly service program.
- Created student application to determine student interest and commitment to service program.
- Coordinate and plan program activities. Participate in weekly sessions.
- Collaborate with organizations to develop partnerships and meet identified needs.
- Founded and led Thanksgiving Food Drive, 2009-2011.

Professional Organizations

- Society for Human Resources Management, Chapter Vice President   Fall 2011
- Toastmasters International, VP Membership, Charter Member   Fall 2011

Activities & Awards

- Alpha Kappa Alpha Sorority, Chapter President   2010-present
- The Lawrenceville School, Class Secretary   2007-present
- Loyola College, Community Service Representative   2009-2011
- Multicultural Service Award   2009
- Green and Grey Society Award (given to 14 seniors nominated by faculty) 2011
- Who's Who Among Students in American Universities & Colleges   2011

73

Degree: BS, Communications, emphasis in Human Relations.

Job Target: Specific position with a specific organization: graduate hall director at Northwestern University.

Strategy: Showcased a well-rounded student leader and capable residential-services worker with the requisite skills to fulfill the job target. The Qualifications list is specifically aligned with the job target.

AIESHA CHAMIN ATLDORE
3351 Pasario Drive
Chicago, IL 60625
214.332.1883   aiesha@aol.com

CAREER OBJECTIVE

Graduate Hall Director at Northwestern University

QUALIFICATIONS

- Three years of experience in residential services in a midsize private university.
- Outstanding organizational skills; excel in managing and coordinating programs and upholding policy.
- Well-liked and respected by students, faculty, parents, and immediate supervisors.
- Valued for strong listening skills, commitment, creativity, and motivation.
- Extensive training in objectivity, diversity, and cultural sensitivity.

EDUCATION

Bachelor of Science—Southern Methodist University (SMU), Dallas, Texas, May 2012
- Major: Communications with emphasis in Human Relations
- Minor: Criminal Justice and Sociology
- Cumulative G.P.A.: 3.87/4.0
- International Study: SMU London School for Scholars, Spring 2011
- Paying 75% of college expenses via scholarships and employment

RELEVANT EXPERIENCE

- Resident Assistant—Laudmore Hall, Southern Methodist University, Fall 2009–Present
  ~ Provide oversight to 45+ residents and staff collaboration to ensure quality and excellence.
- Internship with SMU's Sociology Department Human Relations Chair, Spring 2010.
  ~ Created departmental promotional pieces, delivered PowerPoint presentations, and facilitated alumni relations within the field to expand community-wide knowledge of the department's growth and course opportunities.
- SMU Admissions Department—Work Study Program, Fall 2008–Spring 2009
  ~ Supported efforts of Admissions staff by efficiently performing routine administrative activities.

CAMPUS LEADERSHIP/ACTIVITIES

- Student Foundation—Selected to top leadership organization by SMU Administration, Fall 2010–Present
- Leadership Institute, "The Way of Leadership," a student leadership development conference, Spring 2012
- Criminal Justice Society, Vice President, 2010–Present; Sociology Society, Secretary, 2009–Present
- Speech Communications Honor Society, Member, Spring 2011–Present
- Alpha Pi Tau Sorority, Ambassador, Fall 2008–Present
- Undergraduate Interfraternity Institute Leadership Conference at Pepperdine University, Summer 2010
- Fraternity and Sorority Ambassadors, Spring 2010–Present; *Female Greek of the Year* Award, 2011

Life Motto: "Doing what is popular is not always right; doing what is right is not always popular."

CHAPTER 8

Resumes for Graduates with Advanced Degrees

Resume Number	Degree	Job Target
74	MBA, Global Management	Management trainee
75	MA, Applied Economics	Financial analyst
76	MS, Geography	Resource/environmental analyst
77	MBA	Management consultant
78	MA, Russian, East European, and Central Asian Studies	Intelligence analyst/linguist
79	MS, Printing Management	Graphic arts sales/management trainee
80	MS, Industrial and Organizational Psychology	Training/organizational development position
81	Master of Occupational Therapy	Occupational therapist
82	MS, Occupational Ergonomics	Ergonomist/kinesiologist
83	MA, Special Education	Counselor, teacher, or case manager for special-needs youth
84	Master of Public Health	Medical/pharmaceutical sales position
85	MS Nursing, Family Nurse Practitioner	Family nurse practitioner
86	MA, Photography	Photographer or photographer's assistant
87	MS, Chemical Engineering	Chemical engineer
88	MS, Accounting	Accountant
89	JD	Associate attorney
90	JD	Associate attorney
91	MD	Urologist
92	MD	Physician
93	DVM	Veterinarian specializing in cats

74

Degree: MBA, Global Management.
Job Target: Management training program in a major firm doing international business/finance.
Strategy: Job seeker was transitioning from a career in a collections department to international business upon completion of MBA. Used Career Focus statement to indicate job target and provide a quick overview of suitability for management training program. Highlighted functional skills/job qualifications in a Value Offered section.

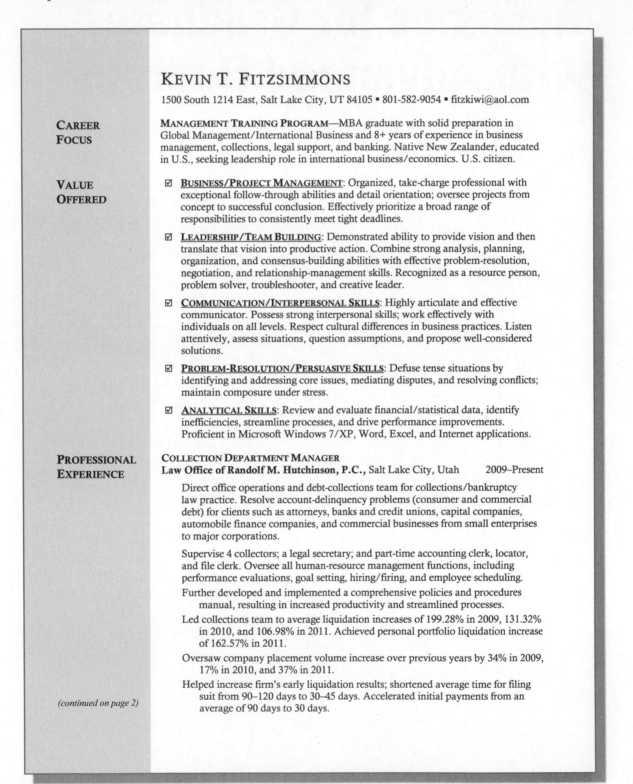

KEVIN T. FITZSIMMONS

1500 South 1214 East, Salt Lake City, UT 84105 ▪ 801-582-9054 ▪ fitzkiwi@aol.com

CAREER FOCUS

MANAGEMENT TRAINING PROGRAM—MBA graduate with solid preparation in Global Management/International Business and 8+ years of experience in business management, collections, legal support, and banking. Native New Zealander, educated in U.S., seeking leadership role in international business/economics. U.S. citizen.

VALUE OFFERED

☑ BUSINESS/PROJECT MANAGEMENT: Organized, take-charge professional with exceptional follow-through abilities and detail orientation; oversee projects from concept to successful conclusion. Effectively prioritize a broad range of responsibilities to consistently meet tight deadlines.

☑ LEADERSHIP/TEAM BUILDING: Demonstrated ability to provide vision and then translate that vision into productive action. Combine strong analysis, planning, organization, and consensus-building abilities with effective problem-resolution, negotiation, and relationship-management skills. Recognized as a resource person, problem solver, troubleshooter, and creative leader.

☑ COMMUNICATION/INTERPERSONAL SKILLS: Highly articulate and effective communicator. Possess strong interpersonal skills; work effectively with individuals on all levels. Respect cultural differences in business practices. Listen attentively, assess situations, question assumptions, and propose well-considered solutions.

☑ PROBLEM-RESOLUTION/PERSUASIVE SKILLS: Defuse tense situations by identifying and addressing core issues, mediating disputes, and resolving conflicts; maintain composure under stress.

☑ ANALYTICAL SKILLS: Review and evaluate financial/statistical data, identify inefficiencies, streamline processes, and drive performance improvements. Proficient in Microsoft Windows 7/XP, Word, Excel, and Internet applications.

PROFESSIONAL EXPERIENCE

COLLECTION DEPARTMENT MANAGER
Law Office of Randolf M. Hutchinson, P.C., Salt Lake City, Utah   2009–Present

Direct office operations and debt-collections team for collections/bankruptcy law practice. Resolve account-delinquency problems (consumer and commercial debt) for clients such as attorneys, banks and credit unions, capital companies, automobile finance companies, and commercial businesses from small enterprises to major corporations.

Supervise 4 collectors; a legal secretary; and part-time accounting clerk, locator, and file clerk. Oversee all human-resource management functions, including performance evaluations, goal setting, hiring/firing, and employee scheduling.

Further developed and implemented a comprehensive policies and procedures manual, resulting in increased productivity and streamlined processes.

Led collections team to average liquidation increases of 199.28% in 2009, 131.32% in 2010, and 106.98% in 2011. Achieved personal portfolio liquidation increase of 162.57% in 2011.

Oversaw company placement volume increase over previous years by 34% in 2009, 17% in 2010, and 37% in 2011.

Helped increase firm's early liquidation results; shortened average time for filing suit from 90–120 days to 30–45 days. Accelerated initial payments from an average of 90 days to 30 days.

(continued on page 2)

74 *(continued)*

KEVIN T. FITZSIMMONS

Page Two

801-582-9054 ▪ fitzkiwi@aol.com

PROFESSIONAL EXPERIENCE
(continued)

COLLECTOR
DiscoverCard, Salt Lake City, Utah   2008–2009

Contacted cardholders to collect consumer credit debt. Consistently exceeded performance objectives. Participated in implementation of quality circles, building teams, boosting morale/motivation, and improving performance.

BUSINESS MANAGER—HORIZON NEWSPAPER
Salt Lake Community College, Salt Lake City, Utah   2005–2008

Sold advertising in 8- to 12-page weekly campus newspaper. Assisted with ad design and copy editing. Developed periodic special advertising features. Managed billing, collections, and budgeting.

Became first Business Manager to completely cover unsubsidized production costs through advertising revenues.

Awarded 1st Place Honors by Columbia Scholastic Press Association in 2006–2007.

Received Outstanding Leadership Award 2005–2006 and Outstanding Service Award 2006–2007.

BANK OFFICER
Westpac Banking Corporation, Dunedin, New Zealand   2001–2005

As Lead Teller, provided commercial/individual bank customers with account transaction assistance. Supervised 4 tellers. Performed back-office functions, including check processing, account reconciliation, cash balancing, and currency exchange.

Presented with Special Recognition Award for reconciling 6-month backlog of Visa/MasterCard transactions that were improperly processed by merchants.

Trained merchants on POS credit-card transactions.

EDUCATION

MBA—Global Management, 2012
University of Phoenix, Salt Lake City, Utah, GPA 3.7

Relevant Coursework: Global Management, Global Marketing, Cross-Cultural Considerations for International Managers, International Financial Management, Business Law, Human Resource Management, Global Business Strategy, International Business Systems, Global Village, International Business Operations, Project Management

BS—Marketing, 2010
University of Utah, Salt Lake City, Utah

AS—Management, 2008
Salt Lake Community College, Salt Lake City, Utah
Who's Who Student in America's Junior Colleges, 2007–2008

75
Degree: MA, Applied Economics.
Job Target: Financial analysis/management.
Strategy: Used course projects, classes, and entrepreneurial experience to demonstrate strong qualifications despite limited job experience.

Meredith K. Holland

2345 NW 151st Street, Vancouver, WA 98685
mholland@gmail.com • 360-294-2570
http://www.linkedin.com/in/meredithholland

SUMMARY

Economic Analyst with MA in Applied Economics and real-world research, analysis, and consulting experience—an effective combination of theoretical and practical knowledge and a solid understanding of how economic principles and policies affect business, social, and political programs.

Key strengths include communication skills, leadership, and the ability to complete projects and deliver results in both individual and team assignments. Proficient in business and statistical software, including MS Excel, SAS, SPSS, and Statistix.

EDUCATION

Master of Arts, Applied Economics   2012
UNIVERSITY OF WASHINGTON, Seattle, WA

- GPA: 3.7 / 4.0.
- University Graduate Scholarship and Assistantship.
- Relevant Coursework: Econometrics, Microeconomics, Macroeconomics, Regional Economics, Cost-Benefit Analysis, International Trade, Quantitative Analysis.

Bachelor of Arts, Economics   2010
SEATTLE PACIFIC UNIVERSITY, Seattle, WA

- GPA: 3.2 / 4.0.
- Selected by faculty committee to participate in SPU study-abroad program; spent four months in London attending Regents College and traveling extensively throughout Europe.
- Resident Advisor, Longworth Hall, 2009–2010.
- Varsity soccer player, 4 years.
- Volunteer Service Award, Washington Special Olympics, 2009.

RELEVANT EXPERIENCE

Co-founder and Principal Investigator: APPLIED ECONOMICS RESEARCH GROUP,
University of Washington Department of Economics   2010–2012

Played a key role in launching consulting practice providing economic analysis for local businesses and institutions. Group grew from initial four founders in 2010 to 10–15 investigators.

Developed consulting proposals and led teams in research, analysis, and report preparation; delivered presentations to client Board of Directors or management team.

- Completed economic analysis for major national retailer exploring entry into the Seattle market.
- Performed employment analysis for regional economic-development organization studying immigrant labor issues.
- Established scholarship fund to channel consulting proceeds to graduate-level economics students.

(continued)

---

75 *(continued)*

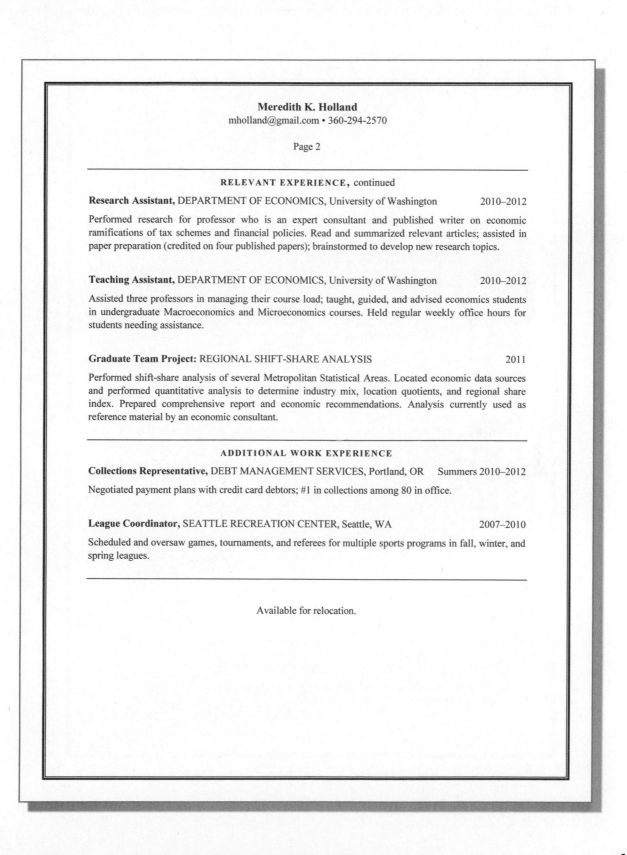

Meredith K. Holland

mholland@gmail.com • 360-294-2570

Page 2

RELEVANT EXPERIENCE, continued

Research Assistant, DEPARTMENT OF ECONOMICS, University of Washington   2010–2012

Performed research for professor who is an expert consultant and published writer on economic ramifications of tax schemes and financial policies. Read and summarized relevant articles; assisted in paper preparation (credited on four published papers); brainstormed to develop new research topics.

Teaching Assistant, DEPARTMENT OF ECONOMICS, University of Washington   2010–2012

Assisted three professors in managing their course load; taught, guided, and advised economics students in undergraduate Macroeconomics and Microeconomics courses. Held regular weekly office hours for students needing assistance.

Graduate Team Project: REGIONAL SHIFT-SHARE ANALYSIS   2011

Performed shift-share analysis of several Metropolitan Statistical Areas. Located economic data sources and performed quantitative analysis to determine industry mix, location quotients, and regional share index. Prepared comprehensive report and economic recommendations. Analysis currently used as reference material by an economic consultant.

ADDITIONAL WORK EXPERIENCE

Collections Representative, DEBT MANAGEMENT SERVICES, Portland, OR   Summers 2010–2012

Negotiated payment plans with credit card debtors; #1 in collections among 80 in office.

League Coordinator, SEATTLE RECREATION CENTER, Seattle, WA   2007–2010

Scheduled and oversaw games, tournaments, and referees for multiple sports programs in fall, winter, and spring leagues.

Available for relocation.

76

Degree: MS, Geography.
Job Target: Resource/environmental analyst.
Strategy: Highlighted functional skill areas in the Value Offered section. Used check boxes to encourage hiring managers to mentally check off the qualifications they are looking for. Packed lots of industry-specific keywords into the resume without harming readability—included plenty of white space.

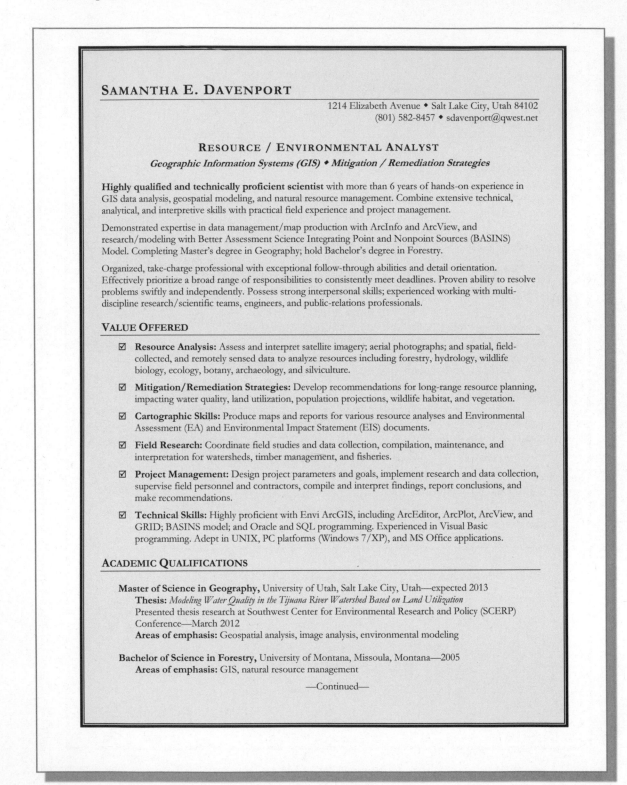

SAMANTHA E. DAVENPORT

1214 Elizabeth Avenue ◆ Salt Lake City, Utah 84102
(801) 582-8457 ◆ sdavenport@qwest.net

RESOURCE / ENVIRONMENTAL ANALYST
Geographic Information Systems (GIS) ◆ *Mitigation / Remediation Strategies*

Highly qualified and technically proficient scientist with more than 6 years of hands-on experience in GIS data analysis, geospatial modeling, and natural resource management. Combine extensive technical, analytical, and interpretive skills with practical field experience and project management.

Demonstrated expertise in data management/map production with ArcInfo and ArcView, and research/modeling with Better Assessment Science Integrating Point and Nonpoint Sources (BASINS) Model. Completing Master's degree in Geography; hold Bachelor's degree in Forestry.

Organized, take-charge professional with exceptional follow-through abilities and detail orientation. Effectively prioritize a broad range of responsibilities to consistently meet deadlines. Proven ability to resolve problems swiftly and independently. Possess strong interpersonal skills; experienced working with multi-discipline research/scientific teams, engineers, and public-relations professionals.

VALUE OFFERED

☑ **Resource Analysis:** Assess and interpret satellite imagery; aerial photographs; and spatial, field-collected, and remotely sensed data to analyze resources including forestry, hydrology, wildlife biology, ecology, botany, archaeology, and silviculture.

☑ **Mitigation/Remediation Strategies:** Develop recommendations for long-range resource planning, impacting water quality, land utilization, population projections, wildlife habitat, and vegetation.

☑ **Cartographic Skills:** Produce maps and reports for various resource analyses and Environmental Assessment (EA) and Environmental Impact Statement (EIS) documents.

☑ **Field Research:** Coordinate field studies and data collection, compilation, maintenance, and interpretation for watersheds, timber management, and fisheries.

☑ **Project Management:** Design project parameters and goals, implement research and data collection, supervise field personnel and contractors, compile and interpret findings, report conclusions, and make recommendations.

☑ **Technical Skills:** Highly proficient with Envi ArcGIS, including ArcEditor, ArcPlot, ArcView, and GRID; BASINS model; and Oracle and SQL programming. Experienced in Visual Basic programming. Adept in UNIX, PC platforms (Windows 7/XP), and MS Office applications.

ACADEMIC QUALIFICATIONS

Master of Science in Geography, University of Utah, Salt Lake City, Utah—expected 2013
    Thesis: *Modeling Water Quality in the Tijuana River Watershed Based on Land Utilization*
    Presented thesis research at Southwest Center for Environmental Research and Policy (SCERP) Conference—March 2012
    Areas of emphasis: Geospatial analysis, image analysis, environmental modeling

Bachelor of Science in Forestry, University of Montana, Missoula, Montana—2005
    Areas of emphasis: GIS, natural resource management

—Continued—

76 *(continued)*

SAMANTHA E. DAVENPORT—Page Two
(801) 582-8457 ◆ SDAVENPORT@QWEST.NET

ACADEMIC QUALIFICATIONS, *continued*

Professional Training:
BASINS Model Training Course—2012
MT/ID GIS Users Conference (ESRI certified training)—2007 to 2011
Cartography for GIS Users—2009
Introduction to GIS Using ArcView—2008
Northwest ArcGIS Users Conference—2007
Watershed Condition Assessment Short Course—2005

PROFESSIONAL EXPERIENCE

RESEARCH ASSISTANT   2011–Present
Department of Geography, University of Utah, Salt Lake City, Utah

- Conduct spatial modeling research using BASINS model in conjunction with Master's thesis project modeling water pollution in the Tijuana River Watershed.

- Edit and create GIS layers using ArcInfo and ArcView software.

- Assess and interpret point and non-point source/water-quality relationship.

- Assess and retrieve spatial and remotely sensed data from San Diego State University, U.S. Geological Survey, U.S. Environmental Protection Agency, and Mexico resource agencies.

GIS SPECIALIST / HYDROLOGIC TECHNICIAN   2005–2011
USDA Forest Service, Fortine Ranger District, Kootenai National Forest, Fortine, Montana

- Compiled digital GIS library analyzing layers of resources in Kootenai National Forest, including timber stands, roads, streams, topography, wildlife habitat areas, archaeological transects, soils, ownership/leases, special-use lands, hunting districts, watersheds, vegetation types, and streams.

- Published analysis maps for EAs and EISs. Designed ArcView template for creation of timber-sale maps and authored users' manuals for foresters.

- Directed data collection, compilation, and interpretation for cumulative watershed effects survey. Prepared water/sediment yield data to be used in spatial model: digitized model-required base layers, overlayed layers to generate additional GIS layers and reports, and edited generated data for completion accuracy.

- Assisted in interpretation of modeled results and field-collected data for use in Integrated Resource Analysis (IRA) and National Environmental Policy Act (NEPA) analysis.

- Collected and maintained water quality and stream morphology data surveying stream channel condition/stability, cross-section, and longitudinal profiles. Processed core samples to determine stream discharge, collected water samples for turbidity and suspended-sediment estimations, and evaluated hydrothermograph data.

TECHNICAL ASSISTANT   Summer 2011
Aqua Terra Consultants, Inc., Sheridan, Wyoming

- Created AutoCAD Map drawings for groundwater-depletion analyses for coal mining. Mapped oil, gas, and water wells.

- Compiled GIS layers to reflect land and mineral ownership and leases based on deed research.

77

Degree: MBA.
Job Target: Management consulting for an Asian company or an American company with business interests in the Asia-Pacific region.
Strategy: Emphasized management-consulting work at the university and business internship experiences because she did not have paid experience in her field.

SUE L. CHENG
telephone: 3399-7744

6E Tower, Hillsdale Bay
Taipo, NT, Hong Kong
e-mail: slcheng@hongkong.net

■ OBJECTIVE

To apply skills and knowledge of e-business, e-government and telecom markets in the Asian-Pacific Region, project-management skills, and cross-cultural communications (Western and Asian) knowledge acquired through experience in diverse business environments.

■ EDUCATION

MBA candidate with concentration in Management of Global Information Technology and e-Commerce Marketing, May 2012
BOSTON UNIVERSITY SCHOOL OF BUSINESS, Boston, MA

Selected Management Consulting Projects:

- Redman Communications, Boston, MA — Conducted comprehensive assessment of business practices of public relations firm. Designed detailed e-business plan for focusing on process improvement and communication strategies, integrating order fulfillment, service delivery, and customer relationship management, resulting in significant reduction in daily operating costs.

- ADI Institute, Boston, MA — Conducted an on-site analysis of the organization's management information systems requirements and designed a procurement system that integrated contracting, accounting, and receiving processes, resulting in a more responsive, user-friendly system with real-time trackable data.

- PacSystems Inc., Boston, MA — Analyzed existing business model and global expansion opportunities for a B2B e-marketplace serving the U.S. packaging industry. Conducted extensive research of major international packaging markets in Asia and Europe. Designed and presented to senior executives region-specific sales/marketing plan for effective market positioning and entry. Commended on research depth and dynamic presentation style.

Awards:

- Case competition winner out of 10 teams in Managers in International Economy class on Steinway's entry strategy to the China market. Professor's comment: *"You made the best presentation on that case ever; no one else was even close."*

B.S. in Communications, summa cum laude, 2010
UNIVERSITY OF RICHMOND, Richmond, VA

■ INTERNSHIPS

CAPITAL CORPORATION, Boston, MA   2012
FORSTERI INTERNATIONAL, Boston, MA   2011

Intern — During MBA program, completed internships related to business outreach, e-commerce marketing, and e-business/e-government analysis. Engagement projects included the following:

Capital Corporation — Conducted market-risk analysis on e-commerce development throughout the Greater China Region (China, Hong Kong, and Taiwan) and identified global market trends, growth areas, and investment opportunities for Aster Technologies, a client of the international investment and consulting firm. Results were published for senior decision makers on Aster's intranet.

Forsteri International — Assessed e-business policy/leadership and e-government readiness in the China market for global technology and policy consulting firm and clients, including Dunston-Patterson, Jones Smythe, and Hamden. Contributed research and analysis to company publication, *"Risk E-Business: Seizing the Opportunity of Global E-Readiness."* Utilized contacts in China and acted as liaison between firm and Chinese Ministry of Information that regulates Internet and telecom development.

Continued on Page 2

77 *(continued)*

SUE L. CHENG
telephone: 3399-7744   Page 2

■ EMPLOYMENT

BOSTON UNIVERSITY, Boston, MA   2010–2012

Project Manager — Multicultural Affairs
Initiated, created, and marketed cultural training initiatives, special events, and educational programs; conducted workshops on cross-cultural issues. Designed department's website and served as webmaster. Coordinated, authored, and produced all office publications.

Accomplishments:

- Revamped, secured funding, and successfully promoted the academic training program. Results: increased participation rate 30% and achieved the highest retention rate organization-wide (34% above national average). Served as consultant to other organizations to establish similar programs.

- Appointed by President to direct the cross-functional strategic planning efforts that resulted in the development of the effective Leadership Training Institute.

- Chosen as internal consultant for the human resources practice in staff recruitment and retention to improve the university's diversity progress.

■ COMPUTER SKILLS

Microsoft Office Suite, SQL, HTML, SPSS, Datatel, NJStar (Chinese Language Software), Compass Marketing Software, and Photoshop.

■ LANGUAGES

Fluent in Chinese (Mandarin and Shanghai Dialects) and English.

78

Degree: MA, Russian, East European, and Central Asian Studies.
Job Target: Intelligence analyst/linguist.
Strategy: Emphasized high-profile position with the US Department of State. Used page 2 to detail relevant volunteer experiences and prior teaching background.

MARIANNA ZILINSKI

606 Highland St. Apt. 12 • Pittsburgh, PA 15122 | 412.555.6901 | mzilinski@gmail.com

ANALYST • LINGUIST
Regional / Media / Intelligence Analysis

New master's graduate with insightful knowledge of the political, economic, cultural, and media landscapes of Russia, East Europe, and Central Asia and a passion for languages and their application for influencing opinions and action. Perceptive leader with a natural ability to build consensus, diffuse tension, and refocus groups and individuals toward productive outcomes. Excel in working with people from all backgrounds and cultures. Recognized for intellectual curiosity, strong communication and presentation skills, and a can-do work ethic.

QUALIFICATIONS

EDUCATION

MA in Russian, East European, and Central Asian Studies
CARNEGIE MELLON UNIVERSITY — Pittsburgh, PA, 2012

BA in Russian Language and Literature / Applied Linguistics (minor in Turkish Language and Literature)
THE OHIO STATE UNIVERSITY — Columbus, OH, 2010

PROFESSIONAL DEVELOPMENT

FLAS Fellowship for Kazakh Language & Central Asian Studies, academic year 2011–2012

ARIT Fellowship for Intensive Advanced Turkish Language & Culture, BOGAZICI UNIVERSITY — Istanbul, Turkey, June–August 2010

WRITING

Undergraduate Thesis: "The changing face of Russian media"
Master's Thesis: "Key political drivers in contemporary Kazakhstan"

LANGUAGES

Russian and Turkish: advanced proficiency • Kazakh and French: intermediate
Uzbek, Azeri, Ukrainian, and Spanish: basic

RELATED EXPERIENCE

US DEPARTMENT OF STATE — Astana, Kazakhstan   August–September 2011
Public Affairs Section Intern
Brought energy and meaningful insights as a team member contributing to all major operations of public affairs section at the US Embassy in Astana. Engaged in organizing official visits, drafting statements and press releases, and using Kazakh language skills to edit translations of daily news highlights. Served as embassy's representative to English-language summer camp for local youth.

- **Wrote statement used by Secretary of State Clinton** congratulating the Republic of Kazakhstan on the 19th anniversary of its constitution. Statement was posted on her website and distributed to local media.
- **Authored successful grant proposal** to send group of wheelchair-bound Kazakhstani volleyball players to the United States for two weeks of training and cultural learning.
- **Researched, analyzed, and drafted report** on status of a new university and its impact on exchange programs, providing a fresh perspective on the policy community's understanding of the project.
- **Co-organized successful performances** of US band Brazzaville. Wrote press release, conducted on-site visits, distributed promotional materials, and escorted the band through Kazakhstan.
- **Stepped up to take over a struggling project** on Martin Luther King, Jr., working with an artist to complete the exhibit on time with high-quality results.

Page 1 of 2

78 *(continued)*

MULTILINGUAL COMMUNITY LEADERSHIP — Columbus, OH
Interpreter (September 2008–October 2009)
Volunteered to provide translation services for group of Ukrainian immigrants living in a Salvation Army retirement home. Applied Russian language skills to facilitate communication between housing program leader and Ukrainian residents. Strengthened Russian conversational skills through regular social visits.

ESL Teacher (January 2007–October 2007)
Instructed adult immigrants enrolled in Rockwood Library ESL program. Developed curriculum and conducted classes for native speakers of Russian, Spanish, and other languages with varying levels of English language proficiency. Incorporated principles of adult learning to enable sustained learning of complex concepts.

ADDITIONAL EXPERIENCE

RAINBOW DAY CARE CENTER — Pittsburgh, PA   2010–2012
Play-based daycare and after-school program serving children aged 1–12.
Lead Teacher
Guided children's activities for one of the most respected day care providers in the Pittsburgh area. Hired as substitute teacher, followed by part-time position for after-school program, and subsequently promoted to full-time position as part of 4-member team with personal caseload of 10 first-graders and overall responsibility for 30 children in K–2 group.

- **Developed system that became schoolwide model.** Improved a child's obsessive behavior by designing a chart that let him evaluate portions of every day, providing ongoing opportunities to succeed.
- **Created a 3-step process to overcome anger management issues,** comprised of 1) stop, 2) walk away, and 3) find a teacher. The process was adopted by coworkers for its success in encouraging productive behavior.
- **Mentored a first-grader with difficulties communicating verbally** by encouraging him to develop his artistic talents, use his work to foster conversation, and eventually overcome his fears.
- **Leveraged a passion for languages to develop literacy skills through an innovative program,** leading children to explore runes and different alphabets and to listen to Kazakh and Russian fairy tales.

WRIGHT CHILD DEVELOPMENT CENTER — Columbus, OH   2006–2010
Educational organization serving 200 children aged 4 months to 6 years.
Student Teacher
Supported lead teachers in classroom setting for children aged 3 to 5, applying principles of Reggio Emilia that empower children to explore their own interests while developing their social and emotional skills. Designed and led small-group projects and communicated student status to parents.

- **Influenced development of new summer program** for grades 1–5 and served as teacher throughout entire summer with support from rotating lead teachers. Transitioned program the next summer to a team of full-time staff.
- **Tapped for a team charged with integrating a special needs child into the classroom,** developing various techniques that enabled him to manage his behavior and interact successfully with peers.
- **Created an original story** that achieved high popularity, resulting in sequels, magic-themed projects, and the staging of a corner of the classroom to enable children to act out their favorite characters.

Degree: MS, Printing Management.
Job Target: Graphic arts sales/management training program.
Strategy: Emphasized graduate degree and involvement in a highly prestigious student organization. Demonstrated sales capabilities and strong organizational skills in work experience. Included experience as a graduate assistant and research fellow to show in-depth technical knowledge in leading-edge areas.

ALBERT DAVIDSON

92 Scottish Place, Apartment #3 ♦ Rochester, New York 14692 ♦ 585-731-9199 ♦ E-mail: aldav23@ur.edu

GRAPHIC ARTS SALES / MANAGEMENT ♦ MANAGEMENT-TRAINEE CANDIDATE

Disciplined and dynamic candidate with Master's degree in Printing Management and BFA in Photography. Exceptional academic record and practical experience in sales, project management, and team leadership. Seeking opportunity to join leading graphic arts firm in an entry-level sales or management-trainee position.

EDUCATION

UNIVERSITY OF ROCHESTER; Rochester, New York
Master of Science, Printing Management   **May 2013**
GPA: 4.0/4.0   *(Anticipated)*

Significant Courses

- Database Marketing   - Sales in the Graphic Arts
- Operations Management   - Trends in Printing Technology
- Print Finishing Management   - Document Processing Languages

Special Projects

Member of four-person team developing estimating software (using Excel) for Variable Data Printing.
Developing business plan and marketing plan for a digital print shop.
Part of two-person team that conducted study of image permanence, comparing liquid and dry toner technologies.

Extracurricular Activities

*Served as **Vice President** of U of R Student Chapter of Association for Graphic Arts Technology (AGAT).*
- Functioned as Project Manager for 15-member student team charged with the concept, design, and production of publication for entry into annual competition. Delegated assignments, ensured equal participation among group members, and followed project from start to finish.
- Arranged seminars with corporate presenters on topics relevant to the graphic arts.

Bachelor of Fine Arts, Photography   **May 2011**
GPA: 3.44/4.0; Graduated with Honors.

Certificate in Business Management   **May 2011**
Three-course concentration in Management Process; GPA: 4.0/4.0.

PROFESSIONAL EXPERIENCE

WEBID.COM; New York, New York
Business Development Manager   **June 2010–Jan. 2011**
Served as outside sales representative for start-up website design firm catering to Fortune 1000 clients.
- Defined target markets and developed strategies for prospecting and qualifying leads.
- Cold-called major accounts and developed relationships with key corporate contacts.
- Established business relationships with blue-chip clientele, including Seagram's, MTV, the New York Jets, and major jewelry firms.
- On track to achieve multimillion-dollar sales goal for first 12 months.

CARL STEVENS; New York, New York
KEN MICHAELS; Brooklyn, New York
Photographer's Assistant (Co-op Assignments)   **2009–2010**
Supported professional photographers in arranging and executing photo shoots.
- Assisted advertising photographer with studio shoots in New York City:
    - Set up studio lighting for catalog shoots.
    - Worked with props and sets.
    - Loaded cameras and maintained equipment.
- Accompanied stock photographer on week-long remote shoot in the Bahamas:
    - Arranged locations and set up shoots.
    - Set up lighting, loaded cameras, and ensured that equipment was ready for shooting.
    - Coordinated scheduling of models.

---

79 *(continued)*

ALBERT DAVIDSON
Resume - Page Two
585-731-9199 ♦ E-mail: aldav23@ur.edu

OTHER RELEVANT EXPERIENCE

UNIVERSITY OF ROCHESTER; Rochester, New York
Fellowship, Professor Rolland Franzen   **Jan. 2012–Present**
Engaged to assist in the revision and updating of "A Guide to Database Printing," a text on the printing industry, with accountability for chapter entitled <u>Variable Data Printing Programs</u>.
- Conduct testing, compile and analyze data, and draw conclusions about various applications.
- Explore how state-of-the-art technologies are being applied in commercial settings.
- Re-draft chapter content (approximately 93 pages) to reflect innovations in Variable Data Printing.

Graduate Assistant, Professor Penelope Barstow   **Aug. 2011–Dec. 2011**
Supported professor in preparing lecture materials and managing grading of assignments for 178 freshman students in "Graphic Media Perspectives" course. Developed collaterals to aid students in completing assignments and assisted students one-on-one in lab setting.

Lab Assistant, Student Computer Lab   **May 2011–Present**
Provide desk-side support to students in computer lab with focus on advanced graphic-arts applications.
- Assist students using Macintosh platforms to scan and print images and documents using a variety of equipment ranging from black & white laser printers to high-end, full-color digital presses.
- Write SOPs for various pieces of equipment in the lab.
- Perform routine maintenance on wide array of computers and peripherals.

TECHNICAL PROFICIENCIES

Macintosh / PC Literate: Adobe Acrobat, Photoshop, Illustrator, InDesign, Dreamweaver; Microsoft Office; BBedit; HTML.

Graphic Arts Equipment: Agfa prepress and inkjet systems; CreoScitex, Epson, and Roland wide-format printers; Xerox digital offset press and production printers; Kodak Approval color proof system; flatbed and drum scanners.

80

Degree: MS, Industrial and Organizational Psychology.
Job Target: OD/training position.
Strategy: With no prior business experience to include, focused on well-rounded internship experience in a corporate OD setting and included a strong profile to capture this graduate's training, knowledge, and skills. The result: a strong first page that has all the essential ingredients to position him for a training/OD role.

GREGORY MARTIN

67 Barkette Road
Tarrytown, New York 10098

(914) 466-9901
martin234@yahoo.com

PROFILE

Organizational Development/Change Management Professional with training and experience that provide a foundation for partnering human resources/OD initiatives with strategic business units to enhance productivity, performance, quality, and service. Core skills include the following:

Project/Program Management—Five years of project management experience that encompasses conceptualization, needs assessment, and planning through execution, postintervention assessment, feedback, and closure. Ability to integrate broader corporate values into functional project plans that yield deliverables aligned with enterprise objectives.

Training & Facilitation/Research—Versed in OD interventions: training, process improvement, team dynamics, meeting facilitation, performance assessment, 360° feedback instruments, coaching, change-management models, and human factors issues. Experience in researching, formulating, and conducting group training, including development of presentation materials. Competent researcher utilizing electronic databases (InfoTrac) and survey methods; trained in performing data analysis using SPSS, ANOVA, t-tests, and others.

EDUCATION

NEW YORK UNIVERSITY, New York, NY
Master of Science in Industrial and Organizational Psychology, May 2012

Selected Projects & Research:
- Transformational-leadership and change-management study.
- Peer-review and organizational-citizenship behavior in relationship to TQM, organizational satisfaction, and employee motivation.
- Study of lean manufacturing, participative management, cell concepts, and flexible structures.
- Onsite studies of workplace safety, human factors, and ergonomics issues.

Bachelor of Science in Psychology, *magna cum laude,* May 2009
Awards/Honors: Provost's Awards (2008, 2009); Outstanding Social Science Award; Psi Chi Honor Society (2009). Self-financed 100% of college tuition and expenses.

EXPERIENCE

KENWORTH CORPORATION, New York, NY
Organizational Development Consultant Intern (2010–2011)
Assisted the internal Senior Organizational Development Consultant in providing proactive OD consulting and interventions to enhance operational and human-resources effectiveness, efficiency, and quality in a Fortune 500 enterprise with 5,000 employees. Supported corporate training and development initiatives—including diversity training, Corporate University offerings, and customer-service training—in coordination with the Human Resources Service centers, Learning and Development Unit, Corporate Library, and Learning Centers.

Program Management, Training & Facilitation

- Planned, managed, and facilitated Manager Information Network, a management peer group from 5 business units sharing best practices and fostering company's commitment to excellence. Initiated intranet-based communication vehicle. Developed organizational structure to allow group to become self-perpetuating.

Page 1 of 2

---

80 *(continued)*

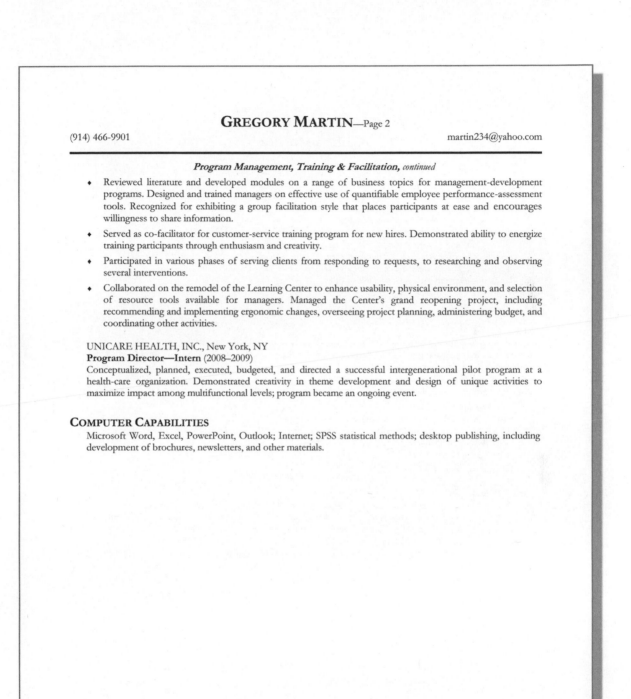

GREGORY MARTIN—Page 2

(914) 466-9901   martin234@yahoo.com

Program Management, Training & Facilitation, continued

- Reviewed literature and developed modules on a range of business topics for management-development programs. Designed and trained managers on effective use of quantifiable employee performance-assessment tools. Recognized for exhibiting a group facilitation style that places participants at ease and encourages willingness to share information.

- Served as co-facilitator for customer-service training program for new hires. Demonstrated ability to energize training participants through enthusiasm and creativity.

- Participated in various phases of serving clients from responding to requests, to researching and observing several interventions.

- Collaborated on the remodel of the Learning Center to enhance usability, physical environment, and selection of resource tools available for managers. Managed the Center's grand reopening project, including recommending and implementing ergonomic changes, overseeing project planning, administering budget, and coordinating other activities.

UNICARE HEALTH, INC., New York, NY
Program Director—Intern (2008–2009)
Conceptualized, planned, executed, budgeted, and directed a successful intergenerational pilot program at a health-care organization. Demonstrated creativity in theme development and design of unique activities to maximize impact among multifunctional levels; program became an ongoing event.

COMPUTER CAPABILITIES
Microsoft Word, Excel, PowerPoint, Outlook; Internet; SPSS statistical methods; desktop publishing, including development of brochures, newsletters, and other materials.

81

Degree: Master of Occupational Therapy.
Job Target: Occupational therapist.
Strategy: Included personal experiences caring for a family member with disabilities as a key qualifier.

Carlena Morales

8713 Lincoln Parkway
Hollywood, FL 33024

954-555-7483
carlena.morales@isp.net

PROFILE

❖ Master in Occupational Therapy with national designation as OTR.
❖ Clinical experience managing full case load and meeting all competencies. Skilled in using a wide range of interventions and therapeutic modalities adapted to meet each patient's unique needs.
❖ Natural-born caregiver. Passion for career in health care germinated over years of caring for others.
❖ Innate ability to anticipate the needs of patients even before they can articulate them.
❖ Reputation as compassionate patient advocate.

EDUCATION

Medical-Professional
Master of Occupational Therapy – Florida International University • Miami, Florida (2012)
Certified Nursing Assistant – Florida National College/Hialeah Training Center • Hialeah, Florida (2008)

Related
Master of Arts in Music Therapy – Florida State University • Tallahassee, Florida
Bachelor of Arts in Arts and Humanities, Cum Laude – Florida Atlantic University • Boca Raton, Florida

Additional Training & Experience
• Completed human subjects education training.
• Collaborated with professor as part of group research project leading to anticipated publication of study.

CLINICAL EXPERIENCE

Level II Fieldwork

Completed evaluations, set goals, implemented treatment plans, evaluated patients for discharge and made discharge recommendations, observed home evaluations, and functioned as part of multi-disciplinary team. Assessed DME needs. Carried full case load and worked with minimal supervision.

Mt. Sinai Medical Center • Miami Beach, Florida (480+ hours)
• Cared for patients with diverse diagnoses in acute rehab setting.

East Ridge Retirement Village • Miami, Florida (480+ hours)
• Provided wide range of OT services and assistance in resident apartments, in the therapy gym, and throughout the facility.

Level I Fieldwork

Observed activities and treatments delivered by OTRs and other health care providers.
Hollywood Hills Rehabilitation Center • Hollywood, Florida (Residential rehabilitative care)
South Florida Jewish Academy • Coconut Creek, Florida (Day school for special needs students)
Pinehurst Rehabilitation Hospital • Delray Beach, Florida (Inpatient for spinal cord injuries)

continued

---

81 *(continued)*

Carlena Morales   carlena.morales@isp.net   954-555-7483

LIFE EXPERIENCE

Family Caregiver (2000–2007)

Provided extensive care to 3 family members diagnosed with serious illnesses. Embraced role of caregiver and advocate. Researched diseases and treatment options. Scheduled and tracked medical appointments. Acted as liaison with medical providers and insurance companies. Delivered in-home treatments when appropriate. Educated family, friends, and classmates on disease process.

- Functioned as primary caregiver to son diagnosed with rare form of leukemia at age 8 until his death at age 13.
- Shared care responsibilities with sibling for father following his cancer diagnosis.
- Provided home care to mother diagnosed with cancer and after fall that required extensive PT and OT treatment. Aided in mother's recovery by effectively assisting with therapeutic exercises at home based on observing clinical treatments. Created adaptive devices to improve functionality.

RELATED EMPLOYMENT

Certified Nursing Assistant (CNA) – Alliance Care • Ft. Lauderdale, Florida (2009–2010)
Home Care Provider – Visiting Angels • Cape Coral, Florida (2008–2009)

- Provided personal care and assistance with activities of daily living for individuals in their homes.

PROFILE

Affiliations   American Occupational Therapy Association (AOTA)
                   Florida Occupational Therapy Association (FOTA)

Certifications   CPR

Languages   English and Spanish (fluent), Portuguese (rudimentary)

Degree: MS, Occupational Ergonomics.
Job Target: A position studying manufacturing processes for the Ontario Worker's Compensation Board.
Strategy: Emphasized education and ancillary research and teaching work, with added value from active participation in university athletics and community involvement. Showed a valuable, well-rounded individual with a unique background capable of teaching, further education, research, and, above all, communicating with people of all backgrounds.

MATTHEW R. JONES, BHK

22 Waverley Lane, Bedford, MA 02157
Home: 781.891.2345 E-mail: mattjones@yahoo.com

OBJECTIVE

ERGONOMIST - KINESIOLOGIST

PROFILE

- Energetic, motivated, and disciplined professional with an outstanding theoretical and practical background in performing physical demands analysis, providing ergonomic assessments, and creating job modifications.
- Task oriented; work methodically to produce consistent quality work; meet objectives within strict time frames. Superior organizer; able to manage concurrent projects with attention to detail and accuracy.
- Articulate; build profitable rapport among clients, supervisors, peers, and other stakeholders.
- Analytical; able to extract pertinent information from a mass of data and produce quality reports for presentation.
- Effective problem solver; thrive in a fast-paced, dynamic, and challenging environment of ongoing change.
- Knowledge of government regulatory compliance relating to WSIB, Health & Safety Act, and other legislation.

EDUCATION

University of Massachusetts, Lowell, MA   2012
MASTER OF SCIENCE—Occupational Ergonomics
- 3.8 GPA
Course modules include

-	Field Evaluations	-	Occupational Biomechanics
-	Physical Agents Evaluation	-	Advanced Biomechanics
-	Design for Injury Prevention	-	Toxicology & Health
-	Human Factors	-	Methods in Work Analysis
-	Workers Compensation (Ontario)	-	Industrial Hygiene & Ergonomics
-	Capstone Course	-	Bio Statistics & Epidemiology

University of Windsor, Windsor, ON   2010
BACHELOR OF HUMAN KINETICS—Movement Science
Course modules included

-	Human Physiology	-	Adolescent Psychology
-	Anthropology	-	Perceptual Motor Control
-	Research & Development	-	Physiology of Exercise
-	Anatomy	-	Human Performance

PROFESSIONAL EXPERIENCE

University of Massachusetts, Lowell, MA   2011–present
RESEARCH ASSISTANT
- Play a pivotal role in a unique case study involving the compilation of data and analysis of multidisciplined health-care workers in four local hospitals. Process includes following workers throughout their daily routine; charting a detailed report every 45 seconds on person's movements; and tabulating daily results into a database.
- Designing a complex ergonomic chart focusing on movement charting for every 45 seconds during a 12-hour shift.

TEACHER ASSISTANT   2011–present
- Facilitate as assistant to Dr. Paul Hawkins, "Occupational Biomechanics" postgraduate module. Oversee the laboratory functions; grade papers and homework.

Page One of Two

---

82 *(continued)*

MATTHEW R. JONES, BHK   781.891.2345 ▪ MATTJONES@YAHOO.COM ▪ PAGE TWO

PROFESSIONAL
EXPERIENCE
...continued

Liberty Mutual Research Center, Hopkinton, MA   6/2011–8/2011
RESEARCH FELLOW
- Awarded the 2011 *"American Society of Safety Engineers"* (ASSE) Research Fellowship.
- Conducted an extensive research project into workers' ability to estimate their grip force, utilizing two common tools: screwdriver and ratchet. Report currently under review by *Professional Safety* magazine.

Doctor Nathan Hanna, University of Massachusetts, Lowell, MA   2/2011–5/2011
RESEARCH ASSISTANT
- Reviewed 68 papers in epidemiologic studies to abstract and tabulate information on ergonomic exposure assessment methods in health care for the head of the exposure and epidemiology assessment team.

General Electric Locomotive, London, ON   10/2009
ERGONOMIC CONSULTANT—Health & Safety
- Conducted, as a volunteer, physical demand analyses for the Chassis Construction Division.

SPECIALIZED
TRAINING

Proactive Ergonomic Concepts, Inc., Windsor, ON   9/2009
Physical Demands Analysis Course
- Introduction to the skills and techniques involved in performing a physical demands analysis.

MEMBERSHIPS &
AFFILIATIONS

Human Factors and Ergonomics Society   2011–present
STUDENT MEMBER

COMMUNITY
INVOLVEMENT

University of Massachusetts, Lowell, MA   2010–present
MEN'S CLUB BASKETBALL TEAM MEMBER

University of Windsor, Windsor, ON   2009–2010
ATHLETE MENTOR
- Conducted presentations to elementary school students with the aim of motivating them to succeed and guiding them in their future choices.
MEN'S VARSITY BASKETBALL TEAM   2010
- Honored for being the *"Most Valuable Player as Team Captain."*
- Recipient of the *"Lancer Award,"* given to an athlete for being an exemplary role model.

Canadian Red Cross Society, Oakville, ON   2005–2007
YOUTH MEMBERSHIP COORDINATOR
- Acknowledged for actively addressing a shortage of youth members. Planned and organized many events; increased membership by 76%.

Big Brothers, Oakville, ON   2005
Big Brother—Appleby College School
- Active participant in the Big Brothers program.

LANGUAGES

Fluent: English, German, Spanish   Proficient: French, Italian

---

83
Degree: MA, Special Education/California Teaching Credential.
Job Target: Counselor, teacher, or case manager for special-needs youth.
Strategy: Drew attention to impressive career through use of keywords in the opening and subsequent paragraphs. Added a graphic element that emphasized commitment to children.

MARIKO K. OZEKI
555 Alamo Court, Signal Hill, California 90806
(360) 278-9256—mozeki@mac.com

PROFESSIONAL QUALIFICATIONS

- ➤ **Counselor, Teacher, and Case Manager for Special-Needs Youth—7 years.**
- ➤ Specialist in diagnosis and treatment of developmental disabilities.
- ➤ Master of Arts in Special Education / California Teaching Credential expected in 2013.
- ➤ Bilingual teaching experience: Spanish / English.

EDUCATION

Master of Arts in Special Education / California Teaching Credential   Expected 2013
California State University, Dominguez Hills, California
Bachelor of Arts Degree in Community Service & Public Affairs   2004
University of California at Los Angeles

PROFESSIONAL EXPERIENCE

SPECIAL-NEEDS INSTRUCTOR   2008–Present
Outreach Training Center, Long Beach, California
Teach community living skills to developmentally disabled teenagers and adults. Prepare and present traditional and multimedia lessons, tailoring them to group and individual needs. Follow up with coaching and lesson assessment. Consult with senior instructors, clinicians, and parents to create comprehensive rehabilitation plans.
- ➤ The Center has placed roughly 80% of our special-needs clients into mainstream society during the past 2 years.

COUNSELOR   2005–2008
California Youth Authority, Corona, California
Counsel and instruct up to 800 juvenile offenders. Recommend youth placements in community jobs or in crisis-intervention or substance-abuse programs. Collaborate with interdisciplinary teams regarding case management of treatment-resistant individuals. Develop and coordinate recreational and social programs.

COMMUNITY SERVICE

BIG SISTER   2010–Present
Big Sisters of South Bay, Long Beach, California
Provide friendship and guidance to adolescents on weekends and on-call.

84

Degree: Master of Public Health.

Job Target: Technical sales: medical/pharmaceutical industries.

Strategy: Created a strong summary highlighting an advanced technical degree in the health-care field, sales experience, experience working in hospital/surgical settings, knowledge of pharmaceuticals, relationship-building skills (particularly with physicians and their staffs), communication skills, and the ability to set and achieve goals.

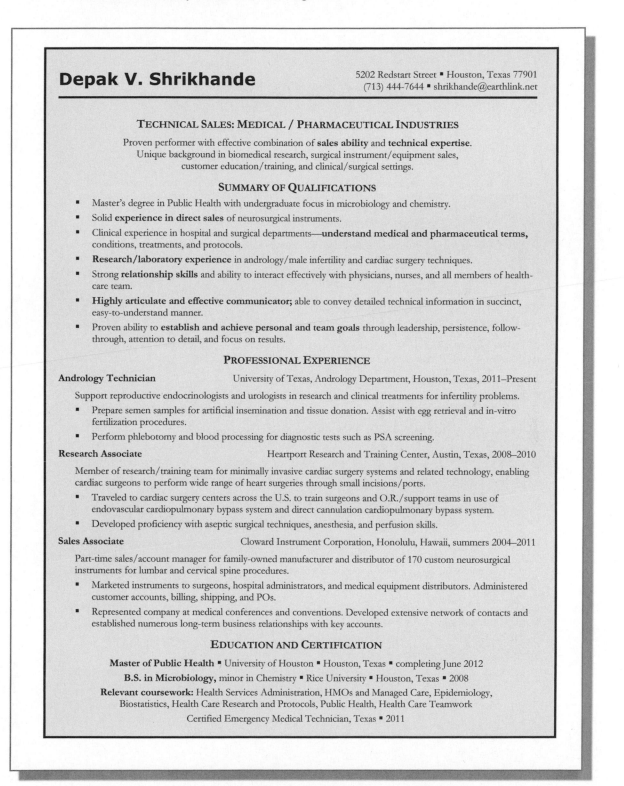

Depak V. Shrikhande

5202 Redstart Street ▪ Houston, Texas 77901
(713) 444-7644 ▪ shrikhande@earthlink.net

TECHNICAL SALES: MEDICAL / PHARMACEUTICAL INDUSTRIES

Proven performer with effective combination of **sales ability** and **technical expertise**.
Unique background in biomedical research, surgical instrument/equipment sales,
customer education/training, and clinical/surgical settings.

SUMMARY OF QUALIFICATIONS

- Master's degree in Public Health with undergraduate focus in microbiology and chemistry.
- Solid **experience in direct sales** of neurosurgical instruments.
- Clinical experience in hospital and surgical departments—**understand medical and pharmaceutical terms,** conditions, treatments, and protocols.
- **Research/laboratory experience** in andrology/male infertility and cardiac surgery techniques.
- Strong **relationship skills** and ability to interact effectively with physicians, nurses, and all members of health-care team.
- **Highly articulate and effective communicator;** able to convey detailed technical information in succinct, easy-to-understand manner.
- Proven ability to **establish and achieve personal and team goals** through leadership, persistence, follow-through, attention to detail, and focus on results.

PROFESSIONAL EXPERIENCE

Andrology Technician   University of Texas, Andrology Department, Houston, Texas, 2011–Present

Support reproductive endocrinologists and urologists in research and clinical treatments for infertility problems.

- Prepare semen samples for artificial insemination and tissue donation. Assist with egg retrieval and in-vitro fertilization procedures.
- Perform phlebotomy and blood processing for diagnostic tests such as PSA screening.

Research Associate   Heartport Research and Training Center, Austin, Texas, 2008–2010

Member of research/training team for minimally invasive cardiac surgery systems and related technology, enabling cardiac surgeons to perform wide range of heart surgeries through small incisions/ports.

- Traveled to cardiac surgery centers across the U.S. to train surgeons and O.R./support teams in use of endovascular cardiopulmonary bypass system and direct cannulation cardiopulmonary bypass system.
- Developed proficiency with aseptic surgical techniques, anesthesia, and perfusion skills.

Sales Associate   Cloward Instrument Corporation, Honolulu, Hawaii, summers 2004–2011

Part-time sales/account manager for family-owned manufacturer and distributor of 170 custom neurosurgical instruments for lumbar and cervical spine procedures.

- Marketed instruments to surgeons, hospital administrators, and medical equipment distributors. Administered customer accounts, billing, shipping, and POs.
- Represented company at medical conferences and conventions. Developed extensive network of contacts and established numerous long-term business relationships with key accounts.

EDUCATION AND CERTIFICATION

Master of Public Health ▪ University of Houston ▪ Houston, Texas ▪ completing June 2012

B.S. in Microbiology, minor in Chemistry ▪ Rice University ▪ Houston, Texas ▪ 2008

Relevant coursework: Health Services Administration, HMOs and Managed Care, Epidemiology, Biostatistics, Health Care Research and Protocols, Public Health, Health Care Teamwork

Certified Emergency Medical Technician, Texas ▪ 2011

85

Degree: MS Nursing, Family Nurse Practitioner.
Job Target: Family nurse practitioner.
Strategy: Set this client apart from the average "new graduate" by highlighting her extensive experience and strong accomplishments in implementing new programs, cutting costs, improving productivity, and developing new business. Condensed 20+ years of work experience so that her most impressive contributions would not be obscured by ordinary responsibilities.

Jennifer C. Powell, RN, FNP

P.O. Box 5578, Towson, MD 21204
(410) 559-2211 ▶ jennpowell@gmail.com

KEY QUALIFICATIONS

▶ Innovative, dedicated **Family Nurse Practitioner** with more than 20 years of nursing experience.
▶ Strong interest in adolescent health issues. Ten years of experience conducting seminars on teen sexuality.
▶ Excellent problem-solving and organizational skills.
▶ Wide range of nursing experience: cardiac, emergency, critical care, home care,
long-term care, oncology, outpatient, and management.
▶ Demonstrated ability to communicate effectively with patients, families, medical staff, and the public.

EDUCATION

Master of Science in Nursing (Family Nurse Practitioner major)   May 2012
Johns Hopkins University, Baltimore, MD; GPA – 3.95

Consistently worked more than the minimum number of clinical practice hours. Clinical rotations provided experience in Women's Health, Pediatric Health, and Adult Health.

Bachelor of Science in Nursing   1990
University of Kentucky, Louisville, KY

HIGHLIGHTS OF PROFESSIONAL EXPERIENCE

Staff Nurse/Team Leader   2008 to present
Baltimore Cardiac Care Center, Baltimore, MD
▶ Serve as a resource on clinical issues for the Office Manager. Assist with the development of clinical policies and procedures. Make recommendations leading to cost savings, increased efficiency, and patient satisfaction.
▶ Assist physicians in understanding ancillary services and utilizing them appropriately.
▶ Helped institute a CHF Nursing Practice. Perform patient assessments and drug titrations under cardiologist supervision.
▶ Facilitate better patient well-being by educating patients and their families about medical conditions and procedures.
▶ Promote teamwork and communication among staff members.

Consultant   2007 to 2009
Johnson County Home Care, Lanham, MD

▶ Conducted Medicare audits and chart reviews that contributed to this agency receiving its first JCAHO accreditation.

(continued)

85 *(continued)*

Jennifer C. Powell, RN, FNP   *Page 2*
(410) 559-2211   jennpowell@gmail.com

HMO Case Manager   2005 to 2008
Emerald Healthcare, Toledo, OH

▶ Accompanied practitioners on rounds and collaborated with specialists on all HMO patients, directly contributing
  to decreased length of stay and improved quality of care.
▶ Assisted patients and families in planning for discharge. Facilitated patient education and satisfaction.
▶ Served on committees that investigated referral standards, morbidity and mortality issues, and appropriate use of
  ancillary services.
▶ Participated in the development of recommendations that shortened the average hospital stay for this practice's
  managed-care population, resulting in annual savings of more than $600,000.

Acting Administrator/ Clinical Supervisor/ Field Nurse   2004 to 2005
Lincoln Home Care, Peoria, IL

▶ Included nursing staff members in marketing luncheons for physicians. This was very effective and contributed to
  a 100% increase in the agency's census.
▶ Spearheaded the relocation of the agency to a building that was close to the hospital and more visible.
▶ Successfully led the office through a Medicare audit. Implemented a campaign to educate physicians about
  Medicare fraud.

ER Staff Nurse/ Medical Telemetry Unit Manager/ Float Pool Coordinator   1999 to 2004
Jefferson County Hospital, Springfield, IL

▶ Established an in-house nursing float pool that reduced hospital staffing costs by eliminating the use of agency
  nurses. Developed float pool policies and procedures.
▶ Managed a 42-bed telemetry unit. Improved employee satisfaction and patient satisfaction. Fostered an increase in
  staff productivity from 90% to 98%.
▶ As a member of the nursing management steering committee, contributed to the successful transition from a team
  nursing care delivery system to a differentiated case management system.

Additional Experience
Also held various Staff Nurse positions (ICU, Oncology Unit, Cardiac Telemetry Unit, Cardiac Rehab Clinic).
Served as Graduate School Teaching Assistant for Nursing Graduate Core Course, "Health Policy & Procedures,"
for two semesters.

PROFESSIONAL AFFILIATIONS & CERTIFICATIONS

Maryland Family Nurse Practitioner License	Maryland State Nurses Association
Maryland Registered Nursing License	CHF Networking Group
American Academy of Nurse Practitioners	ACLS Certification
American Nurses Association	Maryland Primary Health Care Association, Inc.
Who's Who among Students in American Colleges	Sigma Theta Tau Honor Society

86

Degree: MA, Photography.
Job Target: Photographer or photographer's assistant.
Strategy: Included a strong Select Highlights section to bring to the forefront a variety of relevant skills and experiences. Finished the resume with a powerful Accolades section.

HANS VAN DIJK

66 Brattle Place ◆ Cambridge, MA 02138 ◆ 617-353-2406 ◆ hvandijk@gmail.com

---

PHOTOGRAPHER/PHOTOGRAPHY ASSISTANT
Sports Photography / Commercial Photography / Portraiture / Media Arts
≈ Well-versed in all traditional and digital techniques ≈

Offering powerful, dynamic photographs that capture the moment.

UP-AND-COMING PHOTOGRAPHER and candidate for master's degree in photography (expected December 2012) with proven record of success in working with clients to plan and shoot well-received photographs to meet a broad range of commercial (sports, product, fashion, advertising, public relations) and personal needs. World-class triathlete with particular expertise in sports photography; effective in anticipating the moment and capturing spectacular action. Skilled retoucher who is creative in using technology to transform and enhance photos.

SELECT HIGHLIGHTS

- Launched successful freelance career based entirely on word-of-mouth referrals. Earned rave reviews for "awesome" photographs, quickly being dubbed "the guy with the eye."

- Gained business from prominent clients such as Boston Beer Company, Procter & Gamble, Every Brand Apparel, and the Boston Athletic Association, as well as others. Among successes:

  ▷ Shot Red Carpet event for Huntington Theatre Company at the Museum of Fine Arts, capturing the evening's spirit while photographing numerous high-profile attendees.

  ▷ Shot pre-Olympics World Triathlon Championship for well-known sponsor.

  ▷ Served as photographer for the Special Olympics, shooting photos used in fundraising collateral and earning high praise for work.

  ▷ Recorded promotional event for beer company, capturing biker's 3-story jump from mall in South Africa.

- Worked with commercial photographers, in studios and on location, to complete editorial and advertising shoots—covering fashion, food, architecture, and products—in New York and South Africa.

- Hired as assistant, handled retouching responsibilities for prominent catalog for timeless interior furnishings. Successfully handled high volume of work with most retouched photographs going straight to print.

- Shot sports photos accepted for publication in South Africa's largest newspaper.

- Recently featured in *Beantown Magazine*, a local publication promoting art and pop culture of Boston.

EDUCATION

BOSTON UNIVERSITY
Master of Art Degree, Photography, Expected December 2012 (GPA: 4.0)
Bachelor of Arts Degree, Liberal Arts (Photography focus), 2008 (GPA: 4.0)

---

86 *(continued)*

EXPERIENCE

SELF-EMPLOYMENT **2007 to present**
Freelance Photographer
Handled freelance assignments for Boston University, the Boston Athletic Association, and other notable clients.

CONDÉ NAST **2008 to 2009**
Assistant Photographer
Worked with lead photographer on editorial for *Achitectural Digest* magazine. Assisted architectural photographer in photographing Manhattan building for outside client.

BALLARD DESIGNS **2007 to 2008**
Retouching Assistant
Retouched photos used in well-known interior design catalog.

TECHNICAL SKILLS

Film Cameras:	Mamiya rz 67/645, Hasselblad 503 CW/EL, Pentax 67, Nikon F4/5, Canon EOS 3, 4x5, 8x10
Digital Equipment:	Canon 1D/1Ds mark I/II/III, 5d, 40d, Nikon d1x, d70s, and d100/200, Fuji finepix s2
Lighting:	Profoto, Speedotron, Dyna-lite, Broncolor, Arri, HMI, Alien Bees, White Lighting, Hot Lights
Software:	Photoshop, Lightroom, Aperture, Bridge, Capture One Pro, Canon Digital Photo Pro, Photomatix Pro, PTgui, Photo Mechanic, Illustrator, QuarkXPress, InDesign, RapidWeaver, Dreamweaver, HTML (web site design), Microsoft Office, iwork, Mac and PC Operating Systems
Other	RAW processing and color correction, platinum palladium printing, digital printing, photo retouching graphic design

ACCOLADES

"Hans Van Dijk is an up-and-coming Boston-based photographer who has an eye, talent and passion for event and sports photography. Hans uses a unique synthesis of artistic and photojournalistic photography styles to create portraits that are truly memorable."

"Hans' work is powerful, dynamic, and celebrates the moment where light, time, and composition all come together to create a poetic moment."

OTHER HIGHLIGHTS

World-class triathlete (competing for South Africa).
Holder of American and South African passports.

87

Degree: MS, Chemical Engineering.
Job Target: Chemical engineer.
Strategy: Highlighted a distinguishing postgraduate foreign exchange program that provided background in international business to complement recent master's degree.

LEE ANGELO

1308 Granger Street • Nyack, NY 10960 • langelo@hotmail.com • 845-555-8234

PROFILE

Master of Science in Chemical Engineering (2010) with hands-on R&D experience in the international business community. Extensive internship background in the Petroleum, Biotechnology, and Pharmaceutical industries. Resourceful team player with outstanding communication and interpersonal abilities that build trust and promote cooperative relationships among cross-functional teams. Detail-minded, critical thinker knowledgeable in SOP development, FDA and cGMP compliance, and clean room protocol. Intermediate-level fluency in German.

EDUCATION

BRONX COLLEGE, Riverdale, NY
Master of Science in Chemical Engineering, 2010
Bachelor of Science in Chemical Engineering, Minor in Chemistry, 2008
Cumulative GPA: 3.8/4.0

Honors
Bronx College Seamless Master's Scholarship
Gamma Sigma Epsilon, Chemistry Honor Society
Omega Chi Epsilon, Chemical Engineering Honor Society
Epsilon Sigma Pi, Bronx College Honor Society

EXPERIENCE

CONGRESS-BUNDESTAG YOUTH EXCHANGE FOR YOUNG PROFESSIONALS – Jena, Germany
Participant in Government-Funded Exchange Program with Germany (1/2011–1/2012)

- One of 75 participants hand-picked from more than 1,000 applicants throughout the country for program designed to enhance international relations and understanding between the US and Germany.
- The one-year program consists of three parts: an intensive German language training course, an academic study phase, and a five-month internship at a German company.

SCHOTT JENAER GLAS GMBH – Jena, Germany
Research Assistant Intern, Nexterion Microarray Solutions Department (8/2011–1/2012)

- Designed and executed experiments to create and optimize the silane-based surface coating for Schott's upcoming line of Microarray slides.
- Conducted DNA spotting and hybridization runs in conjunction with laboratory quality assurance testing to study the effect of process variables on specific Microarray physical properties.

WYETH PHARMACEUTICALS – Pearl River, NY
Bulk Manufacturing Department (full-time contractual position) (9/2010–5/2011)

- Recruited to participate in project to create an information system to track and organize GMP documentation associated with the manufacture of Prafnar.
- Reviewed and audited batching documentation to ensure compliance with cGMP regulations.
- Studied and organized test results for inclusion in ancillary documents.

Continued....

---

87 *(continued)*

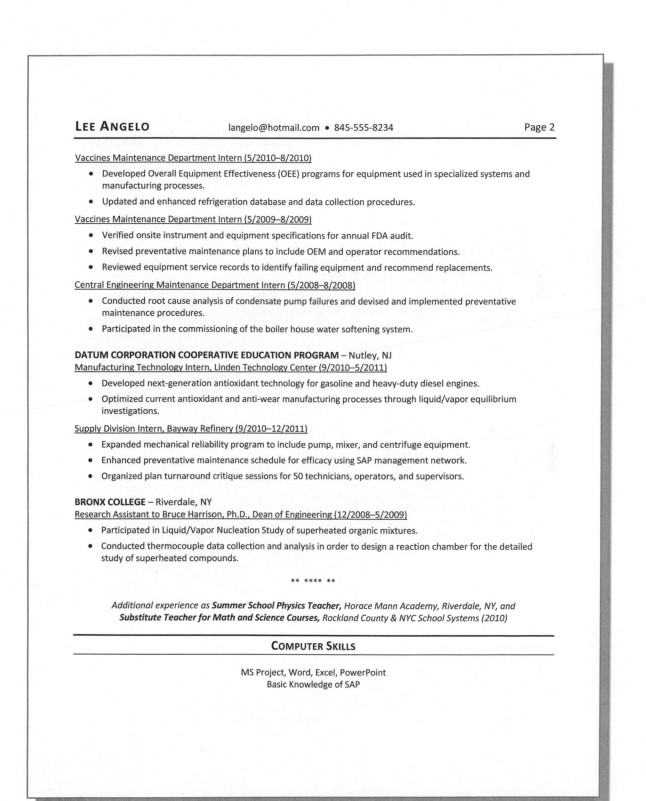

LEE ANGELO   langelo@hotmail.com • 845-555-8234   Page 2

Vaccines Maintenance Department Intern (5/2010–8/2010)
- Developed Overall Equipment Effectiveness (OEE) programs for equipment used in specialized systems and manufacturing processes.
- Updated and enhanced refrigeration database and data collection procedures.

Vaccines Maintenance Department Intern (5/2009–8/2009)
- Verified onsite instrument and equipment specifications for annual FDA audit.
- Revised preventative maintenance plans to include OEM and operator recommendations.
- Reviewed equipment service records to identify failing equipment and recommend replacements.

Central Engineering Maintenance Department Intern (5/2008–8/2008)
- Conducted root cause analysis of condensate pump failures and devised and implemented preventative maintenance procedures.
- Participated in the commissioning of the boiler house water softening system.

DATUM CORPORATION COOPERATIVE EDUCATION PROGRAM – Nutley, NJ
Manufacturing Technology Intern, Linden Technology Center (9/2010–5/2011)
- Developed next-generation antioxidant technology for gasoline and heavy-duty diesel engines.
- Optimized current antioxidant and anti-wear manufacturing processes through liquid/vapor equilibrium investigations.

Supply Division Intern, Bayway Refinery (9/2010–12/2011)
- Expanded mechanical reliability program to include pump, mixer, and centrifuge equipment.
- Enhanced preventative maintenance schedule for efficacy using SAP management network.
- Organized plan turnaround critique sessions for 50 technicians, operators, and supervisors.

BRONX COLLEGE – Riverdale, NY
Research Assistant to Bruce Harrison, Ph.D., Dean of Engineering (12/2008–5/2009)
- Participated in Liquid/Vapor Nucleation Study of superheated organic mixtures.
- Conducted thermocouple data collection and analysis in order to design a reaction chamber for the detailed study of superheated compounds.

** **** **

*Additional experience as **Summer School Physics Teacher,** Horace Mann Academy, Riverdale, NY, and **Substitute Teacher for Math and Science Courses,** Rockland County & NYC School Systems (2010)*

COMPUTER SKILLS

MS Project, Word, Excel, PowerPoint
Basic Knowledge of SAP

Degree: MS, Accounting.
Job Target: Accountant.
Strategy: Positioned this immigrant for success in her new country by showcasing relevant education, experience, and personal attributes that point to success in the field of accounting.

ANGELA CHIN

646-332-9785 ~ angela.chin@baruch.cuny.edu
239 West 110 Street ~ New York, NY 10034

Profile—

- Master of Science in Accounting Student at Baruch College (2013 expected completion).
- Bachelor's Degree in International Economics & Trade.
- Strong analytical and mathematical talents. Won several national and provincial awards in native China.
- Quick, dedicated learner, gaining proficiency in basic Japanese reading and communication in less than 6 months.
- Superior ability to learn and use accounting and statistical software as well as office and design software.
- Teamwork experience and record of working effectively on both group and individual projects.
- Proven ability to set and achieve goals, adapt to new challenges, devise effective solutions, and support/encourage people of all ages, professionally and personally.

Education—

Master of Science in Accounting – Baruch College/CUNY, New York, NY, 2013 (expected)
Bachelor of Economics in International Economics & Trade – Nankai University, Tianjin, China, 2011

Computer Skills—

Accounting: QuickBooks Pro, TaxWise
Statistical Software: SPSS, EViews
Office Software: MS Word, Excel, PowerPoint
Design Software: Photoshop, Fireworks

Languages—

Native: Chinese (Mandarin)
Fluent: English
Basic: Japanese

Internships—

FAR EASTERN ACCOUNTING & CONSULTING, New York, NY
HUDSON RIVER DEVELOPMENT ALLIANCE, New York, NY
    Accountant Intern – Spring 2012
    One of 6 interns chosen from 14 applicants. As the youngest intern with least amount of accounting background, excelled in company's training program alongside interns with 4X the amount of accounting coursework experience.
    - Assisted clients in complying with the latest Office of the Internal Revenue Service (IRS) rules and regulations.
    - Volunteered to prepare tax statements for low-income clients.

NANJING ROAD & BRIDGE TRANSPORTATION ENGINEERING CO., LTD., Xiamen, China
    Accountant Intern – Spring 2011
    Learned company-wide accounting procedures and offered support to the Accounting Staff, including journal entries and cash flow records.

AGRICULTURAL BANK OF CHINA, Xiamen, China
    Accountant Intern – Fall 2010
    Involved in international settlement services, drafting invoices for international clients, and resolving customer issues.

Additional Volunteer Experience—

NAMOZAI NURSING HOME, Bayside, NY – Spring 2012: Visit elderly residents and provide the gift of conversation.
XIAMEN ONLINE VOLUNTEER ALLIANCE, Xiamen, China – 1/2010–8/2011: Supported elderly and elementary-age orphans.

89

Degree: JD.
Job Target: Associate attorney in a private firm.
Strategy: Because of a rather obscure rule, this job seeker was able to "practice law" under the supervision of an attorney. Highlighting this unusual experience was especially important because the law school from which she graduated wasn't accredited.

Allison Bristow

323 Coldstone Court, Montgomery, AL 36100   [334] 207-1255 • allisonjd@juno.com

SITTING FOR BAR EXAM: July 12

CAPABILITIES DONNELLY & SHOREDITCH CAN USE NOW:

- **Communications skills** tested by uninformed clients
- **Research skills** tested by practicing attorneys
- **Presentation skills** tested in court

LAW-RELATED EXPERIENCE:

- **Law Clerk** *later* **Legal Intern**   Smith & Hawken, L.L.C., Wetumpka, Alabama
  Jan 10–Present

EXPERIENCE AS AN ADVOCATE FOR CLIENTS IN COURT

• Bond reduction hearings • Pendente lite hearings • Juvenile court hearings • Sentence reviews • Arraignments • Probation revocation hearings • Administrative hearings • District criminal, civil, and traffic courts • Dependency hearings • Sentencing hearings • Plea hearings

EXPERIENCE PREPARING FOR COURT

• Investigations • Drafting and filing motions • Writing briefs and memoranda • Negotiating plea bargains • Interviewing • Evaluating worth of civil cases • Legal research • Explaining legal rights and evidence

- Successfully defended client in suit against real-estate attorney with a decade of practice. Handled case after only four months of internship.
- Proved in court my juvenile client was not guilty in assault case, even though experienced law officers were witnesses for the prosecution.
- Carried the argument before a tough judge that my client's probation should not be revoked—even though he had tested positive for drugs. Had 15 minutes to prepare this case.

EDUCATION AND PROFESSIONAL DEVELOPMENT:

- J.D., Craft School of Law, Montgomery, Alabama, 12
  Pursued at night while working up to 45 hours a week.
- B.A., Broadcast Journalism, University of Southern Arkansas, Littleburg, Arkansas: 08
- B.S., Business Administration **(Industrial Management),** University of Arkansas, Littleburg, Arkansas: 04
- "Alabama Mediation Training," Resolution Resources, Birmingham, Alabama: 11
  Self-funded, 21 CLE hours.

PROFESSIONAL ORGANIZATIONS: Future Trial Lawyers Association

OTHER EXPERIENCE:

- More than 13 years in various positions in sales, broadcasting, manufacturing, and public relations.

90

Degree: JD.
Job Target: Associate position.
Strategy: Focused on internships and scholarships, placing education up front.

LIZ D. ENGEL

5298 Crow Avenue   212.432.5551
New York, NY 10027   liz@hotmail.com

CAREER FOCUS

Entry-level, Full-time Law Associate
• Corporate • Labor • Civil •

OVERVIEW

❑ Background in analyzing diversified corporate issues and drafting high-quality written documents.
❑ Superior interpersonal skills, able to build strong relationships and conduct liaison.
❑ Exposed to a variety of legal proceedings, research, and processes.
❑ Held several paid internship and clerk positions.

EDUCATION

▪ **Juris Doctor, May 2012**
  Corporate Counsel Certificate, May 2012
  New York University College of Law, New York, New York
  — Dean's List
  — Editor, *Journal of International Relations and Economics*
     Completed a note on the difficulties of prosecuting insider-trading violations

▪ **Bachelor of Arts in Economics and Finance, Minor in Psychology, May 2010**
  New Jersey State University, New Brunswick, New Jersey
  — Graduated with Honors (GPA: 3.8)
  — Dean's List, Golden Key National Honor Society, Summit Scholarship, Brenton Hospital Auxiliary Scholarship, Marcus Scholarship, College Club of Inglewood Scholarship, Athletic Achievement Award

PROFESSIONAL EXPERIENCE

Law Clerk
Michaels, Brenner, Schmidt & Associates, Fairfield, Connecticut   Summer 2012

  ▪ Analyzed diversified corporate issues involving labor, contract, environmental, bankruptcy, and real estate law, and drafted complaints, interrogatories, and legal memoranda for attorneys.
  ▪ Examined the legislative history of the statutes of limitations to clarify intent for specific cases. Thoroughly researched procedures required to commence actions and determined proper jurisdiction to file suits.
  ▪ Actively participated in case discussions, strategy conferences, and settlement negotiations.

Page 1 of 2

90 *(continued)*

LIZ D. ENGEL, PAGE 2   212.432.5551 ▪ liz@hotmail.com

Legal Intern
Law Office of Marsha Bender, Laurel, Maryland   **Summer 2011**

- Drafted complaints, interrogatory responses, and memoranda involving personal-injury claims. Served as an advocate to clients and negotiated settlements in insurance and elder law.
- Conducted legal research. Corresponded with clients and attorneys.
- Participated in real estate closings.

Legal Intern
Honorable Mark L. Williams
Assignment Judge, Criminal Division, Superior Court, Connecticut   **Summer 2010**

- Prepared pre-sentence investigation summaries for court proceedings.
- Worked directly with inmates to procure unawarded jail credit. Reconciled inmate appeals regarding issued bench warrants. Accessed the Promise Gavel Database for inmate verification and case status.
- Observed criminal and divorce trials, voir dire, and mediation proceedings.

Legal Intern
Howard County Probative Services Division, Columbia, Maryland   **Summer 2009**

- Observed child-support enforcement cases and managed pertinent recordkeeping of proceedings.
- Participated in case discussions and analysis with the attorneys and hearing officer.

MEMBERSHIP

American Bar Association, 2012 to Present

TECHNICAL PROFICIENCY

Lexis/Nexis ▪ Westlaw ▪ Library Legal Research ▪ Microsoft Office

91

Degree: MD (completing residency program).
Job Target: Urologist in private practice.
Strategy: Set this candidate apart by including an eye-catching graphic and detailing his earlier career as a naval officer (on page 2) in this otherwise straightforward CV presentation.

JOHN D. ANDENORO, M.D.

Curriculum Vitae

Contact:
801-582-8862 ▪ andenoro.j@mac.com

Residence:
1214 Fenway Avenue ▪ Salt Lake City, UT 84102

Business:
University of Utah Medical Center ▪ 50 Medical Drive ▪ Salt Lake City, UT 84132

SPECIALTY	**Urologic Surgery**	
	Oncology, Stone Disease, Pediatric Urology, Laparoscopic Surgery, Incontinence, Female Urology and Infertility	

EDUCATION

Medical	**Baylor College of Medicine,** Houston, TX **M.D.**	2007
Undergraduate	Washington & Jefferson College, Washington, PA B.A. Biology	1995

MEDICAL TRAINING

Chief Resident	University of Utah Health Science Center Salt Lake City, UT Urologic Surgery	2011–2012
Resident	University of Utah Health Science Center Salt Lake City, UT Urologic Surgery	2009–2011
Resident	University of Utah Health Science Center Salt Lake City, UT General Surgery	2008–2009
Intern	University of Utah Health Science Center Salt Lake City, UT General Surgery	2007–2008

LICENSURE AND CERTIFICATION

Physician & Surgeon	Utah License Number 348070-1205	2007–Present
Board Certification	Applicant to American Board of Urology	in process
Certified	Advanced Trauma Life Support	Current
	Basic & Advanced Cardiac Life Support	Current

PROFESSIONAL AFFILIATIONS

American Urological Association	2009–Present
American Medical Association, Resident Section	2007–Present
Utah Medical Association	2007–Present
American Medical Association, Medical Student Section	2003–2007
Texas Medical Association	2002–2006
Texas Medical Association, Legislation Committee, Medical Student Representative	2004–2006

Continued on Page Two

91 *(continued)*

JOHN D. ANDENORO, M.D.

801-582-8862 ▪ andenoro.j@mac.com

Curriculum Vitae
Page Two

PRESENTATIONS

Andenoro, J., Snow, B., Cartwright, P. "Serum Potassium and Creatinine Changes Following Unstented Bilateral Ureteral Reimplantation." Accepted for presentation at Western Section of the American Urologic Association. Palm Desert, CA. Nov 2012.

Andenoro, J., Snow, B., Hamilton, B., Cartwright, P. "Laparoscopic Renal Surgery in Infants: Is Age a Contraindication?" American Urological Association Annual Meeting. Atlanta, GA. Apr 2012.

Andenoro, J. "Tissue Engineering: Surgical Applications and Urologic Frontiers." University of Utah Division of Urology Grand Rounds. Salt Lake City, UT. Mar 2012.

Andenoro, J., Stephenson, R., Middleton, R. "Biochemical Failure After Radical Prostatectomy: The First 5 Years of the PSA Era." Western Section of the American Urologic Association. Monterey, CA. Oct 2010.

Andenoro, J. "Nephron Sparing Surgery: State of the Art in Open and Laparoscopic Partial Nephrectomy, Cryosurgery and Auto-Transplantation." University of Utah Division of Urology Grand Rounds. Salt Lake City, UT. Jun 2010.

Andenoro, J., Morton, R., Scardino, P. "Immunohisto-Chemical Analysis of E-Cadherin Expression in Prostate Cancer." American Urological Association Annual Meeting. Apr 2007.

RESEARCH PROJECTS

Randomized Survey of Prostate Cancer Screening in Utah	2007
Immunohisto-Chemistry of E-Cadherin Expression in Prostate Cancer	2006

MILITARY SERVICE

Physician	Utah Air National Guard, Rank: Major 151st Medical Squadron, Salt Lake City, UT	2009–Present
Medical Training	Flight Surgeon Training Courses Mass Casualty/Combat Medicine Course	2009 & 2010 2011
Intelligence Officer	United States Navy Reserve, Lieutenant Commander Mine Warfare Command, Corpus Christi, TX Naval Intelligence Service, Houston/Corpus Christi, TX Defense Intelligence Agency, Austin, TX	2002–2007
	United States Navy (Active Duty) Commander-in-Chief, U.S. Navy, Europe London, U.K.	1999–2002
	United States Navy (Active Duty) Fighter Squadron 102 Virginia Beach, VA USS *America*, USS *Theodore Roosevelt*	1996–1999

Degree: MD.
Job Target: Physician.
Strategy: For this foreign medical graduate, highlighted top-of-class status in Egypt, position as chief resident in the United States, and teaching experience to help him stand out from the crowd.

Josef Rahman, M.D.
115 Abernathy Court
New York, NY 10023
(212) 861-2222
drrahman@mci.net

PROFILE

Compassionate, organized physician with well-rounded medical training and solid crisis-management skills. Available for employment in July 2012. Able to work effectively with people of various ages, ethnicities, and socioeconomic backgrounds. Confident and able to learn new skills quickly. Member of American College of Physicians—American Society of Internal Medicine. Special interest in cancer and AIDS.

CERTIFICATIONS & LICENSURE

New York medical license—pending
USMLE
ECFMG
ACLS

EDUCATION

Bachelor of Medicine/Bachelor of Surgery (equivalent to M.D. in the United States)   2005
Asif Medical College, Cairo, Egypt
- Ranked in top 2% of students taking the medical school entrance exam and top 5% of class at Asif Medical College.
- Awarded a full academic scholarship at this prestigious medical school.
- Received "Mr. Team Player" award for demonstrating excellent interpersonal skills.
- Completed internship at Cairo General Hospital. Rotations included pediatrics, surgery, cardiology, emergency medicine, and community health.

Pre-Medical Education
Cairo Junior College, Cairo, Egypt   1996–1998
First in a class of 100 students.

PROFESSIONAL EXPERIENCE

Medical Resident   2010–present
Mount Sinai Medical Center, New York, NY

- Completed clinical rotations in infectious diseases and neurology.
- Selected as Chief Resident.

---

92 *(continued)*

Josef Rahman, M.D.   Page 2
(212) 861-2222 ● drrahman@mci.net

Medical Resident   2008–2009
St. Luke's–Roosevelt Hospital, New York, NY

- Acquired experience in intensive care, coronary care, general medicine, ambulatory care, and emergency medicine.
- Completed clinical rotations in hematology, oncology, nephrology, and intensive care.
- Organized and set up a research project on diabetic ketoacidosis.

Telemetry Volunteer   2007–2008
Rochester Community Hospital, Rochester, NY

- Assisted with patient monitoring in the telemetry department.

Physician   2006
Private Practice, Cairo, Egypt

- Assisted attending physician in caring for patients in the office and hospital.

Senior Intern   2005
Institute of Mental Health, Alexandria, Egypt

- Acquired experience in psychiatric medicine from this 10-week specialty internship.

PRESENTATIONS & TEACHING EXPERIENCE

- Tuberculosis in Immunocompromised Patients, Columbia University conference
- Colon Cancer Screening inservice, Mount Sinai Hospital
- Pneumocystis Carinii Pneumonia inservice, St. Luke's–Roosevelt Hospital
- Diabetics and Genetics, St. Luke's–Roosevelt Hospital

Taught medical students at Mount Sinai School of Medicine:
- Introduction to Clinical Skills, Mount Sinai Hospital
- Preparation for Clinical Medicine, Mount Sinai Hospital
- Ambulatory Medicine, Mount Sinai Hospital
- Advanced Medicine, Mount Sinai Hospital

93

Degree: DVM.

Job Target: Position with a modern animal clinic with special focus on cats and the possibility of being mentored toward an ABVP (American Board of Veterinary Practitioners) certification.

Strategy: Used quotes from clients to add value to this vet's resume and help sell her qualifications to a high-profile hospital in spite of her limited experience in a small-town clinic.

Mary Wiggley, D.V.M.

6399 Bonnett Drive
Lingham, WA 90028
(333) 447-3353
mwdvm@hotmail.com

PROFESSIONAL QUALIFICATIONS

Highly motivated, practice-oriented recent graduate with great interest in personal and practice growth. Team player with special interest in high-quality feline medicine and surgery. Use outstanding communication skills to provide clients with professional and compassionate care. Pursue continuing education to remain current in feline medicine. Intend to pursue ABVP Diplomate certification.

Licensed to practice Veterinary Medicine in the State of Washington—current

PC skills—word processing, spreadsheet, data entry, and AVIMARK software

Member—AVMA, AAFP, and VIN

PROFESSIONAL EXPERIENCE

Associate Veterinarian, Memorial Cat Clinic, Lingham, WA, 2011–present

- Examine feline patients, perform diagnostic tests, create treatment plans, estimate costs, and counsel clients.

- Perform routine surgeries including spays, neuters, abscesses, dentals, and C-sections.

- Rotate with other veterinary clinics to handle weekend and off-hours emergencies.

- *Excerpts from client notes to Dr. Wiggley:*

  "… you see sick animals and their families every day and yet I feel like Rico got 'special' treatment … I couldn't be more pleased or comfortable with the way things were handled."

  "…deeply moved by your depth of understanding for our grief …."

  "Thank you for all your caring and concern … we appreciate you!"

  " … really appreciated all the extra special treatment you gave Frosty …."

  "Thank you warmly for your thoughtfulness and care with Sugar …. Life is full of beautiful people and you are a part of that."

EDUCATION

Continuing Education—VIN classes

D.V.M., Washington State University College of Veterinary Medicine, Pullman, 2010

Pre-Veterinary Medicine/Zoology, Washington State University, Seattle, 2004–2006

B.S., Animal Science, Oregon State University, Corvallis, 2001

OTHER EMPLOYMENT

Technician, Fab 4 & 5, Corvallis, OR, 1994–2004

CHAPTER 9

Resumes for "Average" Students

If you've looked at all of the resumes in this book, you might think that all of them were written for "star performers"—above-average students with exceptional accomplishments. Although it's true that many of these resumes represent students with outstanding qualifications, others simply make the most of every activity and accomplishment and show how these can be valuable to an employer.

To make my point, in this chapter I've selected resumes of "average" students. By this I mean students with GPAs below 3.0 (and thus not featured on their resumes, as recommended in Chapter 2), students who have not been leaders of on-campus organizations, who have not held strong and relevant co-op or internship positions, and who might not have been involved in any campus activities or work experience whatsoever!

I realize that not everyone is an outstanding student in college. Perhaps you fit this category. For any number of reasons, you might have earned grades that are only fair or even poor. Perhaps you had to work to cover the cost of your education. Maybe you started out in the wrong major and either struggled or lost interest. You might have been unmotivated your first year or two and didn't really apply yourself. Similarly, you might have been caught up in the excitement of being away at school and devoted yourself to parties, fun, and friends rather than your studies or any meaningful on-campus involvement. But now you are about to finish school, need to find a job, and indeed do have lots to offer. The resumes in this chapter will show you how to make the most of your college experiences, no matter how "average" you might feel your experiences and qualifications are.

Resume Number	Degree	Job Target
94	BS, Business Administration	Executive assistant
95	BA, Business Studies	Sales position
96	BS, Business Management, Private Recreation	Public relations, product promotion, sales, or recreation position
97	BA, Business Management	Sales and marketing position
98	BS, Biology	Medical/pharmaceutical sales position
99	BS, Marketing	Marketing/advertising position
100	BA, Political Science	International business development position
101	BS, Finance	Financial services sales position
102	BA, Architectural Studies	Architectural resource library manager
103	BS, Human Resource Management	Clerk/administrative assistant
104	BA, Radio and Television	Television, film, or radio production position
105	BS, Recreation, Parks, and Tourism	Hospitality manager
106	AS, Recording Arts	Audio production position

Resume Number	Degree	Job Target
107	BS, Biological Sciences	Laboratory technician
108	BS, Biology	Zookeeper
109	AS, Network Administration	Help desk position
110	BS, Business Administration	Position in marketing or economics
111	BA, Business Management	Management trainee
112	BS, Regional Development	Internship or entry-level position in commercial real-estate development

Degree: BS, Business Administration.
Job Target: Executive assistant.
Strategy: Described in detail two summer jobs, including a stint as a bartender/server that demonstrated customer-service skills and reliability. Highlighted relevant capabilities in the summary.

RACHEL A. WRIGHT

1234 10th Street
Phoenix, Arizona 85019

Phone: (602) 555-1234
E-mail: rawright@hotmail.com

CAREER TARGET: EXECUTIVE ASSISTANT

A reliable and dependable administrative professional with strong multitasking and time management capabilities. Mature and confident in business interactions, with proven communication, interpersonal, and negotiation skills. Demonstrated ability to prepare, analyze, and report data with exceptional attention to detail. Established a reputation for relating warmly to people of different personalities and cultures, generating trust and rapport. Fully proficient in the Microsoft Office Suite.

- Management Support
- Office Administration
- Confidential Assistance
- Client Correspondence
- Customer Satisfaction
- Teamwork & Training
- Telephone Support
- Workflow Prioritization
- Records & Data Management

EDUCATION

Arizona State University, Tempe, Arizona   **Expected Completion 2012**
- Bachelor of Science, Majoring in Business Administration
- Courses include Office Administration, Managerial Accounting, Effective Communications, Project Management, and Interpersonal Relations.

PROFESSIONAL EXPERIENCE

Private Medical Practice, Phoenix, Arizona   **Summer 2011**
Administrative Assistant
Reporting directly to the senior partner, responsible for organizing the doctor's office, classifying patient charts, handling phone calls, filing, and billing. Accountable to manage the Family Health Network program, patient roster, and materials.
- Categorized and compiled a comprehensive patient roster. Successfully completed the entry of 750 patients in the practice within two months of hire.
- Designed the patient correspondence, procedures, and checklists on the Family Health Network Program. Trained and updated staff to ensure program effectiveness and consistency.
- Organized charts for up to 100 patients on a daily basis with virtually 100% accuracy.

Relax Hotel & Conference Centre, Phoenix, Arizona   **Summer 2010**
Bartender/Server
Interacted with customers in a professional manner. Responsibilities included greeting customers, taking reservations, serving, and bartending. Accountable for opening and closing the restaurant, training employees, and balancing cash.
- Commended on a regular basis from supervisors and customers for exceptional customer service and satisfaction skills.
- Assigned to work independently, handle large groups and banquets, and supervise functions due to maturity and reliability.

COMPUTER SKILLS

Proficient in a variety of computer technology and software, including
- Windows and Mac operating systems
- Microsoft Office (Word, Excel, Outlook, and PowerPoint)

Degree: BA, Business Studies.
Job Target: Sales.
Strategy: Expanded a part-time job in sales to include both position duties and accomplishment statements. Added a strong third-party endorsement in the form of a supportive quote from the boss.

BEN GRABER

2345 Roanoke Drive, Houston, Texas 77017
713-457-8990
bengraber@linx.net

CAREER OBJECTIVE

Direct Sales—Entry-level

SALES QUALIFICATIONS

- Recent college graduate who is motivated, goal-driven, and quick to learn new information.
- Successful sales experience with a strong focus on customer service excellence.
- Record of initiative and responsibility; sought by customers to help with their product needs.
- Talent for building rapport with clientele; professional, mature approach; high energy level; liked by others.
- Valued by customers for helpfulness, a caring attitude, and honoring my word.

EDUCATION

Bachelor of Arts in Business Studies
Texas College, Tyler, Texas, 2011
- Major: Marketing with Merchandising Emphasis

EXPERIENCE

WILLOWBY ENTERPRISES, Houston, Texas, Fall 2003–Present
(Part time/full-time throughout college and high school)

SALES AND CUSTOMER RELATIONS

- Position involves selling and merchandising a complete line of specialty clothing products to clients of all ages, types, and backgrounds. Maintain technical knowledge of hundreds of different products sold. Trusted by customers to recommend the right product to meet their specific needs.

Key Accomplishments:

- Contributed to the growth and profitability of the business through successful sales efforts.
- Built a loyal following of satisfied, repeat customers.
- Supported the company's goals and objectives to satisfaction of owner and customers alike.
- Received consistent salary increases based on satisfactory levels of performance.

INTERESTS

Golf, physical fitness, skiing

"Ben is professional, optimistic, and always willing to come in early and stay late."

David Williams III, President, Willowby Enterprises, Houston, Texas

96 **Degree:** BS, Business Management, Private Recreation.
Job Target: Public relations, product promotion, sales, recreation.
Strategy: Used a Creative Expression section in the lower-left column to relate personal pursuits to current job interests. Included a short-term internship at a skate park.

eric hiatt

80 Spencer Lane
Harrisburg, PA 17602

717.574.7190 (h)
717.304.1236 (c)

ehiatt@gmail.com

presenting an eclectic blend of interests and talents

high potential for success in public relations, product promotion, sales, recreation

creative expression
skateboarding
video production
snowboarding
surfing
dirt bike riding
music

filmed and produced the 30-minute video **"shop copy"**: an artistic illustration of skateboarding

profile

- Personable and outgoing; quick to build rapport with people of all ages and socioeconomic, ethnic, and cultural backgrounds.
- Strong oral and written communication skills.
- Naturally inquisitive with a hunger for challenge and intellectual stimulation.
- Analytical thinker with a propensity for research and working with mathematical concepts.
- Determined and willing to risk failure.
- Energized by formulating goals and producing a finished product.
- Enjoy travel and adventure; willing to relocate.

education

Bachelor of Science, **University of Vermont,** Burlington, VT   2012
    Concentration: Business Management—Private Recreation
    Key coursework: Park & Recreation Design; Field Ecology; Tourism Planning; Video/Film Production; Entrepreneurship in Recreation; Resort Marketing & Management; Ski Area Management

Study Abroad, **University of Waikato,** New Zealand
February to June 2011

Paid Internship, **Spirit Skate Park,** South Burlington, VT
February to June 2010
- Worked in tandem with owner, providing sales, customer service, and maintenance support.
- Only employee first year of operation.
- Assisted in variety of day-to-day operations, park monitoring, retail shop sales, merchandising, and promotion.
- Created a demand for a unique skateboarding video; sold 50 copies on first run; currently creating additional copies for retail sale.

technology savvy

- PC & Mac; spreadsheets, word processing, Internet
- Canon GL2 video camera; Final Cut Pro software

summer employment

Conestoga Country Club, Harrisburg, PA—Waiter		2009
Hoffman Auto Supply, Burlington, VT—Delivery Clerk		2008

97

Degree: BA, Business Management.
Job Target: Sales and marketing position.
Strategy: Made the most of academic projects and limited extracurricular activities to demonstrate teamwork and initiative.

JOHN MEADOWS

534 Cherry Lane • Haymarket, VA 22036
H: 703-222-2222 • C: 703-222-2223 • Email: meadows@email.com

CAREER FOCUS & VALUE TO EMPLOYER

SALES & MARKETING

- Business major with a keen interest in a sales and marketing career. Committed to continued learning and the improvement of business-related skills.
- Communication, interaction, and relationship-building skills acquired through work experience, volunteer activities, team sports, and academic projects.
- Computer experience includes MS Office (Word, Excel). Created and managed Excel databases. Completed courses in Web page creation and electronic information exchange. Confident in learning and using new business applications.

EDUCATION & COLLEGE ACTIVITIES

B.A. in Business Management
UNIVERSITY OF VIRGINIA, Charlottesville, VA—2012
- Maintained required GPA to receive Bright Futures Scholarship all 4 years in college.

Associate of Arts with focus on **Business Management**
NORTHERN VIRGINIA COMMUNITY COLLEGE, Fairfax, VA—2010
- Academic Dean's List (2009)
- Bright Futures Scholarship recipient

Academic projects, college activities, and volunteer work:
- Completed several group projects for business classes. Two examples: Built a database for a virtual business (Information Management Systems) and completed a study on the effect of repetitive advertising on consumers (Consumer Behavior).
- Member of Pi Kappa Alpha Fraternity, ranked as UVA's top academic fraternity (2010) and fraternity of the year (2010 and 2011) for grades and philanthropic/community activities.
- Participated in Pi Kappa Alpha charity fund-raisers for *Children's Miracle Network, Christmas for the Kids,* and *Habitat for Humanity.* Member of *Habitat for Humanity* team that built three houses during spring break.
- Participated in intramural sports. Former top seed on Haymarket High School's tennis team.

Relevant business courses:

Organizational Behavior	Cross-cultural Management	Strategic Management & Business Policies
Principles of Purchasing	Contemporary Leadership	Multinational Business Operations
Managerial Accounting	Introduction to MIS	Electronic Information Exchange
Competitive Dynamics	Business & Society	Managing Service Organizations
Consumer Behavior	Web Page Creation	Microsoft Business Applications
Professional Selling	HR Management	Financial Management of Firms

COLLEGE WORK EXPERIENCE

MEADOWS CONSULTING SERVICE, Haymarket, VA—2010
Database Manager—Hired to build Excel database and input data from various sources for an impact evaluation of a state grant to Fairfax County Schools.

HAYMARKET HEALTH AND FITNESS, Haymarket, VA—Summer 2009
Assistant Manager—Interacted with customers to sell memberships, diplomatically resolve customer service problems, and answer questions. Also performed finance and accounting duties.

98

Degree: BS, Biology.
Job Target: Medical/pharmaceutical sales position.
Strategy: Pulled together biology education and science-related work experience plus a variety of part-time sales jobs to position this individual for a new career in pharmaceutical sales after a short stint in a laboratory convinced him to change careers.

Alex K. Rodgers

17 Patterson Street
Somerset, New Jersey 08873   alexrodgers@yahoo.com

Cell   732-821-2905
Home 732-507-3167

Biology major with strong interpersonal and sales skills seeking a challenging position in Pharmaceutical / Medical Sales

SUMMARY OF QUALIFICATIONS
- Several years of experience interacting with a variety of customers while meeting and exceeding sales goals
- Strong knowledge of medical terminology, anatomy and physiology, and pharmaceutical terms
- Excellent rapport-building, presentation, and closing skills
- Experience prospecting clients via cold calling
- Educated in the sciences and adept at learning new processes and information quickly

EDUCATION

Currently pursuing **Certified National Pharmaceutical Representative** designation
Coursework includes Clinical Pharmacology, FDA Laws, Effective Pharmaceutical Sales Techniques

B.S., Biology, with a minor in Chemistry, 2011
Georgetown University, Washington, DC

PROFESSIONAL EXPERIENCE
SCIENTIFIC EXPERIENCE

Bio-Tech Systems Inc., Branchburg, NJ   2011–Present
Technician
- Perform stability functional testing of raw materials and test kits for HIV, HCV, DNA, and blood-screening products.
- Analyze, maintain, and validate test data using LIMS system.
- Participate in routine lab maintenance and ISO implementation.
- Monitor testing reagent status and equivalency using SAP and LIMS.
- Generate data to support shelf-life extensions.

Bio-Life Plasma Service, New Brunswick, NJ   2011
Laboratory Technician
- Worked effectively in a high-volume laboratory.
- Tested plasma for HIV antigen, HIV antibody, Hepatitis B, and Hepatitis C.
- Completed tests within strict time schedules under the Standard Operating Procedures.

SALES EXPERIENCE

The Shoe Boutique, Washington, DC   2010–2011
Sales Associate
- Led sales team with the highest units sold per hour; consistently exceeded all sales quotas.
- Interacted effectively with a wide customer base and assisted customers in determining appropriate gift choices.
- Assigned to provide sales assistance to several high-profile sports figures.
- Maintained excellent record of financial accuracy at day's close.

TGI Friday's, Washington, DC   2007–2008
Server
- Effectively up-sold menu items, resulting in increased sales for establishment.
- Interacted with customers in a professional and courteous manner.
- Handled questions and problems effectively; handled financial transactions accurately.

Civic Group, New Brunswick, NJ   2005–2006
Telemarketer
- Made cold calls and established rapport within a very short period of time to effectively close sales and meet sales goals.

99

Degree: BS, Marketing.
Job Target: Marketing/advertising position.
Strategy: Devoted most of the space on the resume to part-time work experience and one relevant internship.

NITA K. SHANE

11 Stanton Avenue • Corning, CA 95973 • 530-789-1568 • nita@hotmail.com

MARKETING/ADVERTISING PROFILE

Motivated, talented professional offering a bachelor's degree in marketing, diverse experience, and a solid understanding of marketing and advertising strategies. Experience in conceptualizing, planning, promoting, and executing multifaceted projects. Customer-focused communicator with proven ability to understand customer needs and a commitment to satisfaction and prompt service. Top producer, willing to go the extra mile to meet deadlines and achieve company goals. Expertise includes

- Conceptual Planning
- Strategy Development
- Project Management
- Web-Based Marketing
- Marketing Penetration
- Competitive Analysis
- Advertising Campaigns
- Media/Client Relations
- Ad Copy Creation

EDUCATION AND TRAINING

B.S. Marketing with Minor in Communication, California State University, Sacramento—2010

Certificate of Completion, Media School, Grey Advertising, San Francisco, CA—2011
Won award for best innovation and creativity for media project. Developed marketing campaign for new product by focusing on the wants/needs of our target audience and by creating product awareness through proper placement.

Foreign Languages: Fluent in Punjabi and have an understanding of Hindi.

EXPERIENCE

GREY ADVERTISING, SAN RAFAEL, CA—2011

Media Coordinator

Contributed to research, analysis, and recommendations designed to guide clients in the selection of effective marketing strategies. Responded to project-specific and general client questions and requests on a daily basis.
- Increased visibility by continually monitoring online campaigns to ensure proper placement and accessibility.
- Communicated among all departments to ensure smooth, on-time delivery of marketing campaign.
- Planned and organized buying for interactive media.

TALYOR MOTORS INTERNSHIP, SACRAMENTO, CA—2010

Advertising Associate Intern

Developed and implemented an informative event at CSUS campus. Guided development of advertising campaign and theme development. Coordinated talent search and auditions for product commercials. Contacted community sponsors and local radio stations for advertising and entertainment.
- Targeted more than 200,000 impressions—developed public service announcements, press releases, flyers, banners, and bulletins to promote event participation.
- Met all deadlines and created an outstanding event with attendance exceeding 3,000 students.

STATE OF CALIFORNIA, DEPARTMENT OF HEALTH SERVICES, SACRAMENTO—2007 to 2008

Student Assistant/Analyst

Maintained and updated provider database for Med-Cal applications. Acted as contact for direct-mail marketing. Provided customer qualification screening and satisfactory resolution of case issues.

AFFILIATIONS

Member of American Marketing Association (Advertising Director 2010), California State University Chapter

---

100

Degree: BA, Political Science.
Job Target: International business development.
Strategy: Used an eye-catching format to call attention to class projects, internship and work experience, and educational qualifications.

FRED MOSBACH

3592 Bogart Avenue, Apartment 1J • Columbus, Ohio 43201

FredJD@homespun.com • 614-306-6636

FOCUS: International BUSINESS DEVELOPMENT

- **Classically educated team player;** significant travel to Europe, Asia, and the Middle East.
- **Strong crisis management skills;** able to steer and support operations through volatile situations.
- **Dedicated to global affairs;** recognized for willingness to learn with ability to succeed in diverse arenas.
- **Proven record of effectively managing multiple tasks** without compromise to quality; employ innovation, creativity, and enthusiasm when approaching projects.
- **Proficient with Microsoft Word and Excel.**

EDUCATION

THE OHIO STATE UNIVERSITY ... Columbus, Ohio
Bachelor of Arts in Political Science, 2011
Treasurer ... Delta Chi Fraternity (March 2010 to February 2011)

REPRESENTATIVE PROJECTS

Labor & Business: Contributed to group project requiring business decisions/conclusions made for Barrier Toys' handling of unions and employment in Germany and Sweden; strategies included methods of communicating with media and advertising to improve image of company, use of lobbyists to communicate with international governing bodies, and comprehensive action plans to improve workplace image for employees.

International Affairs: Produced several major documents defining methods to improve democratic process in Italy; documents focused heavily on theories based on active political parties, historical settings, and nature of Italian political state.

WORK HISTORY

STATE OF OHIO SENATE—Senate Page: Displayed professionalism, workflow management skills, and motivation while participating in sessions and committee meetings with responsibility for allocating bills, generating documents, and assisting senators and reporters with special projects; simultaneously assisted senators with delivery of packages to governor's office, Ohio House of Representatives, and Ohio Department of Education. Columbus, Ohio (September 2010–December 2010)

COVER TO COVER—Sales Associate: Enhanced business development and maximized profit potential with dedicated customer service, visual merchandising, shipment processing, overstock/damaged inventory returns, inventory sourcing, and store restock and cleanup. Performed managerial duties including store opening/closing, cash/credit handling, bank deposits, post office runs, data management, and store closings. Within months of hire, assumed increased responsibility for managerial activities. Columbus, Ohio (January 2008–August 2010)

Additional operations and business development assignments at **FedEx** (June 2007–September 2007); **Victoria's Secret** (November 2006–January 2007); **Gap, Inc., Warehouse** (June 2006–September 2006); **Gap** (August 2005–November 2005); **Kroger** (September 2004–August 2005); and **Young's Nursery** (June 2004–August 2004).

101

Degree: BS, Finance.
Job Target: Financial services sales.
Strategy: Emphasized an on-campus investment club that provided a good source of relevant experience, even though his involvement was very part-time.

DAVID MARTIN

29224 Jones Avenue NE | East Lansing, MI 48824 | 517-461-9706 | davidmartin@david.com

FINANCIAL SERVICES CANDIDATE

Driven, intelligent, hardworking professional pursuing entry-level opportunities in the **Financial Services** industry. Demonstrated success utilizing sound customer-service techniques, solid relationship-building talents, and proficient communication skills. Recognized for being a team player who is eager, enthusiastic, and focused. **Core strengths and abilities include**

- ♦ Financial Analysis
- ♦ Presentation Creation
- ♦ Customer Service
- ♦ Securities Research
- ♦ Performance Analysis
- ♦ Business Development
- ♦ Market / Sector Knowledge
- ♦ Stock Trading / Investing
- ♦ Leadership / Team Building

EDUCATION

Bachelor of Science in Finance—Michigan State University; East Lansing, MI   **Graduated 2011**
Minor in International Business—Copenhagen Business School; Denmark

Key Coursework: Portfolio Theory and Investment; Corporate Finance; Cost and Managerial Accounting; Strategic Management and Company Analysis; Financial Institution Analysis (Brokerage Houses, The Stock Exchange, Banks, Corporate Mergers); International Marketing; International Investment

FINANCIAL SERVICES EXPERIENCE

JAGUAR INVESTMENT FUND; Michigan State University   *Technology Sector Analyst*   **2010–2011**
- ♦ Assisted with managing and selecting technology-sector investment opportunities to grow $1M+ investment fund 6% in 2010.
- ♦ Conducted securities and sector research; created and delivered financial and investment presentations.

ADDITIONAL WORK HISTORY

SEARS; East Lansing, MI   **2009–Present**
Sales Associate
- ♦ Achieved top sales position in Men's Sportswear Department as well as fourth place in storewide sales competition.

USA FITNESS; East Lansing, MI   **2008–2009**
Personal Trainer
Recruited to provide one-on-one fitness training to clients after creating a customized weight and diet plan.
- ♦ Recipient of "Outstanding Customer Service Award."
- ♦ Achieved recognition as top trainer in nutritional supplement sales.

JOHNSON, BLACK, DRAKE, EDWARDS; East Lansing, MI   **2007–2008**
Office Assistant
Provided assistance to attorneys, performing research projects and organizing the file room.

MOORE-JACKSON MARTIAL ARTS; East Lansing, MI   **2005–2007**
Assistant Instructor
Instructed students ranging in age from 10 to 55 years old and assisted with daily operation efforts, including accounting, student retention, and recruitment activities.

TECHNOLOGY SKILLS INVENTORY

Word • Excel • PowerPoint • Outlook • HTML • Java

102

Degree: BA, Architectural Studies.
Job Target: Architectural resource library manager.
Strategy: Pulled together a diverse educational background to show strong qualifications for the target position.

JUSTIN RHODES

721 W. 26th Street ♦ Oklahoma City, OK 54923 ♦ 250-481-3862
justindrhodes@hotmail.com

ARCHITECTURAL RESOURCE LIBRARY MANAGER

Strong organizational and problem-solving skills useful for managing complex and diverse systems of information. Ability to communicate effectively at all levels of organization, achieving thorough comprehension of issues and requests. Talent for utilizing databases and research information with positive end results. Service orientation.

Industry knowledge a plus, possessing a Bachelor of Arts in Architectural Studies.

EDUCATION

University of Oklahoma School of Architecture 2011
Bachelor of Arts: Architectural Studies; Emphasis: Music

Architecture: Programs include construction techniques and materials, freehand drawing, architectural acoustics, design theory, computers, history of the city, and historical study from ancient to modern. Experience with presentation boards, project finish books, and furniture specifications.
Design Project: 200-seat multipurpose concert hall with calculations for reverberation times.

Music: Research and historical study of music with emphasis on Latin American, Masterworks, Jazz, and Rock. Worked independently on piano study and was a member of chorale, men's glee, and Collegium Musicum choirs.
Paper: "The Buena Vista Social Club"

Liberal Arts: Avant-garde coursework including *The Geography of Wine,* which explored architecture through a geographical eye and its pertinence to wine.
Paper: "Architecture of the Vineyard"

University of Maryland–Peabody Conservatory of Music Fall 2010
Semester class focus: *Breaking Musical Barriers.* Final project culminated in original composition for solo piano.
Composition: E-Flat Smoothie

TECHNICAL SKILLS

Hardware: Apple and Personal Computer
Software: MS Office Suite: Word, Excel, PowerPoint, Outlook; AutoCAD; Adobe Illustrator, Photoshop

WORK EXPERIENCE

Golf Discount of Oklahoma City, Oklahoma City, OK 2005–Present
Customer Service, Inventory, Sales
▹ Perform daily customer relations and telephone service, meeting the needs of 100+ clients weekly.
▹ Receive and record inventory, anticipating client requests and providing in-demand merchandise.
▹ As direct vendor contact, build knowledge of product quality, dependability, instruction, and cost, ultimately strengthening and securing sound professional relationship.

Law Offices of R. Andrew Williams and Ray Wholfe, Oklahoma City, OK Summer 2010
Legal Assistant
▹ Designed, created, and executed interior decorating project; completed under assigned budget.
▹ Performed video documentation validating unsatisfactory workmanship of refurbished building.
▹ Wrote and edited client chronologies and brochures for pending lawsuits.

INTERESTS/HOBBIES

Avid musician with 19 years of piano, 5 years of guitar, and a self-produced and performed album, *Fairy Tales Aside.* Interest in and support of photography and painting continue to sharpen and fine-tune creative skills.

103
Degree: BS, Human Resource Management.
Job Target: Clerk/administrative assistant position.
Strategy: Included comments from supervisors and made the most of this student's work-study experience.

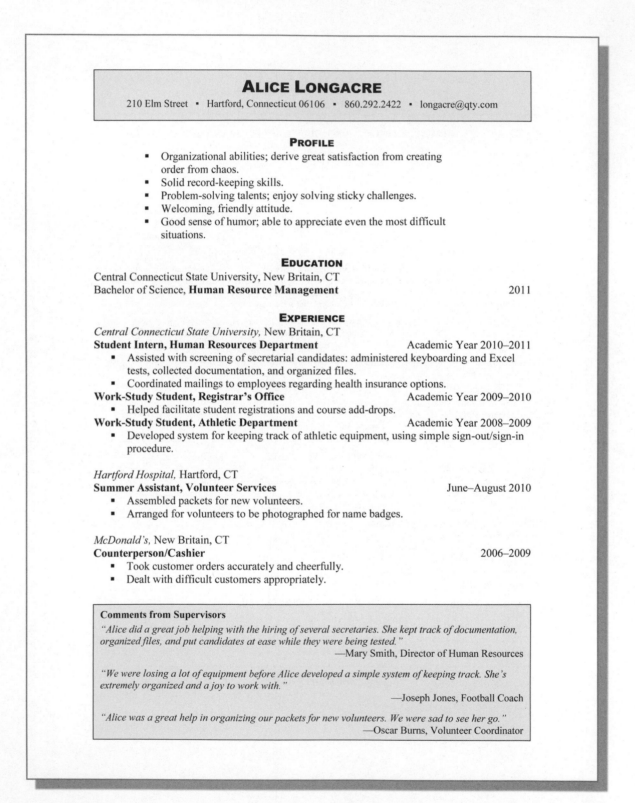

ALICE LONGACRE

210 Elm Street • Hartford, Connecticut 06106 • 860.292.2422 • longacre@qty.com

PROFILE

- Organizational abilities; derive great satisfaction from creating order from chaos.
- Solid record-keeping skills.
- Problem-solving talents; enjoy solving sticky challenges.
- Welcoming, friendly attitude.
- Good sense of humor; able to appreciate even the most difficult situations.

EDUCATION

Central Connecticut State University, New Britain, CT
Bachelor of Science, **Human Resource Management**   2011

EXPERIENCE

Central Connecticut State University, New Britain, CT
Student Intern, Human Resources Department   Academic Year 2010–2011
- Assisted with screening of secretarial candidates: administered keyboarding and Excel tests, collected documentation, and organized files.
- Coordinated mailings to employees regarding health insurance options.

Work-Study Student, Registrar's Office   Academic Year 2009–2010
- Helped facilitate student registrations and course add-drops.

Work-Study Student, Athletic Department   Academic Year 2008–2009
- Developed system for keeping track of athletic equipment, using simple sign-out/sign-in procedure.

Hartford Hospital, Hartford, CT
Summer Assistant, Volunteer Services   June–August 2010
- Assembled packets for new volunteers.
- Arranged for volunteers to be photographed for name badges.

McDonald's, New Britain, CT
Counterperson/Cashier   2006–2009
- Took customer orders accurately and cheerfully.
- Dealt with difficult customers appropriately.

Comments from Supervisors

"Alice did a great job helping with the hiring of several secretaries. She kept track of documentation, organized files, and put candidates at ease while they were being tested."
—Mary Smith, Director of Human Resources

"We were losing a lot of equipment before Alice developed a simple system of keeping track. She's extremely organized and a joy to work with."
—Joseph Jones, Football Coach

"Alice was a great help in organizing our packets for new volunteers. We were sad to see her go."
—Oscar Burns, Volunteer Coordinator

Degree: BA, Radio and Television.
Job Target: Television, film, or radio production position.
Strategy: Emphasized extensive hands-on involvement with two college radio stations.

Macey M. Ash
1991 Manchester Ave., Appling, GA 30802
Home: (706) 541-9991 | mm_ash@jitaweb.com

DJ / ASSISTANT PRODUCER OF SHORT DOCUMENTARIES / PRODUCTION MANAGER
with a skill set applicable to television, film, and radio positions

---

Professional with production-management and on-air experience that flows into audio and digital editing, operations management, staff training and coaching, and copywriting and editing.

Wrote and narrated documentaries, commercials, and news stories in coordination with topical and timely world events. Researched and verified information for stories to ensure factual newscasts and other on-air details. Authored, produced, and voiced commercial/promotional copy. Collaborated with managers and subordinates to provide creative guidance and discuss production changes. Participated in the entire production process, from concept and planning to quality assurance and airing.

PROFESSIONAL EXPERIENCE

ASSISTANT PRODUCTION MANAGER, FALL/SPRING, 2009–2010
College Radio Station, University of South Carolina, Columbia, SC

- Oversaw the production of music programs, news, interviews, and infotainment talk shows created by the production department; assessed for quality and accuracy.

- Assisted with hiring, directing, and supervising production personnel, which also involved selecting, training, and coaching new hires who possessed little or no experience creating high-quality radio programs.

- Met with managers and subordinates to collaborate on operations, production improvements, and delegation of duties. Troubleshot production quality (station IDs, show promos, underwriting, PSAs, and sound effects).

- Applied a hands-on supervisory style with students and recommended new software and hardware upgrades that enhanced sound quality; received recognition from the campus newsletter.

ASSISTANT PRODUCER, 2007–2008
Georgia University & State University, Georgia Media Productions, Milledgeville, GA

- Assembled and shot storyboards; selected graphics, props, and backdrops for visual appeal; and rotated audio/visual requirements in relation to footage and specs.

- Supported the production department with directing and producing several short documentaries: "Campus Living," "Classes to Addiction," and "Making Decisions."

- Researched and interviewed individuals and experts; wrote and edited content.

- "Campus Living," a 12-minute documentary, is currently used as an informational and educational video within the college recruitment department.

EDUCATION

B.A., Radio and Television, 2011
University of South Carolina, Columbia, SC

HARDWARE & SOFTWARE

Mac/PC; Cool Edit Pro, Nuendo, Avid Xpress, Logic, Final Cut Pro

---

105

Degree: BS, Recreation, Parks, and Tourism.
Job Target: Hospitality management position.
Strategy: Showcased the significant impact this student had on the small bed-and-breakfast where he completed a short but meaningful internship.

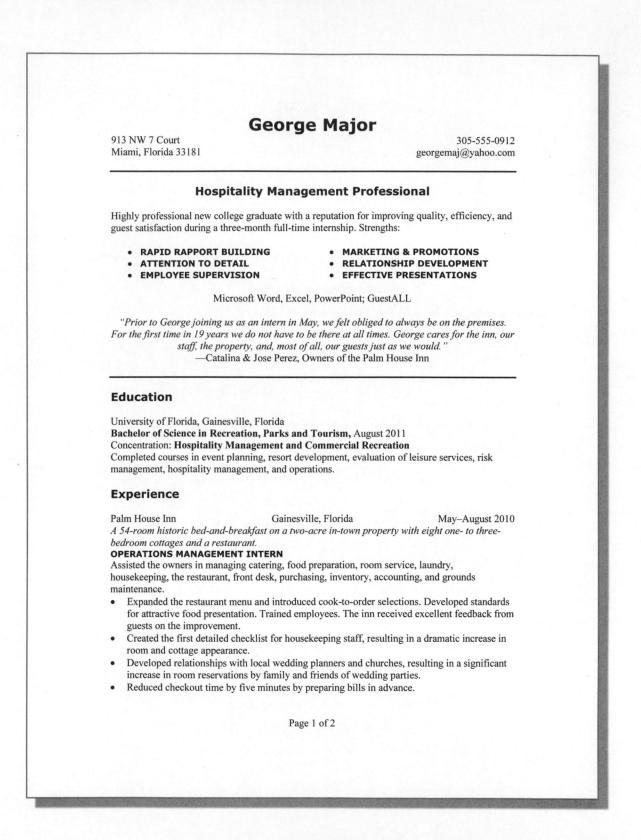

George Major

913 NW 7 Court
Miami, Florida 33181

305-555-0912
georgemaj@yahoo.com

Hospitality Management Professional

Highly professional new college graduate with a reputation for improving quality, efficiency, and guest satisfaction during a three-month full-time internship. Strengths:

- **RAPID RAPPORT BUILDING**
- **ATTENTION TO DETAIL**
- **EMPLOYEE SUPERVISION**

- **MARKETING & PROMOTIONS**
- **RELATIONSHIP DEVELOPMENT**
- **EFFECTIVE PRESENTATIONS**

Microsoft Word, Excel, PowerPoint; GuestALL

"Prior to George joining us as an intern in May, we felt obliged to always be on the premises. For the first time in 19 years we do not have to be there at all times. George cares for the inn, our staff, the property, and, most of all, our guests just as we would."
—Catalina & Jose Perez, Owners of the Palm House Inn

Education

University of Florida, Gainesville, Florida
Bachelor of Science in Recreation, Parks and Tourism, August 2011
Concentration: **Hospitality Management and Commercial Recreation**
Completed courses in event planning, resort development, evaluation of leisure services, risk management, hospitality management, and operations.

Experience

Palm House Inn   Gainesville, Florida   May–August 2010
A 54-room historic bed-and-breakfast on a two-acre in-town property with eight one- to three-bedroom cottages and a restaurant.
OPERATIONS MANAGEMENT INTERN
Assisted the owners in managing catering, food preparation, room service, laundry, housekeeping, the restaurant, front desk, purchasing, inventory, accounting, and grounds maintenance.

- Expanded the restaurant menu and introduced cook-to-order selections. Developed standards for attractive food presentation. Trained employees. The inn received excellent feedback from guests on the improvement.
- Created the first detailed checklist for housekeeping staff, resulting in a dramatic increase in room and cottage appearance.
- Developed relationships with local wedding planners and churches, resulting in a significant increase in room reservations by family and friends of wedding parties.
- Reduced checkout time by five minutes by preparing bills in advance.

Page 1 of 2

105 *(continued)*

George Major
305-555-0912 • georgemaj@yahoo.com

Resume, page 2

Alachua County Visitors
& Convention Bureau (VCB)   Gainesville, Florida   August–December 2009
VOLUNTEER
- Promoted the bureau as a marketing resource for local restaurants. Visited the owners of about 30 downtown restaurants after 5:00pm and encouraged them to participate in the "Downtown Dine Around" for convention participants.
- Wrote menu highlights and designed coupons for restaurants to place in the VCB planner.
- Chartered buses to take convention participants to downtown restaurants, clubs, and events.

Cocopelli Sandwich Shop   Gainesville, Florida   2005–2007
ASSISTANT MANAGER
- Supervised five employees. Ordered and inventoried supplies. Maintained security on supplies to prevent shrinkage. Opened and closed the shop and made bank deposits.
- Prepared meals for guests and developed a reputation for building repeat business through superior customer service.

Certifications

State of Florida, Certified Food Handler
Basic Cardiac Life Support (CPR)
First Aid Certification

Affiliations

Leisure Education and Parks Students, 2009–Present

Activities

Culinary arts, gardening, piano, stained glass, soccer, and tennis

106

Degree: AS, Recording Arts.
Job Target: Audio production position.
Strategy: Detailed class projects and provided an extensive list of equipment knowledge. Provided a summary of work experience that emphasized many of the traits employers value.

Isabella Cakskid

8384 Stanton Avenue • Cincinnati, OH 45222
(513) 245-4211 • isabella222@gpnet.com

Skilled **audio production** professional qualified by *Recording Arts degree,* creative talent, and hands-on experience in a recording studio setting. Skilled in all facets of pre- and post-production, from sound system and microphone placement to editing and mixing. Prior experience in business has provided exceptional interpersonal, conflict resolution, and leadership skills. A good listener and effective communicator. Organized and attentive to detail; efficient in coordinating multiple projects, managing time, and meeting deadlines. Technical skills include operation of Antares Auto-Tune Plug-In, calibration of 24-track tape machines, cable repair, and a wide range of audio editing and audio post-production duties. Well-qualified for an entry-level or intern position involving the following:

- Broadcast Engineering
- Programming
- Mixing
- Foley Editing
- Music Production & Music Editing
- Sound Design & Editing
- Sound Effects Editing
- Recording Engineering

PROFESSIONAL TRAINING

ANDERSON COMMUNITY COLLEGE
Associate of Science Degree in Recording Arts   June 2011
Completed comprehensive program with emphasis on creative and technical skills associated with audio production.

Relevant courses:

**Advanced Audio Workstations • Audio Post-production • Audiotronics • MIDI • Multimedia Audio
Recording & Mixing Consoles • Session Recording • Music Theory • Songcraft • Sound Dynamics**

#2 in graduating class for Project Mix Competition. Worked with a group to record and mix a song, which was subsequently judged by a group of industry professionals.

Recreated a scene from a movie, including all dialogue and sound effects. Used DigiDesigns Pro Tools with a Pro Control to record all dialogue, Foley, and sound effects. Edited and blended sounds while viewing scene, using a variety of outboard effects units and plug-ins.

Recorded a CD for a local band. Successfully recorded and mixed all tracks within allotted time. Used AMEK 9098 to record onto analog tape, which was then dumped into Pro Tools for editing and mixing.

Gained hands-on experience with the following software and equipment: **Software:** Pro Tools, Ulysses, Logic, Nuendo. **Boards:** 72-Input AMEK 9098I Console, 80 Input SSL 9000J Console, Sony DMX-R-100, Soundcraft Ghost, Mackie Digital 8 Buss. **DAW:** Pro Tools (HD, TDM, and LE Systems), Steinberg Nuendo, Logic 6. **Multi-track Recorders:** Studer A-827, Tascam MX2424. **Effects Units:** Lexicon (960L, PCM 70, PCM 80); TC Electronics System 6000, 2290; Eventide H3000 Harmonizer; Eclipse. **Compressors and DQs:** Focusrite (F2, F3), Tubetech LCA3B Compressor CL1B Compressor, PE1C EQ, LA-2, LA-4.

EXPERIENCE

All positions required excellent communication and organizational skills, a high energy level, and a customer-focused approach. Demonstrated flexibility, a willingness to do what it takes to meet business objectives, and a strong work ethic.

CENTRAL TRUST BANK, Cincinnati, OH   10/08–Present
Teller—Cross-sell all banking products/services. Consistently exceed sales objectives. Train new employees.

KING-KWIK MINIMART, Covington, KY   3/07–10/08
Cashier—Handled/processed cash, checks, and credit-card transactions. Trained new employees. Significantly increased revenue from video rentals by reorganizing video department.

TACO BELL, Cincinnati, OH   6/05–3/07
Shift Leader—Supervised 8 crew members in all aspects of restaurant operation. Oversaw food production, sanitation, customer service, and inventory control. Balanced cash registers; prepared bank deposits.

107

Degree: BS, Biological Sciences.
Job Target: Laboratory technician.
Strategy: To overcome the fact that this student had no relevant work experience or college extracurricular activities, summarized classroom learning under specific areas of knowledge that are relevant in lab positions.

Brenda Cox

939 South Gramercy Place, Indianapolis, IN 46239
Residence: (317) 787-4885 • E-mail: brenda.cox@sbcglobal.net

LABORATORY TECHNICIAN

*Recent college graduate seeks to apply formal training in Biological Sciences
to begin career in a Medical Laboratory performing analyses and critical tests.*

EDUCATION

Bachelor of Science in Biological Sciences (BS)
UNIVERSITY OF INDIANAPOLIS, Indianapolis, IN 2011

QUALIFICATIONS

- Project Management
- Customer Service
- Vertebrate Histology
- Laboratory Equipment

- Research / Analysis / Problem Solving
- Teamwork
- Tissue Slides
- Southern Transfer & Gene Detection

RELEVANT TRAINING / COURSEWORK

- **Microbiology:** Morphology, cultivation, and biochemical activities of microorganisms. Survey of viruses, bacteria, blue-green algae, fungi, and their diversity in natural environments.
- **Genetics:** Nature and function of genetic material with emphasis on transmission and population genetics. Exceptions to and extensions of Mendelian analysis, gene mapping, quantitative genetics, and the change of gene frequencies with time.
- **Human Parasitology:** Aspects of parasitology, including epidemiology, diagnosis, and identification of parasites in three major categories: protozoology, helminthology, and anthropodology.
- **Submicroscopic and Macroscopic Chemistry:** Structure and properties of atoms and molecules and physical and chemical behavior of large collections of atoms and molecules.
- **Organic Chemistry:** Principles, theories, and applications of the chemistry of carbon compounds.
- **Quantitative Analysis:** Chemical methods of analysis covering traditional as well as modern techniques and equipment; emphasis on calculations and interpretation of analytical data.
- **Laboratory Medical Microbiology and Immunology:** Identification of etiological agents of disease; bacteria, fungi, and viruses using cultural and immunological methods.

WORK EXPERIENCE

Team Member, **Lockwood's Tropical Fish, Inc.,** Greenwood, IN, 2010–Present
- Package wholesale orders.
- Maintain healthy environment for tropical fish.

Cook / Customer Service, **KFC,** Broad Ripple, IN, 2005–2010
- Filled customer orders and prepared food.

Degree: BS, Biology.
Job Target: Zookeeper.
Strategy: Blended class experiences, an internship, and extracurricular activities to paint a picture of someone with consistently strong interest in animals and the outdoors.

JEREMY POPLAR

2958 Elm Avenue, Apartment C • Olympia, Washington 98501
Home: (360) 222-1313 • jeremypoplar624@yahoo.com • Cell: (816) 444-1616

CAREER OBJECTIVE
Zookeeper

Self-motivated college graduate offering **science-based education** with experience and hands-on skills in supervision and customer service. Strong work ethic evident in focused perseverance to finish projects and accomplish objectives. Team player.

EDUCATION

Bachelor of Science, Park University, Kansas City, Missouri, 2011
- Major: Biology with Emphasis in Zoology / Minor: Chemistry
  - Courses: Herpetology, Invertebrate Zoology, Ecology, Computer Applications
- **Internship:** Biology Seminar Lab Assistant, Fall 2009
  - Taught "Photosynthesis" and "Dissection of the Pig"; graded student papers.
- Celebration 2010—An Interdisciplinary Undergraduate / Graduate Symposium
  - **Presentation:** "Road-Kill Effect on the Wild Mammals of Western Missouri," based on research paper detailing two-month automobile-trip class project comparing type and number of animals killed on highways vs. country roads.
- Extracurricular activity: River Wildlife Club, member for two years

EXPERIENCE

Shift Manager, Buster's Big Boy, Kansas City, Missouri   9/09 to 12/10
- Supervised and trained two to three wait staff at any one time. Investigated and resolved customer complaints. Cooked and served food.

Kitchen Assistant, Applejack Restaurant, Kansas City, Missouri   6/09 to 9/09
- Delivered food orders to diners' tables. Cleaned kitchen.

Dishwasher, Shasta Restaurant, Kansas City, Missouri   3/09 to 6/09
- Assisted with food preparation. Sanitized dishes.

Cook, Burgers-to-Go, Kansas City, Missouri   9/08 to 6/09
- Prepared fast-food orders, working effectively in fast-paced environment.

Groundskeeper Assistant, Park University, Kansas City, Missouri   9/07 to 9/08
- Maintained college campus grounds utilizing commercial lawn care equipment.

ADDITIONAL INFORMATION

- Partially financed college expenses with part-time employment while studying.
- Proficient with Microsoft Word, PowerPoint, and Excel.
- Hobbies include hiking, fishing, and reading.

109

Degree: AS, Network Administration.
Job Target: Help desk position.
Strategy: Matched deep-seated interest in problem solving, mechanics, and mysteries to current goal of working at a technical help desk.

JOE DETONEZ

1234 25th Street, Edmonds, WA 98117
(206) 592-2022 • joed@gmail.com

CAREER TARGET: HELP DESK POSITION

SUMMARY OF QUALIFICATIONS

Intuitive 2011 graduate in networking administration. Strong diagnostic, logic, observation, and analytical skills: innate ability to discern irregularities in a situation. Broad interest in computer hardware, security, and forensics. Proven ability to handle multiple projects and address customer needs. Adept at reading and interpreting technical documentation and manuals, demonstrated by ability to maintain high-end automobiles. Learn new technologies quickly.

Proficiencies include the following:

Business Skills	**Technical Skills & Training**
• Customer Service	• Network Admin: LAN/WAN
• Problem Solving	• A+, Installs, Upgrades, Assembly
• Inside Sales	• Linux, UNIX, Windows, Mac OS
• General Office	• Computer Forensics
• Training	• Windows Workstation

EDUCATION

South Seattle Community College
A.S., Network Administration, 2011
Coursework: Computer Forensics, Windows and Windows Workstation, Linux/UNIX, A+ core certification classes: Active Directory, Server, TCP/IP, Network Plus, technical writing

Graduate, Tyee High School, Federal Way, WA. Tech-Prep Program.

WORK EXPERIENCE

Porter, Bellevue Motors, September 2008–present
Detailer, Shtronz Airport Detailing, April 2007–February 2008
Lot Attendant, Jaguar of Kirkland, December 2005–April 2007
Valet, At Your Service Valets, March–June 2005 and November–December 2005
Customer Service Representative, Hollywood Video, June 2004–February 2005
Customer Service Representative, Taco Bell, July 2002–August 2003
Office Assistant/Copy and Print Room Helper, Lane Powell Bryant, August–November 2002

COMMUNITY SERVICE

Participated in a wide variety of fund-raising and community activities, including
• Lakeside High School / Southend Food Bank / Friends of the Library Book Sale

INTERESTS

Avid interest in mysteries, criminal psychology, and police work.

110

Degree: BS, Business Administration.
Job Target: Position in marketing or economics.
Strategy: Combined job activities with key class projects in one meaty Professional/
Educational Experience section.

BARBARA GIBSON

1234 North Shore ▪ Parkville, Missouri 64152
816.522.1256 ▪ gibsonbarbara@kc.rr.com

QUALIFICATIONS SUMMARY

- Educated and experienced in **Marketing, Business, and Economics.**
- Motivated worker contributing to a winning outcome using project-management skills.
- Personable and team-focused with a consultative approach.
- Computer skills: MS Word, Excel, PowerPoint, Publisher; familiar with Access.

EDUCATION

Bachelor of Science in Business Administration—Marketing Concentration, 2011
Park University, Parkville, Missouri

Economics Coursework:
Macroeconomics, Microeconomics, Managerial Economics, Intermediate Economics

---

PROFESSIONAL / EDUCATIONAL EXPERIENCE

PRINTING EXCELLENCE, Kansas City, Missouri, Summer/Winter 2010
EXECUTIVE SUPPORT ANALYST
- Day-to-day initiatives involved highly consultative interface with key decision-makers.
- Challenged with initial design of an brochure for a Printing Excellence account; customized brochure for five additional accounts with company-wide distribution.
- Pinpointed and turned around accounts-receivable problem, analyzing addresses and serial numbers of 350 machines to reduce monthly billing errors to zero.
- Instrumental during Sprint Corporation's "Move Booths," performing instructional services to 500+ employees over 5-day period.

NORTH SHORE GOLF CLUB, Parkville, Missouri, Summer 2007
GOLF COURSE MAINTENANCE ASSISTANT ▪ ASSISTANT GOLF CART ATTENDANT
- Promoted to Golf Course Maintenance Assistant tasked with upkeep of company's first impression to customers—visual grooming of professional course, a #1 priority.
- As Assistant Golf Cart Attendant, assumed front-line customer-service role preparing golf carts for play and greeting/serving golfers to ensure repeat business.

PARK UNIVERSITY, Kansas City, Missouri, 2006 to 2010
MANAGEMENT INFORMATION SYSTEMS PROJECT
- Member of project team tasked with research of target company's information systems.
- Interfaced with COO to gain understanding of company processes and objectives.
- Presented findings—company needed to update hardware/software—to a receptive COO.

PERSONAL SELLING PROJECT (This project impacted 45% of class grade.)
- Originated sales proposal and presented to classmate and professor; earned an "A" grade.

FORECASTING PROJECT
- Tracked/reported on 2 years of company's (Apple Computers) regression and trendlines.
- Analyzed 4 years of statistics/regression for company's (Printing Excellence's) revenues.

111

Degree: BA, Business Management.
Job Target: Management trainee.
Strategy: Capitalized on a strong and relevant internship plus college projects to show capabilities and potential. Included performance review quotes, at the end, to provide a strong endorsement of his innate qualities and work ethic.

REES DONOVAN TYLER

5555 Lexington Avenue, Apt. C • Maryville, Minnesota 55113
612-501-5555 • reesd9@hotmail.com

BUSINESS GRADUATE

Strong interpersonal skills and experience gained from education, internship, and positions as part of academic and customer service–oriented teams. Hands-on group experience examining marketing practices of a local business, developing an entrepreneurial business plan, and designing strategic promotion plan.

Computer Skills: Proficient: Microsoft Word, Excel, PowerPoint ~ User Skills: Microsoft Access

EDUCATION

BACHELOR OF ARTS, BUSINESS MANAGEMENT, Luther College, Decorah, Iowa 2011

Relevant Coursework:
❑ Financial Management • Financial Accounting • Marketing/Guerrilla Marketing • Sales, Promotion, and Advertising
Management Information Systems • Human Resource Management • International Management • Investments

Team Projects:
❑ Developed and presented an entrepreneurial business plan (including mission statement, distribution of ownership, competitive analysis, financial plan, marketing plan, and more).

❑ Examined marketing practices of two-year-old business, gaining "real-life" experience as part of Guerrilla Marketing team. Suggestions offered to owner (many adopted): develop concrete marketing plan and tracking tool, create customer database, conduct competitive analysis, and improve professionalism.

❑ Repositioned American Express Blue card by creating copy platform outlining advertising objectives, target audience, major selling points, creative strategy, and promotion plan.

International Experience: "Entrepreneurship in a Tourist-Based Economy," Canary Islands, Spain (1/10)

INTERNSHIP EXPERIENCE

JOHN ANDERSON FINANCIAL GROUP, Minneapolis, Minnesota   (Summers) 2008 to 2010

Financial Advisor Intern—Shadowed financial advisor during meetings, learning customer-service skills and nuances of financial services business. Researched market funds, prepared paperwork, and entered data into computer.
❑ Created a new marketing campaign, organizing binders for each client.

WORK EXPERIENCE

MY GARDENER, Burnsville, Minnesota   April 2011 to Present

Gardener / Landscape Assistant—Work directly with company owner on a 4-person team to maintain or improve landscapes for an affluent client base.
❑ Building on professionalism, gained respect of owner, offered opinions, and accepted additional responsibilities.

WINTER PARK RESORT, Winter Park, Colorado   October 2010 to April 2011

Lift Operator—Supervised use of ski-lift equipment, ensuring skiers got on and off lift safely. Monitored equipment for mechanical problems. As a resort ambassador, greeted guests, anticipated needs, and provided information about facilities and services (including snow conditions, trails, weather conditions, and hours of operation).
❑ Performance review quotes: "... Rees's work is accomplished ahead of time and needs no correction... record of attendance is excellent... we can count on Rees... makes an effort to see that customers are satisfied. Thank you for being flexible under changing conditions... Excellent professional appearance... works well with others..."

Degree: BS, Regional Development.
Job Target: Internship or entry-level position in commercial real-estate development.
Strategy: Built a strong Traits and Skills summary and Qualifications list to offset lack of relevant experience or stellar academic record.

Fred E. Smith, Jr.
520-998-4134
fsmith1990@hotmail.com

6521 E. Drachman
Tucson, AZ 85719

OBJECTIVE

Internship in commercial development and real estate investment.

TRAITS AND SKILLS

Customer-driven and people-oriented. Effective communicator with excellent verbal and interpersonal skills. Honest and hard worker. Quick learner with demonstrated ability to work well with the public under stressful conditions and smoothly resolve any conflicts that may arise. Excellent at multitasking and completing projects on target. Have the ability to train others.

QUALIFICATIONS

- Able to maintain a daily schedule.
- Enjoy heavy customer contact and handling.
- Strong communication skills with peers and team members.
- Readily comprehend instructions, rules, and regulations whether written or verbal.
- Able to provide leadership in varying situations.
- Good organization and time-management skills.
- Function well in cooperative team situations.
- Maintain professional demeanor under stress.
- Experienced traveler.

UPPER-DIVISION COURSES

Economic Geography	Computer Cartography	Introduction to Planning
Advanced Applications—Remote Sensing	Principles and Practices in Regional Development	Population Geography

TECHNICAL AND COMPUTER PROFICIENCIES

Excel	PowerPoint	IDRISI
ArcMap	Word	Collaboratus

EDUCATION

University of Arizona—B.S., Regional Development, 2011

High School—The Kent School, Kent, CT, 2006

WORK HISTORY

A variety of part-time jobs while supporting my college experience:

PCZ Enterprises—Tucson, AZ	Rebuilding Historic Homes	2009 to present
Famous Sam's—Tucson, AZ	Door Security	2009
Starpass Golf Resort—Tucson, AZ	Waiter	2008
Blackjack Pizza—Tucson, AZ	Delivery Agent	2008
Wendy's—Phoenix, AZ	Customer Service Rep.	2007
Circle-K—Phoenix, AZ	Customer Service Rep.	2007
Prime Masonry—Phoenix, AZ	Commercial Construction	2006

CHAPTER 10

Resumes and Strategies for Nontraditional Students

How do resume writing and job search strategies differ for nontraditional students, those who finish their college educations later in life? Whether you've earned your educational credentials to enter a new profession or to advance your career in your present field, you offer a wealth of experience that traditional new grads do not. So it might seem that your resume would be very different from those presented thus far in this book.

But in reality, all good resumes are based on the same principle of presenting your strongest qualifications and value to employers as these relate to your career goal. As a nontraditional student, you do have more years and more experiences to draw from than most new grads. Your resume might look a bit different and will probably include a heftier section for your work experience. Yet the exercises, activities, strategies, and ideas presented throughout this book will work just as well for you as they will for a younger, less experienced graduate.

When preparing your resume, start with a clear understanding of your job target and the required skills and qualifications. Then evaluate all of your past experiences—your jobs, recent college education, extracurricular activities, volunteer and leadership roles in the community, hobbies, and other activities of your life. Look for specific examples that demonstrate the skills you want to use, and include these in your resume.

Don't overlook the fact that a strong work history can give you a definite edge in your job search. Even if your experience is unrelated to your current goals, you can use your work history to show your work ethic, reliability, and other skills that are always in demand, no matter what type of work you do: leadership and initiative; communication skills; interpersonal skills; organization, time management, planning, and follow-through skills; and problem-solving abilities.

When evaluating your work history, look for small assignments and special projects that allowed you to engage in activities related to your current goals. Use these examples as evidence of your skills, even if they were short term or not really "part of your job." And be sure not to overload your resume with details of your job activities that will position you squarely as what you "used" to be, not what you have become or how you want to be perceived.

Review the resumes in this chapter, taking careful note of the strategies the resume writers used to position newly qualified graduates for their new careers. Some of the resumes feature strong and detailed experience sections, while others use functional headings to call out skills that were gained through a variety of experiences. Remember that there are no rules for where and how you must present your background, and you don't have to include everything. Picture yourself in your next job and make sure your resume qualifies you for that job, no matter how or in how much detail your prior experience is presented.

Resume Number	Degree	Job Target
113	BA, Psychology	Pharmaceutical sales position
114	BA, Business Administration	Retail manager
115	BA, English	College public relations position
116	BLS (Bachelor of Liberal Studies) in Business, emphasis in Human Resource Management	Entry-level position in human resource management
117	Certificate in Human Resources (recent); BSW (prior)	Human resources position
118	BSW (most recent) along with two associate degrees and GPN/LPN training	Administrative support position in social work/social services
119	BA, International Business/Marketing/Economics	Economist
120	MS, Physician's Assistant	Physician's assistant
121	BS, Business Administration	A position in banking, investment, or finance
122	AS, Computer Science	Help desk/computer support technician
123	BS, Business Administration	MIS position

113

Degree: BA, Psychology.
Job Target: Medical or pharmaceutical sales.
Strategy: Emphasized the two areas of strength this candidate brings to her goal: medical knowledge (from experience as a medical assistant, EMT, and military hospital worker and college science courses) and sales and customer service skills (from her jobs as a bartender).

ELLYN C. MUDRA

14 Callea Road, Apt. 45 • Chicago, IL 60604 • (312) 223-9841 • ellynmudra@hotmail.com

JOB TARGET: PHARMACEUTICAL SALES

PROFILE
- Enthusiastic, motivated medical professional with excellent rapport-building skills.
- Wide variety of clinical experiences: Family Practice, Obstetrics & Gynecology, Asthma, Allergies, Neonatal.
- Positive business relationships with 40+ medical practices in the Chicago area.
- Proven ability to identify problems and implement solutions.
- Strong communication and negotiation skills.
- Member of the American Psychological Association.

EDUCATION & TRAINING
Bachelor of Arts in Psychology—Pre-Med concentration (expected December 2011)
University of Illinois, Chicago, IL
- Courses include anatomy & physiology, chemistry, organic chemistry, and microbiology.

Emergency Medical Technician Training (2002), Jacksonville, NC

Hospital Corpsman Training (2001)
U.S. Naval School of Health Sciences, San Diego, CA

MEDICAL EXPERIENCE
Medical Assistant (2006–present)
Allergy Relief Center, Chicago, IL
- Contribute to the high level of patient compliance and patient satisfaction in this clinic.
- Conduct patient education. Utilize patient education and persuasive ability in explaining the benefits of immunotherapy to patients who are afraid of shots.
- Administer allergy injections. Determine appropriate dosages within guidelines provided by physicians.
- Train new medical assistants and front-office staff.
- Organize patient records and ensure accurate documentation of injections given by other staff members.

Emergency Medical Technician (2002–2004)
Onslow County Rescue Squad, Jacksonville, NC

Hospital Corpsman (1999–2003)
U.S. Naval Hospital, Camp Lejeune, NC
- Provided patient care, including administering medications and intravenous therapy, performing venipuncture, assisting with minor surgeries, and assisting with Cesarean sections.
- Developed an admission checklist for infants that decreased staff errors and increased efficiency.
- Conducted patient education, including neonatal care.
- Volunteered for position of Forms Control Supervisor. Ensured availability of more than 400 forms that were used hospital-wide. Managed a budget of $30,000. Developed a database to efficiently keep track of forms.
- Trained nurses and other corpsmen. Taught co-workers to use monitoring equipment.

SALES AND CUSTOMER SERVICE EXPERIENCE
Bartender (2005–2009)
The Fun Place, Chicago, IL / Woody's, Chicago, IL
- Developed and maintained a loyal customer base through rapport-building and excellent service.

AWARDS
- Chosen as Honor Recruit out of a Basic Training class of 85 members. This award recognizes superior commitment, integrity, and teamwork (2001).
- U.S. Army Reserve Scholar/Athlete Award (2000).

114

Degree: BS, Business Administration.
Job Target: Retail management.
Strategy: Created a functional section highlighting relevant skills; supported retail industry target with a Relevant Employment Highlight section.

Steven Toner
1547 London St., Fredericton, NB J0A 2E4
(741) 894-1234 ♦ toner@gmail.com

RETAIL BUSINESS MANAGER
Hands-on experience in sales and customer service.

Broad-based knowledge of all aspects of business and store management encompassing ability to develop ongoing client relationships with individual attention to detail. Superior communication and bookkeeping proficiencies. Positive attitude and ability to adapt to fast-paced environments. *Relevant capabilities:*

Operations Management	Merchandising / Store Setup	Customer Relations
Selling Techniques	Conflict / Time Management	Cash Management
Promotions / Advertising	Supervision / Training	Opening / Closing Routines

HIGHLIGHTS OF SKILLS & QUALIFICATIONS

MANAGEMENT SKILLS
- ✓ Instrumental as leader and motivator of team achieving "Most Improved Section" award for two consecutive years.
- ✓ Acted as complaint resolution point, solving even the most complex of difficulties quickly and efficiently to the satisfaction of all involved.
- ✓ Participated in strategic corporate planning, including organizational direction, staff hiring & scheduling, and purchasing of stock.

FINANCIAL & BOOKKEEPING KNOWLEDGE
- ✓ Directed all bookkeeping and payroll functions, including weekly and monthly financial reporting to directors' level.
- ✓ Strong academic preparation within degree program.

CUSTOMER SERVICE EXPERTISE
- ✓ Recognized as "Best Employee of the Week" while working as a front-line representative of Value Store, a national retail chain.
- ✓ Acknowledged for superior customer retention in a highly competitive retail arena.
- ✓ Demonstrated attention to clientele needs through launching of customer-driven delivery system.

RELEVANT EMPLOYMENT HIGHLIGHT

Senior Salesperson—Value Store, Moncton, NB, 2006–present

Operationally responsible for entire franchise store, covering more than 2,000 square feet of retail space. Main product includes high-end hair-care supplies servicing salons throughout the area. Given full authorizing responsibility in the absence of the owner. Demonstrated extensive knowledge in retail management, including maintenance, security, purchasing, merchandising, administration, bookkeeping, warehousing, and distribution. *Highlights of accomplishments:*

- ➢ Assisted in increasing store revenues to $487K, achieving regular bonuses based on improving year's monthly projections by +10%.
- ➢ Led staff in major year-end inventory, assuring quality monitoring and recording over all corporate stock.
- ➢ Assumed responsibility for hiring and training new staff members, as well as the daily supervision of up to 5 customer-service representatives.

EDUCATION

Bachelor of Business Administration, *St. Thomas University,* Fredericton, NB, 2011

"Putting customers first is a lost art in retail today...but not in my store!"
Work philosophy from Steven Toner — 2011

115

Degree: BA, English.
Job Target: College public relations—entry-level.
Strategy: For this new graduate in her early 50s, used a functional approach to eliminate dates; downplay prior unrelated experience; and draw from her mix of professional, volunteer, and college projects.

CHRISTINA MORAN

18 Apple Street, Nyack, NY 10568
(845) 359-4532
chris_moran@email.com

OBJECTIVE

Key member of a **college public relations** team contributing my 14 years of professional experience, passion for academia, and proven writing and organizational skills.

EDUCATION

Bachelor of Arts, English, May 2011
Saint Thomas Aquinas College, Spring Valley, NY
Alpha Sigma Lambda Honor Society

RELATED SKILLS AND ACHIEVEMENTS

Writing & Editing
- Created advertising copy for the *Friends of the Branch Library* newsletter to help generate funds for building a new library.
- Wrote a weekly report on the status of international shipments for the president of ABC Baby Toys.
- Wrote an A-grade, 20-page thesis on "William Butler Yeats: The Impact of His Passion for Mysticism and Maude Gonne on His Poetry."

Coordinating & Communicating
- Tracked international shipments of infant and construction products and reported status to management. Followed through to ensure orders were delivered on time.
- Researched orders held in customs and facilitated clearance by maintaining daily contact with the New York Port import broker.
- Communicated materials delays to contractors and negotiated acceptance of partial shipments to job sites.
- Coordinated visitors to Nyack Hospital while working as a volunteer.

Computer Applications
- Proficient with Microsoft Office, Internet navigation, and e-mail.
- Used a proprietary software program to track shipments.

CAREER HISTORY

Volunteer, Friends of the Branch Library & Piermont Thrift Shop, Piermont, NY

Import Control Specialist, ABC Baby Toys, Orange, NJ

Assistant to General Import Manager, Building Supplies, Inc., New York, NY

Budget Control Specialist, New York University Geological Observatory, Spring Valley, NY

116

Degree: BLS (Bachelor of Liberal Studies) in Business, emphasis in Human Resource Management.
Job Target: Entry-level position in human resource management.
Strategy: Featured degree and coursework applicable to the position; downplayed prior unrelated work history.

Jalice Thompson

3310 Farnsworth Avenue
Hartford, Connecticut 06120
Home: (203) 811-5432
Email: jalicet@mail.com

FOCUS

Entry-level position in **Human Resource Management** where academic foundation, along with business background and strengths in customer service, will be of value.

EDUCATION

Wesleyan University, Middletown, CT
2012, **Bachelor of Liberal Studies in Business with emphasis in Human Resource Management**

Coursework included recruiting, classification, human resource policy, compensation, benefits, performance appraisal, employee relations training, and planning.

Quinnipiac University, New Haven, CT
Undergraduate coursework in Business
Dean's List

PROFILE

- College graduate with an emphasis in Human Resource Management.
- High confidence in professional abilities.
- High interest in organizing human resource programs and projects that will attract and retain employees.
- Skilled user of MS Word, Excel, and PowerPoint.
- Lifelong learner, constantly updating skills.
- Known for high work ethic…work at a project until it is completed satisfactorily.

EMPLOYMENT HISTORY

2006–2011, **Claims Specialist I,** Aetna Insurance, Hartford, CT

Demonstrated customer service skills. Cited for high work productivity. Specialized in setting up systems to organize projects, including back-up plans.

2004–2005, **Family care and undergraduate studies.**

2002–2004, **Owner/operator,** Licensed Family Day Care Service, Middletown, CT

Developed and delivered programs to help young children learn basic skills. Managed all aspects of a small business, from planning to accounting.

117

Degree: Certificate in Human Resources (recent); BSW (prior).
Job Target: Human resources position.
Strategy: Used the profile to highlight aspects of HR that relate to her background as well as her recent HR certification.

Jane L. Morrissey

22 Mattabessett Road • Woodstock, VT 05411 • 802.885.9654 • Janelmor@aol.com

Summary

- **Accomplished and Dedicated Human Services Professional** qualified for opportunity demanding experience in recruiting, interviewing, hiring, training, mediating, and evaluating; key skill development in designing and facilitating training programs addressing wide range of requirements. Expert editorial and Microsoft Word/Excel/PowerPoint abilities.

- Very effective communication and interpersonal skills; irreproachable professional ethics.

- **Human Resources Certificate** (90 classroom hours … Springfield Community College, Springfield, VT — 2011) … successfully completed coursework in **Compensation, Benefits, Labor Law, Recruiting, Interviewing, Hiring, Training and Development,** and **Documentation.**

Professional Experience

1998–Present
BREWSTER CHILDREN'S SERVICES • South Woodstock, VT
Foster Parent Developer, Resources Dept. (2004–Present); **Foster Care Worker** (1998–2004)
Responsible for identifying, recruiting, screening, and evaluating participant families. Use effective case-management skills, serving as agency liaison among key stakeholders and support personnel as well as through representation at court hearings and intervention during emergencies.
- Provide ongoing development to participants, including orientation and pre-service training.
- Negotiate effectively with social welfare organizations and professionals to procure services; maintain confidential assessment records, detailed case notes, and psychosocial summaries.
- Utilize highly effective motivational strategies working with challenging and occasionally unmotivated audiences. Credited with creating increased professionalism and commitment to program objectives among participant foster families. Draw on excellent interpersonal skills in cultivating and maintaining relationships among all parties.
- Positively managed responsibilities throughout merger with another agency that doubled households of foster parents served (from 200 to 400).

Distinctions …
- Recognized for significantly decreasing turnover and improving morale among foster parents through design and implementation of innovative development programs; selected/purchased relevant materials to complement hands-on program. Number of attendees participating increased substantially while turnover rates stabilized.
- Planned, implemented, and directed such successful specialty programs as recruitment events and holiday parties; continued to coordinate and monitor ongoing recognition dinners on regular basis.
- Initiated, wrote, and launched quarterly publication of newsletter; authored articles for agency-wide newsletter.
- Developed and implemented caseload-management applicant-processing and tracking system.

Complementary Career Background includes freelance and newspaper writing/editing as well as administrative skills. Developed, investigated, and authored many feature articles for local newspaper; edited textbooks for medical publishing house.

118

Degree: BSW (most recent) along with two associate degrees and GPN/LPN training.
Job Target: Administrative support position in social work/social services while he pursues his MSW.
Strategy: Positioned for job target by emphasizing blend of health-care experience (10 years) and administrative support for a government agency (although 10+ years ago) plus the recent BSW degree. Focused primarily on "value offered" skills and education while putting less emphasis on actual nursing experience by using a modified functional approach.

MATTHEW DORRIS

Email: mattdorris@hotmail.com

1321 Paxton Circle
Whites Creek, TN 37080
Home (615) 746-3941

Goal — Administrative position with a social services agency.

Recent B.S.W. graduate with ten years of experience providing hands-on health care to a diverse patient population plus three years of experience in accounting and administrative support for a state agency. Recognized for leadership qualities and abilities—given responsibility for training and supervising others. Possess strong analytical and organizational skills that complement interpersonal abilities.

VALUE OFFERED:

➤ **Project Management / Supervisory Skills:** Able to set priorities—efficiently manage progress of work and competing demands. Effectively direct people to high levels of performance.

➤ **Strong Communication Skills:** Articulate in both written and spoken communications—effectively convey ideas and information to professionals at all levels.

➤ **Computer Abilities:** Experienced with word processing (MS Word) and spreadsheet (Excel) applications. Confident in learning and using new technology.

Education

BACHELOR OF SOCIAL WORK—3.6 GPA—Member, Pinnacle Honor Society   2011
Vanderbilt University—Nashville, TN

ASSOCIATE OF SCIENCE IN NURSING—3.5 GPA   2004
Tennessee State University—Nashville, TN

GRADUATE PRACTICAL NURSE (GPN)—3.9 GPA—Class Valedictorian   2001
Nashville Memorial Hospital School of Nursing—Nashville, TN

ASSOCIATE OF APPLIED BUSINESS MANAGEMENT—3.7 GPA   1996
Member, Phi Theta Kappa Honor Society
University of Kentucky—Lexington, KY

Career Highlights

HEALTH CARE EXPERIENCE:
Provide high-tech nursing services for hospital, rehabilitation, geriatric, psychiatric, and nursing home patients. Administer prescribed medications and treatments. Experienced in medical and postsurgical care; upper airway and tracheotomy care; IV therapy; and care of feeding tubes, catheters, and dressings. Supervise and manage work assignments of five to six technicians. Educate patients and family members on medications and diet.

Charge Nurse RN, VILLAGE GREEN CONVALESCENT CENTER, Madison, TN	2009–Present
Staff Nurse RN, SUMNER REGIONAL MEDICAL CENTER, Gallatin, TN	2007–2009
Staff Nurse / Pool Nurse RN, NASHVILLE MEMORIAL HOSPITAL, Nashville, TN	2004–2007
Staff Nurse LPN, VANDERBILT UNIVERSITY MEDICAL CENTER, Nashville, TN	2002–2004
Pool Nurse LPN, BAPTIST HOSPITAL, Nashville, TN	2001–2010

ADMINISTRATIVE SUPPORT EXPERIENCE:

Account Clerk, KENTUCKY BOARD OF PAROLES, Lexington, KY   1997–2001

➤ Maintained accurate records of payments collected from parolees; audited travel claims; coordinated meetings for parole officers; and created financial reports, graphs, and spreadsheets.

➤ Trained and supervised new account clerks. Reported to Accounting Manager.

119

Degree: BA, International Business/Marketing/Economics.
Job Target: Economist.
Strategy: Played up applicable experience gained while attending school.

Matt A. Elder

111 Kenzie Street, Welling, WA 82222
(330) 333-1133
MAElder@yahoo.com

ECONOMIST

Motivated, goal-oriented professional possessing acute business insight, strong conceptual and people skills, and demonstrated ability to provide financial and management analysis that results in successful operational plans and effective management practices.

QUALIFICATIONS SUMMARY

- B.A., International Business / Marketing / Economics
- 10+ years of practical experience in multi-level sales and financial analysis (grocery industry)
- Strong analytical, problem-solving, multitasking, and time management skills
- Focused—Persistent—Determined—Consistent—Ultra organized
- Team player attitude—enjoy teaching and empowering others to improve skills and abilities
- Mac and PC proficient with Excel, Word, Web page design

EDUCATION / PROFESSIONAL DEVELOPMENT

B.A., International Business / Marketing / Economics—2011
State University, Welling, CA

Consumer's Choice Courses: Company-Specific Management; Time Management; CPR/First Aid
Associated Grocers: Black-n-White Advancement Program

PROFESSIONAL EXPERIENCE

Store Manager, Black-n-White Grocery, Welling, CA   9/10–present
Provide direction and daily management to locally owned grocery store generating approximately
$4 million annual sales. Challenged to turn store from negative to positive bottom line.

Solutions:
Set in motion a system of manager accountability—increased accuracy in purchase-to-sale reporting.
Analyzed and corrected P&L—created double-check system.
Created, developed, and implemented Performance Appraisal Format.
Created, developed, and implemented Labor Tracking Spreadsheet.
Created, developed, and implemented Gross Points Spreadsheet for tracking overall gross margins.

Results:
- Cut quarter losses by 50% in one quarter after 2+ years of steady losses.
- Stabilized positive work environment and increased employee retention and productivity.

Checker, Night Stocker, Sunnyland Black-n-White, Welling, CA   2000–2010
Exercised innate ability to learn management with no training or mentoring—wrote grocery schedule
(60% labor)—trimmed schedule to produce right amount of labor in ratio to amount of sales.

Solution: Developed spreadsheet to determine labor-to-sales ratio.

Result: Implemented schedule and significantly increased cash flow, cut costs, and increased profit.

Produce Assistant / Checker, Community Food Cooperative, Welling, CA   1999–2000

Checker, Night Stocker, Welling QFC, Welling, CA   1995–1999

Checker, Courtesy Clerk, Stocker, Westate Albertsons, Welling, CA   1992–1995

"...in four months...he has given the store a sense of direction... paved the way for better performance...much more positive environment to work in."
Produce Manager,
Black-n-White Grocery

"...demonstrated an eagerness to learn...fair and thoughtful...treated everyone with dignity and respect...I appreciated his enthusiasm, effort, and willingness to take on responsibility."
PE Teacher/Tennis Coach,
Welling High School

OTHER EXPERIENCE

Soccer Coach, Welling Soccer Association
Tennis Coach / Cross Country Coach, Welling High School
Junior Achievement, 8th Grade
Welling Rotary

120

Degree: MS, Physician's Assistant.
Job Target: Physician's assistant.
Strategy: For this nontraditional new graduate starting a new career at age 60, the resume focuses on his medical experience and summarizes his 30-year upper-level-management work history in one sentence so that it won't intimidate hiring managers (a real problem with his previous resume).

Barry D. Hargrove, PA-C

781 Forest Lane ◆ Palmdale, CA 93591 ◆ (661) 445-0922 ◆ bdh1000@yahoo.com

SUMMARY OF QUALIFICATIONS

Energetic, dedicated **Physician Assistant** with strong interpersonal skills. ◆ Emergency Medical Technician background. ◆ Proven ability to work effectively with people of various ages, cultural backgrounds, and socioeconomic statuses. ◆ Long-time interest in medicine and desire to assist those who are suffering physically or emotionally. ◆ Provide high-quality medical care with an emphasis on treating patients as unique and valuable individuals. ◆ Well-developed organizational skills. ◆ Fluent in Spanish language.

EDUCATION

Master of Science — Physician Assistant   2011
Lancaster University, Lancaster, CA

Clinical rotations included

Internal Medicine	Family Medicine	Urgent Care
Surgery	Pediatrics	Psychiatry
Neurology	Obstetrics & Gynecology	Urban Clinic
Radiology	Outpatient Medicine	Emergency Medicine
Critical Care	Geriatrics	Long-Term Care

Participated on a four-member team that researched the cultural competence of allied health graduate students in ethnically diverse urban environments.

PROFESSIONAL EXPERIENCE

Resident   2010–2011
Antelope Valley Medical Center, Lancaster, CA

◆ Provided care to patients in orthopedic clinic.
◆ Obtained history and physical for new patients. Wrote admission notes and pre-op orders.
◆ Performed pre-surgical evaluations and scheduled OR time.
◆ Wrote post-op orders and provided follow-up care to patients after surgery.
◆ Treated orthopedic trauma patients in busy emergency department.
◆ Collaborated with physicians in all aspects of patient care. Participated in rounds.

---

120 *(continued)*

Barry D. Hargrove, PA-C   Page 2
(661) 445-0922 ◆ bdh1000@yahoo.com

EMT Instructor/CPR Instructor   2000–2009
<u>Riverside Emergency Medical Services</u>, Riverside, CA

- ◆ Taught classes of up to 120 EMT students.
- ◆ Treated students with respect and communicated an expectation of success. This was reflected in consistent student achievement on state exams.
- ◆ Received 4 Outstanding Instructor awards.
- ◆ Served as a resource to the Program Director for management issues and decision making.

EMT-D   2005–2006
<u>Beaumont First Aid Squad</u>, Beaumont, CA

- ◆ Provided emergency care on an as-needed basis. Attended fire calls.

EMT-D   2000–2005
<u>Moreno Valley First Aid Squad</u>, Moreno Valley, CA

- ◆ Administered emergency care to patients throughout community, which included a high number of trauma and myocardial infarction cases.
- ◆ Elected to offices of First and Second Lieutenant.
- ◆ Often on standby during local high school and college athletic events.

<u>Prior employment</u> was in management and provided experience in planning, human resources management, time management, working effectively on a team, and problem solving.

CERTIFICATION & LICENSURE

Physician Assistant Certification
California Physician Assistant License
BLS
ACLS

Have extensive and diverse Continuing Medical Education—details available upon request.

Degree: BS, Business Administration.
Job Target: A position in banking, investment, or finance.
Strategy: Capitalized on seven years of grocery/management experience, specifically the ability to offer leadership, build relationships, and provide customer satisfaction. Demonstrated productivity, the ability to meet objectives, and a progression from courtesy clerk to grocery manager.

ERIC H. KATAYAMA

92-9876 Kukui Street • Mililani, Hawaii 96789
E-mail: ekatayama@onlinealoha.com
Tel: (808) 245-1234

Seeking Mid-Entry-Level Position in...

BANKING / INVESTMENT / FINANCE
Relationship Building, Customer Service Excellence, and Leadership
Enhancing Organizational Success Through Customer Satisfaction

---

Recent college graduate offering academic credentials in Finance and Business Administration—worked full-time while pursuing education. Seven years of practical experience satisfying customer needs and developing productive working relationships. Verifiable record of sound management skills.

> *"Eric has a strong desire to succeed and pays close attention to details. He has excellent interpersonal skills and will be an asset to any organization."* Store Manager, Foodmart

EDUCATION & TRAINING

Finance Major—B.S., Business Administration, 3.1 GPA
University of Hawaii, Honolulu, Hawaii, 2011

Zenger Miller Frontline Leadership
Management Training, 2003

EXPERIENCE

Foodmart, Inc., Kailua, Hawaii — 2003 to Present

Grocery Manager (May 2006 to Present)
Oversee store operations on nightly basis, personally supervising up to 40 employees. Handle grocery department orders totaling 40% of store sales. Train new employees and develop managers in training.

- Consistently lead store to profit-sharing goals, regularly finishing in top 15% of Western Division for customer-service benchmarks.
- Sustained department productivity levels despite staff reductions of 30+%.
- Set all-time store sales record for 2009.
- Promoted from…

Stock Clerk / Cashier (July 2004 to May 2006)

- Consistently received above-average evaluations from supervisors.
- Charged with entire store when no managers available.
- Selected to handle grocery-department ordering.
- First in two years to be promoted from **Courtesy Clerk** (June 2003 to July 2004).

COMMUNITY INVOLVEMENT

Treasurer, Mililani Leeward Community Board
Participant, Foodmart Employee Fundraiser Cookouts
Coordinator, Kailua Foodmart Softball Team

TECHNICAL SKILLS

Microsoft Office
Quicken and QuickBooks
10-key calculator

Degree: AS, Computer Science.
Job Target: Help desk/computer support technician.
Strategy: Emphasized coursework and used employment and personal activities to showcase intangible qualities such as leadership, customer service, and training abilities.

Dwayne Prescott
1226 Rambling Way, Columbia, MD 21044
410-997-7555 Home ▪ dpres18@yahoo.com

OBJECTIVE

Help Desk / Computer Support Technician position

PROFILE

✓ Recent computer-degree graduate with proven organizational abilities.
✓ Demonstrated track record of achieving goals in a team environment.
✓ Highly motivated and dependable—able to take responsibility for projects.
✓ Proven skills in problem solving and customer service.

EDUCATION

Columbia Community College, Columbia, MD   2010–2011
A.S., Computer Science
Computer courses completed in
✓ Networking Essentials   ✓ Windows Workstation
✓ A+ Certification   ✓ Administering Windows Workstation
✓ Intermediate Word   ✓ Windows WorkStation Core Technologies
✓ Beginning Word   ✓ Windows Workstation Support By Enterprise
✓ Beginning Access   ✓ Beginning Business on the Internet
✓ TCP / IP protocol   ✓ Beginning Dreamweaver

University of Maryland, College Park, MD   2009–2010
General first-year coursework in Bachelor's Degree program.

EMPLOYMENT

The Cutting Edge, Laurel, MD   2009–2011
Receptionist/Cashier

▪ Successfully handled front desk and 3 incoming telephone lines for busy, upscale hair salon with 15 stylists. Greeted and logged in steady stream of customers, coordinating appointments with hairdresser availability.

▪ Developed cooperative, team-oriented working relationships with owners and co-workers in this 18-station salon.

▪ Managed customer problems and complaints with tact and attention to prompt customer service. Commended by owners for resourcefulness.

▪ Gained experience in opening and closing procedures, cash register receipts, counter sales, light bookkeeping, and telephone follow-up.

Columbia Aces Soccer Camp, Columbia, MD   2008, 2009 Summers
Trainer / Coach

▪ Assisted Women's Soccer Coach in 200-participant practice-intensive soccer camp. Worked with individuals, as well as teams, to improve their attitude and resulting soccer performance.

ACTIVITIES & AWARDS

Maryland Mavericks Soccer Semi-Pro Team—Center Half   2006–2010
✓ Team consistently ranked in top 10 semi-pro teams in the nation.

Wilde Lake High School Soccer Team   2006–2009
✓ Co-captain of team that won the State Soccer Title in 2008.
✓ Recognized as one of the top three mid-fielders in the state in 2009.

123

Degree: BS, Business Administration
Job Target: MIS position.
Strategy: Created a strong, comprehensive summary of education, computer skills, and other professional abilities. Used work experience to provide supportive evidence of diversity of skills.

GEORGE A. PORTER

1555 Nottingham
Mt. Pleasant, MI 48888

577.727.7749
georgeaport23@gmail.com

PROFESSIONAL QUALIFICATIONS

A dedicated and resourceful young **MIS Professional** offering a unique combination of knowledge and skills in a variety of areas. Creative and enthusiastic, with proven success in building and managing relationships with peers, coworkers, customers, and the general public. Excellent attendance with employers and school. Confident, decisive, and committed to professional growth and opportunity. Dependable, self-motivated, hardworking, and a quick learner. Experience includes

Analytical & Problem-Solving Skills • Oral & Written Communication • Customer Service • Team Participation
Community Outreach • Leadership • Computer Troubleshooting • Project Planning & Coordination • Reporting

EDUCATION

BACHELOR OF SCIENCE IN BUSINESS ADMINISTRATION
CENTRAL MICHIGAN UNIVERSITY, Mt. Pleasant, MI, 2011
• Major: *Management Information Systems*

COMPUTER SKILLS

Systems & *Languages*	Windows Workstation Visual Basic	MS Windows ASP/HTML	CDS Systems Visual IFPS-Plus	COBOL Oracle PL/SQL
Software	MS Office	MS Project	WordPress	Networking TCP/IP

RELEVANT EXPERIENCE

GREEKTOWN CASINO / SOARING EAGLE CASINO & RESORT, Detroit & Mt. Pleasant, MI   2010–2011
COMPUTER TECHNICIAN
Duties included updating customer accounts, tracking customer comp points, and producing customer gambling activity reports. Also provided system maintenance and troubleshooting, as needed.

OTHER EXPERIENCE

B & D CONSTRUCTION, Bloomington, IN   2007–Present
INSTALLER
Work effectively with teams to install pool liners in commercial pool systems.

GREEKTOWN CASINO / SOARING EAGLE CASINO AND RESORT, Detroit & Mt. Pleasant, MI   2005–Present
DEALER
Oversee various casino games played by the public. Responsibilities include setting up and paying of complicated wagers, game protection, customer relations, and the handling of large currency transactions.

SOLID CONCRETE, INC., Howell, MI   2000–2005
CONCRETE CUTTER/CORE DRILLER
In charge of specialty equipment and company vehicles. Serviced clients in a professional and efficient manner, consistent with company values.

Resume Development Worksheet

Use Chapter 2 to guide you through each step of completing this worksheet and then drafting and polishing a great resume. Even when your resume is completed, keep these worksheets; they'll come in handy every time you update your resume or adapt it for a different job target.

Resume Development Worksheet

Header/Contact Information

Name _____

Home or school address (if local to job) _____

_____

Cell phone number (or other reliable phone number) _____

E-mail address (permanent and professional sounding) _____

_____

Professional online profile or web portfolio URL _____

Objective, Goal, or Target Statement

_____

_____

_____

Skills Summary (Evidence of Core Qualifications)

_____

_____

_____

_____

Education

Graduate Degree

Name of school, city, state _____

_____

Degree, year earned _____

Major _____ GPA (if 3.0 or higher) _____

Major coursework (if needed to describe unusual major or flesh out resume) _____

_____

_____

Academic honors _____

_____

Thesis or other special projects _____

_____

Scholarships/fellowships _____

_____

Extras _____

_____

Undergraduate Degree

Name of school, city, state _____

_____

Degree, year earned _____

Major _____

Minor (if relevant to your career target) _____

GPA (if 3.0 or higher) _____

GPA in major (if significantly higher than overall GPA) _____

Major coursework (if needed to describe unusual major or flesh out resume) _____

_____

_____

Academic honors _____

_____

Scholarships _____

_____

Co-op or internship experience (may appear here or in "Experience" section) _____

_____

_____

Special projects, team projects, thesis _____

_____

Extracurricular activities/leadership activities _____

_____

Volunteer activities _____

_____

International study _____

_____

Extras _____

_____

Additional Training/Certification

High school experience (if notable and relevant) _____

_____

_____

Experience (Employment and/or Co-op or Internship)

Company name, city, state _____

_____

Job title, dates of employment _____

_____

Summary of job duties _____

_____

Accomplishments/highlights/contributions _____

_____

_____

Company name, city, state _____

_____

Job title, dates of employment _____

_____

Summary of job duties _____

_____

Accomplishments/highlights/contributions _____

_____

_____

Company name, city, state _____

_____

Job title, dates of employment _____

_____

Summary of job duties _____

_____

Accomplishments/highlights/contributions _____

_____

_____

Additional Information (important things that don't fit the other categories)

_____

_____

Find a Professional Resume Writer

If you need professional assistance with your resume or with any aspect of your job search, contact one of the experts who contributed to this book! With a wealth of experience writing resumes for clients in many different and very challenging circumstances, these writers know how to make the most of your experience (however limited), your education, and your unique qualifications.

In updating the resume samples for this third edition of the book, I turned immediately to the expert ACRWs—Academy Certified Resume Writers—who are graduates of the rigorous Resume Writing Academy program that I co-lead. I knew their work would be top-notch and up-to-date, and I wasn't disappointed!

Special thanks to the following ACRWs for their contributions:

Carol Altomare
World Class Résumés
Flemington, NJ 08822
Phone: (908) 237-1883
E-mail: carol@worldclassresumes.com
www.worldclassresumes.com
Resumes: 19, 35, 59, 86

Lorraine Beaman
JLB Career Consulting
426 Del Oro
Davis, CA 95616
Phone: (530) 219-9651
E-mail: jlbcareers@sbcglobal.net
www.jlbcareers.com
Resumes: 14, 17, 20, 22

Janet Beckstrom
Word Crafter
1717 Montclair Ave.
Flint, MI 48503
Phone: (810) 232-9257
E-mail: janet@wordcrafter.com
www.wordcrafter.com
Resumes: 3, 5, 6, 33, 81

Ann Boyer
P.O. Box 1143
Fair Oaks, CA 95628
Phone: (916) 942-9207
E-mail: aboyerconsult@aol.com
Resume: 26

Renée Green
Passionate Coaching & Career Services, LLC
Phone: (763) 807-1850
E-mail: renee@greenpassionatecoaching.com
http://greenpassionatecoaching.com
Resume: 43

Lesa Kerlin
LEK Consultants
1703 Meadow View Dr.
Kirksville, MO 63501
Phone: (660) 626-4748
E-mail: lesa@lekconsultants.com
http://lekconsultants.com
Resumes: 32, 34, 51

Anne Kern
ReachHire Resume Service
P.O. Box 942
Atco, NJ 08004-0942
Phone: (856) 261-1097
E-mail: reachhire@yahoo.com
www.reachhire.org
Resume: 49

Mary Schumacher
CareerFrames LLC
517 Nova Way
Madison, WI 53704
Phone: (608) 242-1879
E-mail: mary@careerframes.com
www.careerframes.com
Resumes: 38, 78

Marjorie Sussman
Dover Productions
Phone: (201) 941-8237
E-mail: marjorie1130@gmail.com
www.visualcv.com/marjoriesussman
Resumes: 70, 87, 88

And continuing thanks to the following writers whose work is again featured in this edition of the book:

Sheila Adjahoe
The Adjahoe Group
Resume: 116

Lynn P. Andenoro
My Career Resource
Resumes: 74, 76, 84, 91

Jennifer Nell Ayres
Nell Personal Advancement Resources
Resume: 52

Ann Baehr
Best Resumes of New York
Resume: 37

Carla Barrett
Career Designs
Resume: 99

Jacqui D. Barrett
Career Trend
Resume: 110

Rima Bogardus
Garner, NC
Resumes: 85, 113, 120

Arnold G. Boldt
Arnold-Smith Associates
Resumes: 15, 69, 79

Carolyn Braden
Hendersonville, TN
Resumes: 40, 54, 118

Martin Buckland
Elite Resumes
Resume: 82

Diane Burns
Career Marketing Techniques
Resumes: 55, 90

Camille Carboneau Roberts
CC Career Services
Resume: 45

Lisa Chapman
Chapman Services Group, LLC
Resume: 101

Freddie Cheek
Cheek & Associates
Resumes: 9, 62, 68

Fred E. Coon
Stewart, Cooper & Coon
Resume: 112

Norine T. Dagliano
ekm Inspirations
Resume: 96

Dian R. Davis
Career-Dreams
Resume: 7

Michael Davis
Centerville, OH
Resume: 107

Kirsten Dixson
KirstenDixson.com
Resumes: 18, 115

Nina K. Ebert
A Word's Worth
Resumes: 12, 65

Cory Edwards
Partnering For Success, LLC
Resume: 72

Debbie Ellis
Phoenix Career Group
Resumes: 1, 41

Michelle M. Fleig-Palmer
University of Nebraska-Lincoln
Resume: 48

Joyce Fortier
Create Your Career
Resume: 123

Louise Garver
Career Directions, LLC
Resumes: 67, 77, 80

Rosemarie Ginsberg
Career Planning Solutions
Resume: 46

Sharon Graham
Graham Management Group
Resume: 94

Susan Guarneri
Guarneri Associates
Resumes: 23, 39, 61, 122

Alice Hanson
Edmonds Community College
Resume: 109

Erika C. Harrigan
Success Partners
Resume: 98

Peter Hill
P.H.I. Consulting
Resume: 121

Gay Anne Himebaugh
Seaview Resume Solutions
Resume: 2

Lee Hogaboom
Power Punch Resume
Resume: 102

Gayle Howard
Top Margin Career Marketing
Resume: 66

Lynn Hughes
Lubbock, TX
Resumes: 29, 30

Deborah S. James
Leading Edge Resume & Career
Services
Resume: 57

Marcy Johnson
Story City, IA
Resumes: 13, 58, 111

Bill Kinser
To The Point Resumes
Resume: 16

Cindy Kraft
Executive Essentials
Resume: 31

Louise Kursmark
Best Impression Career Services,
Inc.
Resumes: 4, 10, 27, 28, 75

Lorie Lebert
The LORIEL Group
Resumes: 11, 63

Kathleen McInerney
Career Edge, Inc.
Resume: 105

Jan Melnik
Absolute Advantage
Resume: 117

Nicole Miller
Ottawa, Ontario
Resume: 114

Meg Montford
Abilities Enhanced
Resume: 108

Doug Morrison
Career Power
Resume: 42

Ellen Mulqueen
Hartford, CT
Resume: 103

Helen Oliff
Turning Point
Resume: 50

Don Orlando
The McLean Group
Resumes: 60, 89

Teresa L. Pearson
Meriden, KS
Resumes: 24, 47

Michelle Mastruserio Reitz
Printed Pages
Resume: 106

Barbara Robertson
Rensselaer, IN
Resume: 71

Teena L. Rose
Resume to Referral
Resume: 104

Janice Shepherd
Write On Career Keys
Resumes: 21, 93, 119

Karen M. Silins
A+ Career & Resume, LLC
Resume: 56

Billie Ruth Sucher
Billie Sucher & Associates
Resumes: 73, 95

Karen Swann
TypeRight
Resume: 53

Roleta Fowler Vasquez
Wordbusters Resume & Writing
Services
Resumes: 8, 83

Jean West
Green Cove Springs, FL
Resume: 97

Sharon Williams
JobRockit, Inc.
Resumes: 25, 44, 64

Janice Worthington
Worthington Career Services
Resume: 100

Linda Wunner
A+ Career & Resume Design
Resume: 36

Index